The Making of Tesco

www.**transworldbooks**.co.uk

THE MAKING OF TESCO

A Story of British Shopping

Sarah Ryle

BANTAM PRESS

LONDON • TORONTO • SYDNEY • AUCKLAND • JOHANNESBURG

TRANSWORLD PUBLISHERS
61–63 Uxbridge Road, London W5 5SA
A Random House Group Company
www.transworldbooks.co.uk

First published in Great Britain
in 2013 by Bantam Press
an imprint of Transworld Publishers

A CIP catalogue record for this book
is available from the British Library.

ISBNs 9780593070444 (hb)
9780593072387 (tpb)

Addresses for Random House Group Ltd companies outside the UK
can be found at: www.randomhouse.co.uk
The Random House Group Ltd Reg. No. 954009

The Random House Group Limited supports the Forest Stewardship Council (FSC®),
the leading international forest-certification organization. Our books carrying the
FSC label are printed on FSC®-certified paper. FSC is the only forest-certification scheme
endorsed by the leading environmental organizations, including Greenpeace.
Our paper procurement policy can be found at
www.randomhouse.co.uk/environment.

Typeset in 11.5/15pt Minion by Falcon Oast Graphic Art Ltd.
Printed and bound in Great Britain by
CPI Group (UK) Ltd, Croydon, CR0 4YY

2 4 6 8 10 9 7 5 3 1

Contents

CHAIRMEN and CEOs mentioned in the text

Sir Jack Cohen
Founder, 1919.
Chairman
1947–1970.
Life President
1970–1979

Hyman Kreitman
Chairman
1970–73

Sir Leslie Porter
Chairman
1973–1985;
Non-Executive
Chairman
1985–1987

Lord MacLaurin
Managing Director,
1973–1985;
Chairman
1985–1987;
Non-Executive
Chairman
1987–1997

David Malpas
Managing Director
1987–1997

John Gardiner
Chairman
1997–2004

Sir Terry Leahy
Chief Executive
1997–2011

Sir David Reid
Chairman
2004–2011

Philip Clarke
Chief Executive
2011–

Richard Broadbent
Chairman 2011–

Author's Note

Over and above the usual acknowledgements, it is important to describe the role in this book of an incredible archive of oral history in the making.

Tesco itself is impoverished in terms of its historical archive: perhaps its people were too busy looking forward to preserve the past. So an invitation from the British Library's National Life Stories team, some nine years ago, to contribute to its sound archive was welcomed and accepted.

Over the course of several years a collection amounting to more than three hundred hours of memories was created. The lead interviewer, Niamh Dillon, spoke to Tesco people who had been at Board level and on the shop floor, in offices and warehouses. I have contributed additional interviews. The archive – dubbed internally the 'Tesco tapes' – chronicles the successes and failures of one of Britain's best-known businesses. But it is more than that. It is a history of people and of shopping.

Nobody at Tesco was keen on a corporate history told largely from Annual Reports and newspaper cuttings: what would that add? Tesco, though, gets a lot of attention: to let its own people describe its journey seemed to be an interesting idea.

Thanks to National Life Stories, it has been possible to do this. The Tesco tapes are a small part of the larger oral-history programme, 'Food: From Source to Salespoint', which covers food production, manufacturing and consumption in the UK. Within this collection the biographical recordings with Tesco's staff are the largest body of interviews with a single retailer.

Each recording was frank and even funny, insightful and sometimes inconsistent: above all, very human. It would have been wonderful, if overwhelming, to be able to include them all.

Where the 'Tesco tapes' could not paint the whole picture, this book relies on more conventional sources, including Annual Reports, Sir Jack Cohen's autobiography and the one other book written about the company twenty years ago.

Like the oral archive, the story told here is subjective in places as it relies on individual memories. There might be some distortions and conflicting interpretations of events, but these are what make history so compelling and engaging. The intention here has been to share the recollections as they are, with a reasonable attempt to set them in context and cross-check inconsistencies. I have looked for stories and quotations that kept the history moving. Several different books could have been written from the same archive. All the contributors who are included can be heard in full at the British Library.

This book can never be a definitive version of events – but claims to be definitive are in any case always suspect. Developments postprint will probably cast a new light on elements of this story, because that is what time does. The views and observations in this book merit reading in their contemporary context. The Tesco tapes record Tesco's story only as far as January 2012.

What follows is an attempt to convey some of the humanity behind the journey of a corporate entity: this is Tesco's story for its people and, mostly, by its people.

Foreword

'When you get to be as big and as successful as Tesco has become, people put a sort of sheen on the journey – as if the place we got to was inevitable. But it really wasn't. I think it's important that Tesco's story is told honestly because there were moments when we could just as easily have gone the other way.'

Sir Terry Leahy, former chief executive[1]

'For ninety-three years, Tesco has been serving customers in this country. In the life of the company, we are all only here for a short while. But in our time together, we can touch the lives of millions of people and make as big a contribution as any politician or government. It's an incredibly precious responsibility that we hold.'

Philip Clarke, chief executive[2]

Tesco today is one of the UK's most talked-about businesses, operating in fourteen countries at the start of 2012, serving 50 million customers every week and employing half a million people.

It is a long way from the obscurity of the single market stall in Hackney that Jack Cohen set up nearly a century ago on his return to Civvy Street after the First World War. Were he here to read it, Jack might have raged about the bad publicity; he would also have known that Tesco had survived greater trials in the past. Known in his lifetime as 'The Old Man', 'Jack the Nagger' and 'Slasher Jack', he was never part of English society, but by the time he died in 1979 he had transformed his own and his family's standing beyond recognition and changed the face of British shopping.

This is the human story of that journey. It includes the wheeling and ever so slightly dodgy dealing of the early days, such as sand-papering rust off tins of fruit and taking incentives from sales reps. Then there was the South v. North conflict; the boardroom battles at the top; the long, often terror-filled, weeks for the middle ranks; and the woeful treatment of shop-floor and warehouse workers before major changes made employee-satisfaction a sincere aspiration.

Much has been written about Tesco by outside observers and this story draws on some of those perspectives, because how others have seen Tesco has influenced its growth. The majority of the book's material, though, is derived from an incredible store of more than 300 hours of recorded interviews with people who have been close to the heart of the business and whose stories form part of the British Library's National Life Stories oral-history project. Former chief executives Lord MacLaurin and Sir Terry Leahy are among the Tesco leaders who spoke at length for the archive. Dame Shirley Porter may never have worked at Tesco but as Jack Cohen's younger daughter and Leslie Porter's wife, she was part of the Cohen clan and nobody else can provide their viewpoint today.

The interviews not only place Tesco firmly in its social context but also paint a parallel picture: the changing habits of British consumers. Tesco's tale is a social story as well as a business epic. One after another, Tesco's bosses have required resolute observance of customers' wants and needs at any given moment, learning the hard way that being a step behind can be catastrophic. Tesco has also consistently crossed social and geographical boundaries; before the internet, this was as rare in British retail as in British society in general. Tesco is for everyone, they say. When no other supermarket group would invest in a store on a sink estate Tesco would, yet Tesco is also on some of the smartest high streets in the land, albeit in a discreetly toned-down black-and-white livery.

A snapshot of Tesco is a snapshot of society at any given point. At its checkouts, baskets containing Finest balsamic vinegar or organic milk follow baskets holding frozen chips and cola; often the same basket will have a mix of the best and the basic. Tesco Finest and Tesco Value are the UK's biggest brands at the time of writing.

Tesco's size worries some interest groups. It took sixty years for the company really to make a mark, but then only another thirty for it to achieve the sort of size we see today. Society, too, has experienced a speeding-up of change, driven largely by technology that is never 'new' for more than a couple of months at a time. Tesco in many ways has become a lightning conductor for objections to all kinds of changes that have transformed Britain. Those objections – and Tesco's responses – form a sort of social history in themselves.

The tendency for Tesco staff to count their career with the company in decades influences the way this story is told. From Sir Jack Cohen's family firm onwards, loyalty to Tesco is notable. Winning and maintaining loyalty – from staff and customers – is not so much a thread running through its timeline as a great, thick rope. Staying power is highly prized, as Leahy told more than one interviewer. He joined in his early twenties and stayed for thirty-two years before retiring in February 2011. His successor, Philip Clarke, is the son of a Tesco store manager, so the business has been part of his life for almost as long as he can remember. Many of the people in this book have had lifelong careers with the company too, and this is one of the traits that Tesco's leaders have in common. The fact that it is possible to count Clarke's predecessors on one hand across nine decades is significant. 'A baton was chiselled out by Jack Cohen in Hackney,' says Clarke. 'It was handed to [Hyman Kreitman, then to] Leslie Porter, then to Ian MacLaurin, then to Terry Leahy and now I have got it for a while.'[3]

Each chief executive leaves the stamp of his personality on first hundreds, then thousands and now hundreds of thousands of staff. This story describes those personalities, as well as the company's triumphs and errors, because the business is built on people with all their human strengths and weaknesses. There are occasional digressions to capture a flavour of individual life stories from the

British Library archive, giving us a glimpse of British society at different moments in history and so telling us a bit about the families that Jack Cohen and his successors were serving. That in turn explains some of the decisions that Tesco's leaders made.

Many of the personal stories in this book are of social mobility. It is no exaggeration to say that many of the people who made Tesco began life with little more than a roof over their heads and what would nowadays pass for one square meal a week. It invites derision now to talk about how successful people began with nothing – but the truth is that some of Tesco's most influential leaders came from families where money couldn't be found to buy shoes. Many more have travelled the less extreme journey from having just about enough to living lives of considerable comfort. The current boss, Philip Clarke, is a case in point. Like Leahy, Clarke was made on Merseyside. Leahy, from the blue Evertonian side, has roots in an Irish Catholic family whose home was a council-owned prefab. Clarke, from Liverpool's red side, started maybe one notch up thanks to his store-manager father. The north-west of England is famed for facing out to the rest of the world through the port of Liverpool. No accident, perhaps, that Leahy and Clarke have been so influential in exporting Tesco far and wide – geographically and digitally.

Tesco employs 500,000 staff across the globe in thirteen countries (having withdrawn from Japan since the start of 2012). It opened its thousandth store in Central Europe in 2011. It serves 50 million customers every week. There are share schemes and pensions, industry-leading rates of pay for store workers and millions of pounds for charities and community schemes – from night classes in South Korea to football coaching for kids in the UK, or game-changing amounts of money for research into disease and disability.

Outsiders see Tesco's success in two-dimensional terms, focusing on the financial facts and figures. 'Because Tesco is so big, most people have an opinion that they have formed from second- or third-hand reports,' Leahy reflected. 'They don't actually know us. People who have personal experience of Tesco, as customers or as suppliers or as groups we work with, have a positive view for the most part. Yes, in a business with hundreds of thousands of staff, we'll get things wrong. That's human. We try to put that right and above all we learn from our mistakes.'[4]

Clarke, almost a year into his stewardship in January 2012, explained that the reason he has overcome an aversion to the microphone or television camera is that the more open Tesco people are, the less general misunderstanding there is. He is the first Tesco director to blog and podcast, because he wants Tesco people to feel able to talk about the business with confidence in their own communities and to engage equally easily with concerns and praise.

How, then, did Tesco get from Jack Cohen's barrow in Hackney to the hypermarkets in Hungary and Thailand and the home-delivery business serving customers from Cheshire to the Czech Republic? Has it been the result of hard graft? Luck? Subterfuge? How has Tesco succeeded where other British companies – and retailers in particular – have stalled? How did it overtake Sainsbury, the unchallenged leader for six decades? How did its people respond to setbacks across the last ten decades such as inflation and profit warnings? What impact did political and social upheaval – from war to national industrial turmoil – have on shops? What did a traditionally bricks-and-mortar retailer do for customers who increasingly began to shop online? Here is Tesco's story told for the first time by people with first-hand knowledge.

Chapter 1

The Poor Shall Be Fed: Jack's Bargain-barrow Beginnings

'We are a company that looks forward so it is interesting to stop and look back, to remember why things worked, why things happened and when. Your daily life is looking forwards and hitting targets so we tend not to look back too much: probably not enough, because the past can be a good guide to the future. Learning from what you did well and what you didn't do well and why.'

Sir David Reid, Tesco non-executive chairman 2004–2011[1]

Pretty much anybody who would remember Jack Cohen's first retail venture is long gone. We need to imagine the single barrow in deepest Hackney's Well Street in 1919 and the twenty-year-old who stood beside it. He was small of stature, as so many children of London's crowded East End would have been, but reportedly mighty of voice. He may have looked fierce – his nose was squashed due to an untreated break in childhood and subsequent repair job by a military hospital that removed a piece of bone to help his breathing.

Born on 29 October 1898, in a modest East End house, Jacob was two months premature and coated in the caul, which was supposed to mark out a child for good luck. According to Jack's biography, *Pile It High, Sell It Cheap*, Jack was saved only by a quick-thinking aunt who removed the caul and so prevented his suffocation. The house in Sander Street was packed with siblings and ruled by an autocratic father, Avroam, a tailor who had 'married up' a few social levels within the Jewish immigrant pecking order. The family moved to the area just south of the London Hospital on Whitechapel Road; Jacob's school was in the same road, Rutland Street (now named Ashfield Street). He failed to shine at school and his early life would have been fairly mundane, with few sparkling moments. Fresh food was a limited luxury, and days out of polluted London were almost unheard of. In 1915 he lost his mother, Sime, to whom he was close. His father remarried a lady whom his daughters Shirley and Irene and their cousins only ever knew as 'Mrs Howdoyoudo', which Shirley recalls they took to be an indication of their father's opinion of his stepmother.

In 1914 Europe had embarked on a war fuelled for the first time by mass-produced weaponry and motorization. Young Jacob enlisted, arriving at Aldershot Barracks on 7 March 1917; he had opted for the Royal Flying Corps, the precursor to the RAF, and started out sewing the canvas on barrage balloons. He went into the First World War as a hard-working Jewish East Ender with fairly limited horizons, but he came out a different person, according to his daughter, Shirley. When his boat, the *Osmanieh*, sank at Alexandria on New Year's Eve 1917, he would have drowned but for a nurse who kept him afloat. As well as the fighting, he encountered a range of people he might never otherwise have come across. As 64535 Air Mechanic Cohen, J., he also met anti-Semitism, possibly for the first time. Shirley says his response was to assimilate as best he could: 'He lost a lot of what he was brought up with in the air force'.[2]

By the time the war ended, Jack had tasted a life beyond the tailoring mapped out for him by Avroam. Yet he had not displayed much talent for anything else and there were few choices available to a twenty-year-old with no education in the economic slump that followed the First World War. Wartime industries went into reverse and 2.1 million men returned from the front to find their jobs had either disappeared or been taken by men spared conscription, or by women. Civil unrest, race riots, the Battle of Wood Green (just up the road from Hackney) and youngsters attacking the police made headlines then as nowadays. The scary spectre of the Russian Revolution of 1917 provoked genuine fear that revolution would reach British shores. Spanish flu was lethally rampant. Even the once-safe tailoring option looked shaky because the rag trade was in decline, dented as demand for uniforms vanished. For Jack, prospects were poor; but there was one avenue that seemed to him worth exploring. Before the war he had tasted market life on a stall run by his brother-in-law, Morris Israel: perhaps that could be his route out of either penury or, possibly even more depressing, grinding out piecework for his father.

Shirley believes that her father was driven. 'He had a reason for getting out of what he was doing. Life was tough. It was hard in those days. If you didn't work, you didn't get paid. There was nobody sitting there with a welfare cheque. Who would want to live badly? He'd seen another world in the Air Corps, apart from the overcrowded world of the East End tenement. I think he succeeded at first from sheer hard work, enormous energy and dedication. And he had luck. You need luck in anything. He was always battling, always fighting. He had charisma. He had vision. He was prepared to cock a snook at the establishment.'[3]

Jack did get a handout of sorts at the end of the war: having survived two bouts of malaria as well as the ship-sinking, he came back to London exactly two years after he had joined up and received the lump sum given to service personnel as they left the forces. Jack collected his £30 'demob' money – a decent sum in 1919 – spent it on a consignment of NAAFI goods, hired a barrow and headed for Well Street, a busy market site between London Fields and Hackney Common and only two streets south of his family home at 26, Darnley Road. He persuaded an established trader to let him use part of her pitch for a shilling and from it he sold £4 of Maconochie's Paste, Lyle's Golden Syrup and a supply of Nestlé's canned milk that had been labelled for French troops, making £1 profit on his first day.

Most of Jack's stock continued to be sourced from the NAAFI stores based around London's Eastcheap. He looked for stock that was cheap because it was hard to sell. He also explored other street markets to find new outlets. His biography describes a serious young man. Your typical market trader drank, smoked and swore. Jack did none of these. He worked very, very hard and, with the help of young nephews and cousins, set up stall five days a week.

Costermongering was not what Avroam had in mind for his son at all, and he particularly objected to the growing mounds of stock that were gradually colonizing his back-room workshop at Darnley Road. But Jack loved it. Dame Shirley Porter recalls that even three or four decades later, when Jack had become John and moved to a mansion in Finchley, her father loved to take his girls back to the East End to see the traders and eat lunch at Bloom's.

'We went to Petticoat Lane every Sunday unless we were going picnicking,' she says. 'We'd drive "Down the Lane". He'd plonk the car somewhere – out we'd tumble – "Hello Jack" – "Hello! Here I am and here are my girls." I was happy saying hello, but my sister was older and she felt more embarrassment because he was so proud of us.

'The market was very vibrant, there were stalls either side. China, glass, clocks, food – costermongers shouting out and calling out and sometimes he'd stop and shout out with them: "Buy one get one free." Then we'd go to Bloom's for marvellous food – chicken soup, salt beef, tongue – it was a warm, hot atmosphere – and it would be "Hello Jack" everywhere. People wanted to speak to him. It can be upsetting for children but I didn't mind it. I liked all the excitement.

'We'd be there for several hours, then we'd go and see the place where they sold dogs that had been found. Then back we'd go home. It was a social outing, a sort of reunion. He knew all of them. He spent years in the market. There are still people today who remember him who were little children then. There were lots of different people. I just remember the vibrancy, the warmth, the shouting, the colour, all the goods and particularly the bagels and the smoked salmon and the lady with the pickled herrings and cucumber.'[4]

For Jack, the excitement, the smells and the direct contact with his customers were invigorating. He was entirely comfortable living on his wits and just on the edge of the establishment.

The single market stall soon became a series of stalls; in his first three years Jack was operating out of a number of London's many street markets: Hammersmith, Hoxton, Chatsworth Road in Hackney, Bermondsey and Caledonian Road near King's Cross as well as Well Street. At a time of chronic unemployment – 2 million by the summer of 1921 – the markets kept many families alive.

It would be illegal today, but back then trade associations existed to fix prices on more than a third of consumer goods.[5] Nor would those associations sell to street-market traders, who instead bought salvaged – often a euphemism for damaged – produce and goods. Traders were often chased off their pitches and Jack himself was detained at Hammersmith Police Station for obstruction; his future mother-in-law had to bail him out.

Jack learned that the establishment did not always work well for customers. He also found that even dented tins or packets could be retailed if you marketed them at the right price.

To begin with Jack ran his market stalls hand to mouth, but by November 1920 he was able to set up a bank account. He was soon turning over more than £100 a day in some of the markets – Caledonian Cattle Market was the first place he hit this milestone – and had to find an alternative to his father's back room at Darnley Road, so in 1922 he rented a lock-up half a mile north up Mare Street on Clarence Road. That filled up. Two years later he moved to a bigger storage place under the railway arches in Upper Clapton Road, nowadays known as Murder Mile despite regeneration schemes and a wave of middle-class home-owners. It was the beginning of Jack's journey along the A10, away from crowded Hackney, through Edmonton and finally to Cheshunt, Hertfordshire, where Tesco is still headquartered.

By the time he was holding stock at Upper Clapton Road, Jack was operating out of six street markets and had bought a horse and cart. He also had a converted ambulance in which to move his stock around, which was particularly useful as one of the markets he had branched out into was Surrey Street in Croydon. By January 1924 he had felt economically secure enough to marry Sarah 'Cissie' Fox, at the Hackney Synagogue. The couple moved into a flat in Gore Road, Hackney. On their marriage they received £130 from friends and relatives and Jack used the money to buy soap at £15 a ton, which he then sold at £20.

Cissie was the daughter of Polish Jewish émigrés, Benjamin and Annie Fox (anglicized from Fuchs). Benjamin made suits for Aquascutum. Shirley Porter recalls that her mother's family was considerably further up the immigrant Jewish social scale than her father's and that they were very patriotic. 'They felt Britain had welcomed them in and given them freedom. They were British Jews,' she says.[6] 'He was fortunate in that he married my mother. She kept him grounded. They argued. He would say she was always nagging, though people called him Jack the Nagger because he was always nagging and insisting. They were different people, but they made it together.'[7]

Six markets – in Hoxton, Hammersmith, Hackney, Islington, Bermondsey and Croydon – meant Jack had to delegate. In the summer of 1924 he advertised for salesmen. This brought him his first experience of being ripped off, as the traders supposedly working for him picked up their consignments of soap and disappeared with the cash. After that he found it was easier to trust relatives and hired his nephew, Mossie Vangar, and his brother-in-law Harry Fox. One of the boys he took on at Croydon, however, Jim Harrow, stayed with Cohen for the rest of his working life, such was the loyalty Jack inspired and prized.

It was around this time that, on one of his many buying forays, Jack met T. E. Stockwell, a partner at Torring and Stockwell, which sold blended tea. It was Jack's habit to re-brand products that he repackaged and, according to the account he gave his biographer,[8] they decided there and then that the tea would be called TESCO – 'TES' for T. E. Stockwell and 'CO' for Cohen. Jack bought 500 chests and sold 400lb on his first day. He had his first big hit.

The bank manager who set up the account told Jack that there were too many businesses registered to people called Jacob Cohen, so Jack altered his name to John Edward. Whether as Jacob, Jack or John, he bought tea at ninepence a pound in bulk then repackaged it in half-pound packets that housewives could afford at sixpence. TESCO tea was such a hit that other traders wanted in on the action. Jack, who worked only on the shake of a hand, had built up a solid relationship with T. E. Stockwell and began to buy enough of the tea to sell it to the other traders himself. The first year – 1925 – was not successful in terms of profit, however, as Jack extended credit to too many of his fellow market traders. Turnover on his six stalls had shot up but he was just £30 better off at the end of the year than he had been twelve months earlier. He was doing well enough to buy his first car – a Morris Oxford – but decided that next year he would trade for cash only.

Jack's biggest challenges were external. The National Federation of Grocers and Provision Dealers' Association, in effect an early union for small traders, was cross about the street markets. The coster-mongers undercut shop prices and, although this ensured survival for families on or below the poverty line, the London County Council eventually passed a bill in 1927 seeking to curb the markets.

Perhaps Jack felt that the time was ripe to boost his respectability: tackling the establishment did not preclude aspiring to have a bit of what his economic or social superiors took as their right. They moved to a semi-detached house in Gunton Road, Hackney, close to the railway arches lock-up. Clapton railway station stood at one end of the street, North Millfields recreation ground at the other. There were views over Walthamstow Marshes that seemed positively bucolic to the London-bred eye. The house was called Southdene, and Shirley was born there on 29 November 1930 (her older sister Irene had been born on 22 October 1926). In 1930 business was doing so well that Jack struck a deal with Cyril Carter of Amalgamated Dairies for 500 cases of New Zealand Snowflake canned milk. It cost him £250 and was so popular with London housewives that he ordered a further 87,000 cases at a profit of

3 shillings a case. This was Jack's second big hit after TESCO tea. Again, he sold from his six market stalls, but also sold cases to other traders, wholesale, from his warehouse in Upper Clapton Road. By now he was selling an array of products, in packets and tins, that ranged from biscuits from Russia to jars of Keiller's jam whose lids had torn; Jack put paper lids and elastic bands on them for resale.

Jack was proficient at mental mathematics, but was never going to win awards for bookkeeping. Two events were to underpin his embryonic business and lay the foundations for today's Tesco. First, he hired Albert Carpenter, from a food merchant's firm, who fought hard to order the paperwork in a tiny office at the Upper Clapton Road warehouse. Second, possibly deciding that if he couldn't beat the small shops' trade association he would join them, in November 1930 he opened his first indoor stall at Tooting Arcade, South London. It was called The Bargain Centre and set up with Sam Freeman; Jack invested £500.

If the years immediately after the First World War had been hard, 1930 was harder still. Though handouts were available, they were severely stigmatized in pre-Welfare State Britain and ordinary families were barely coping with the fallout from the Wall Street Crash of 1929. Then as now, press reports suggest that the chattering classes were obsessed with the notion that 'dole-ites' had money to burn while hard-pressed, hard-working, middle-class families went without.

Jack dealt in groceries that he priced and repackaged for the end of metropolitan British society that was otherwise ill-served. Salvaged stock – from tinned salmon to tinned fruit – could be repackaged and sold at prices housewives could afford. By selling lots of stock at low margins, the business continued to thrive and in May 1931 Jack opened a second store, named Jax, in Chatham, Kent, in partnership with his nephew Jack Vangar.

He was by no means the only grocery trader doing well. During the 1930s the number of retailers who had ten or more branches rose by 44 per cent. Companies with twenty-five branches or more increased by 68 per cent and by 1939 the Co-operative, the biggest by far, had 24,000 shops, a rise of 150 per cent in two decades. Jack, meanwhile, had Bargain Centres of London (at Tooting Arcade), Jax (at Chatham) and then he opened Bargain Centres (Dartford) with a family friend, Mick Kaye. This would become Pricerite in 1938 and Jack held his 50 per cent stake until the 1950s: his biographer says business relations had soured though personal relations remained comfortable.[9]

Industrial Britain may have been in decline, but new economic prospects were opening up, driving different social developments. Well-to-do suburbs were appearing, featuring spacious, light homes with three or four bedrooms, indoor bathrooms and neat gardens. They were near golf courses and stations that ran fast trains into London for the professional fathers. Middle-class women did not generally go out to work once they had children; they shopped for groceries every day and fitted committee or church work around managing the home and the family. Also, new industries manufacturing motor cars, chemicals and electrical goods were creating jobs in areas around London and in the Midlands. Women worked in those factories, rushing home to get tea on the table for six o'clock and stocking up on groceries on Friday nights with the weekly pay packet. Model villages and so-called New Towns sprang up. The 1930s aspirational housewife turned her gaze away from the street markets. She wanted to visit a proper shop, on a proper high street, where she could buy a better, brighter range of groceries.

In this environment, it was no coincidence that Jack chose routes through the new suburbs when he took his family out on day trips. He was searching for sites, with the dream of reaching a hundred stores.

This was also the point at which Jack made one of his most important hires – an eighteen-year-old school-leaver called Daisy Hyams, who would become known as 'the legendary Daisy Hyams', a feared buyer at Tesco and its first woman Board director. Even at eighteen her job was not a menial one – she joined Jack at the Upper Clapton base to bring order to the stock and takings, dishing out stock to the market traders and overseeing deliveries to the new shops. She collected the takings and banked them in Mare Street's Midland Bank (to whom Jack remained loyal when the takings could be counted in many millions).

A decade after he had set up stall in Well Street and turned over £4, Jack's business had outgrown his haphazard way of working. It was time to get professional.

Chapter 2

Shopping through the Darkest Hour: Jack on the Home Front

'We'd be going along and he'd suddenly say "This looks like a good place for a shop!" and he'd leap out and chat a few people up.'

Dame Shirley Porter[1]

As the thirties dawned, Jack's enterprises had generated annual sales of £119,000. He had cash in hand of £929 and his bank balance was £2,000 in 1931. The milestone of audited books was achieved on 1 January 1932 and had come about as a direct result of Jack buying a shop site at Burnt Oak, in the London borough of Barnet, south of Edgware, which he had spotted when he was out scouting for sites with his elder daughter Irene. It was one half of a fruit shop at 54 Watling Street and he made an offer in September 1931. This could not be done on the shake of a hand, so Jack found a lawyer, Bernard Lazarus, who advised buying the site with a mortgage. The lender advised an accountant and, through Lazarus, Frank Cooper was found. He was horrified that a business turning over £119,000 was not registered. He sorted out the books and arranged the formal separation of Jack the individual from Jack's business.

Jack established two companies: Tesco Stores Ltd and J. E. Cohen and Company Ltd. The first was the retail side; the second was the wholesale division. Each entity had paid-up capital of £100 and each had the same two directors: John Edward (Jack) and Sarah (Cissie)

Cohen. The business was called Tesco after the tea which, along with Snowflake milk, was its most important product. The tea wholesaler, T. E. Stockwell, had registered the brand in 1924 and transferred it to Jack for nothing.

The very first store to bear the Tesco fascia, at Burnt Oak according to Cohen's authorized biography, did, however, break Jack's mould in one very important way. After he bought the site, he traded in Burnt Oak as he did the other stalls and covered shops: groceries were auctioned in bundles. Thanks to the arrival of a new recruit, Thomas Freake, who had managed shops in Islington, all this changed. He said customers should be able to see straight away what was on offer, and to achieve this he built pyramids of the products. So began the pile it high, sell it cheap approach that Tesco maintained for the following four decades. Jack put Freake in charge at Burnt Oak – and also at Green Lanes, which he acquired at around the same time – and sales at the store doubled. On 24 January 1934 Tesco Stores was registered as a private company.

Tesco Stores Ltd – still the supermarket's trading name in the UK – boasted a warehouse, a couple of market stands, six pitches and two small shops. The tiny team's universe was quite unlike the one inhabited by the best-known retailers of the day, who were J. Sainsbury, the Co-operative – which then had 24,000 stores – and a chain called International. They were the smarter side of grocery retail. Jack's ideas for his small shops, roofs apart, barely differed from the way he ran his market stalls. His shops had roll-down shutters at the front and a trader stood by the stock, shouting out the offers.

Jack saw opportunities anywhere and everywhere he passed through. As the early thirties' Depression gradually gave way to growth, the new industries – electricals, chemicals and motor – meant new factories and large housing estates. House-builders looked then, as now, for retailers to anchor the high streets that served their new developments. Jack Cohen was not always first choice, but he struck up relationships that enabled him to acquire sites at Elm Park, Wimbledon, Enfield, Staines, Ealing, Hornchurch,

Croydon and Watford. The neat ring around London happened by accident as much as by design. There was little strategy involved: Jack loved a property deal in the way he loved picking up a consignment of dented tins. He was after an attractive proposition at a great price.

Dame Shirley Porter remembers how, when she was a small girl, family trips mingled leisure with business. 'We'd be going along and he'd suddenly say "This looks like a good place for a shop!" and he'd leap out and chat a few people up, have a look around, go into the local estate agent. That's how he bought quite a lot of shops: by feel, by instinct, by smell. For many years it was like that: how many people live in the area, what's the socio-economic grouping, who else is here? He was right then because the suburbs were popping up everywhere and there were new people and all you had to have was confidence and faith. He was doing his own market research.'[2]

For Jack's staff, operating these shops was hard work. The lorry would arrive and boxes would be unloaded one by one. Food could not always be put straight into the shop, as sometimes it had to be prepared or repacked – from pats of butter to packets of tea. Then there were the hours. Managers opened early, then simply stayed open for as long as they could. Many women had to wait for their husbands to get home on a Friday evening with the week's wages before they could get the shopping in, so that meant trading at 9 p.m., notwithstanding the 1928 Shops Act having limited opening hours. Late-night shopping is nothing new.

His growing chain of shops in the suburbs – there were forty Tescos by 1935, though some of those acquired from other retailers didn't display the name immediately – did not mean Jack had lost his market-trader mentality and it certainly did not calm antipathy from the big manufacturers towards jumped-up barrow boys. Makers such as Cadbury, Kellogg's, Heinz and Beecham had Resale Price Maintenance protecting their sales and profits. Certain house-hold staples were off-limits for Tesco and its customers. Jack was buying, and selling, large volumes of lines that manufacturers could not shift through regular outlets. Sweets from a Keiller factory at Plaistow, Upton Park, which had shut; elastic tape that had no stretch; baked beans from Leningrad: Jack's customers got them repackaged at keen prices.

The business was doing well and Tesco opened a new head-quarters, Tesco House, in 1934. It was at Angel Road, Edmonton – despite its name, an unlovely section of what is now known more prosaically as the North Circular Road, roughly between the present A10 underpass and the Lea Valley Viaduct. In 1934 the offices transcended their ordinary surroundings with a little West End glamour: furnishings were by Heal's. In addition, the ten trucks and vans were given a Tesco livery. The warehouse employed twenty-four men.

In the same year, Cohen moved his family from Gunton Road, Hackney, to Chessington Avenue, Finchley – just a ten-minute drive west along the North Circular from Jack's Angel Road HQ but a world away for the family. Large, elegant homes were being built on what were then Finchley's green acres, where a self-made man could stretch out and let his family breathe pure air. The home that Shirley Porter remembers was in the latest art deco style, with every modern luxury and, like Tesco House, was kitted out by Heal's – maybe Jack got a good discount on a bulk purchase.

Tesco's early success brought the Cohen family a sort of status and some of the trappings traditionally reserved for British aristocracy. There were beautiful dolls and teddy bears for the girls, who were brought up emulating the little princesses, Elizabeth and Margaret Rose. Where a stately home would have a billiards room, Jack had a large games room with a dartboard and a snooker table (a game which Shirley got rather good at). Certainly the recollections of his employees and family suggest that Jack and Cissie loved the luxuries and the lifestyle that success could bring. The Cohens were an ordinary family living an extraordinary life.

By 1938, Tesco's profits stood at £105,000 and were growing year on year. Then came war. For the Cohens, it started a little early and, had they had less luck, it could have ended very differently for them.

Porter recalls the summer of 1939, when she was not quite nine.

'We were in the south of France and we went to this hotel and when we woke up in the morning there weren't any people around. They had all gone. We got into the car – it was a Sunbeam Talbot. The chauffeur had come too. There was a famous bandleader, Joe Loss, there with his wife. They didn't have any means of transport [so] we all piled in this car. Off we went, day and night. My parents realized terrible things were happening. We finally arrived at Dieppe, which was absolutely crowded with people. We were very lucky. We got on the last ship that left France.'[3]

Safely across the Channel in their recently acquired seaside bungalow at Worthing, the family was listening to the radio with friends, along with most of the country, when war was declared.

'There was an awful feeling,' Porter recalls. 'Chamberlain made his speech. We were at war. I burst out crying.' The young Cohen sisters took to sitting on the beach at Worthing, waiting for the Germans.

On the eve of the Second World War, Jack had nearly 100 shops. His approach to buying products remained exactly as it had been when he ran market stalls: whether it was tinned milk or red salmon – another great seller for Jack, who re-branded it with some 'Red Glow' labels he had bought cheap from a printer who had no other home for them – the point was to get a great price and buy lots of it. This bulk-buy tactic had an unforeseen benefit when rationing was introduced. Retailers were allocated scarce goods based on their pre-war purchasing patterns, deemed an acceptable guide as to where customers had chosen to shop. Daisy Hyams unearthed cardboard boxes full of purchase orders covering the previous three years and dispatched them to Whitehall's officials, who were based by then in north Wales. The paperwork showed that Tesco bought and sold large volumes, which meant it was allocated a healthy share of available goods. When the government asked citizens to register with a grocer in order to receive rationed goods from January 1940 onwards, Tesco's range and volume of goods not yet on ration swung a fair few housewives its way. The other significant factor was the location of the new shops in the suburbs and on estates. It was a virtuous circle: the more demand, the more supply the government granted.

The equality of rationing – the sense that everybody was getting more or less the same, affluent or not – possibly broke down some of the pre-war tendency to be picky about a retailer's pedigree.

Jack had spotted his customers' need for fairness a year before the government, as it happened. In the months after war was declared, Tesco introduced a points system for registered customers for goods even before they were officially rationed. This helped customers to feel that they were being treated fairly. The Ministry of Food introduced a similar system in 1941 and Cohen was one of the retailers brought on to the Ministry's Food Trade Emergency Committee.

The government's system of allocating rationed goods to retailers was partly responsible for the rise in Tesco's fortunes during the war years. By 1941, profits were £131,000. By 1942, there were so many shops that the forward-thinking Thomas Freake had taken on three inspectors to keep tabs on them.

Jack's family was by now very, very wealthy. His daughters, being brought up to be 'perfect little English ladies', clothed at Harrods, Fortnum and Debenhams, were sent off to boarding school. War meant school evacuation away from the south coast to Cornwall, where they watched dog fights off Land's End as well as knitting scarves for sailors on the Atlantic convoys.

'We were probably very precious, cosseted, spoiled little girls,' Porter admits. Yet she loathed the nice, English, upper-middle-class boarding schools she attended. She says they turned her from a happy child into a rebel. She was finally allowed to leave by Jack, after he argued with the headmistress: he took the view that Shirley had been denied the head girl's post, and her name in gilt on wooden panels, because of her surname.

'Trade was looked down on,' she explains. 'It wasn't quite nice to be a shopkeeper. Perhaps that's why we were different. Fay Courage was there – she'd have come from the brewing family. For some reason that was acceptable – old money and brewers were acceptable but grocers, pile it high and sell it cheap, were not.'[4]

She lived for the holidays and home, where life was full of surprises. To the family's astonishment, their regular electrician, with whom Shirley used to make models of Spitfires in a Golders Green workshop, was arrested, tried and convicted for the murder, dismemberment and aerial dumping into the sea of an underworld boss. The double life of tradesmen aside, home was interesting because it was interwoven with the expanding, occasionally exotic and always novel developments at Tesco.

For Jack, business and home life were inextricably intertwined: business was pleasure and pleasure was business. When he bought a nice country farm in a pretty corner of Essex at Maldon around 1940, it was no accident that his purchase included Goldhanger Fruit Farms. Before too long, the fruit farm was supplying Tesco's shelves with bottled jam and frozen fruit – a novelty then – as well as providing country weekends for friends and family.

'It was not grand at all. It was a proper thirties, ordinary house. But we had horses,' Shirley remembers. Somewhat incongruously, visitors would be conveyed to the 'ordinary' house from the stations at Colchester or Chelmsford in a pony and trap. The Cohens liked to have Sunday lunch at the local pub with the landlords, Mr and Mrs Offord. Jack plucked the parts of life he liked, whether or not they matched up.

Even on holiday, he was at work. After the war he took Shirley to South Africa and to southern Europe, where her schoolgirl Italian came in handy negotiating for cherries and tomatoes. 'He couldn't speak the language and I couldn't add up,' she remembers, adding that he characteristically struck up lasting friendships with suppliers.

All those who remember him say that Jack had no interest in pretending he was anything other than a Hackney boy made good. 'He taught us Second World War songs and he had rude ones, such as "Dan, Dan the lavatory man",' says Shirley, adding that her father's repertoire of blue jokes and songs drove her mother mad. He never changed his accent. 'The East End was where he started and he never forgot it or put on any airs or graces. He had that nasal twang. He used back-slang. You took the first letter of a word and put it at the end and added an "a". I don't know if it was to do with "Watch out – the police are coming", but certainly it was used in the East End by the market boys. Other people couldn't understand, so we found it great fun. The only time I ever heard [my parents] use Yiddish was "*Nisht mit der kinder*" [Not in front of the children].'[5]

Jack, being working class like his customers, knew well what basic goods they wanted and he sold them at prices most established grocers would not entertain. The result was that, as the 1940s continued, Tesco consolidated its position as a profitable purveyor of basic products to ordinary English housewives. Personally, the Cohen family was enjoying unimagined affluence and, snobbery notwithstanding (not many society doors would open to an East End Jewish grocer), even some social status. Jack and Cissie's charitable work brought a visit from Lady Churchill to Chessington Avenue, where they hosted an auction in aid of the Russian Ambulance Service: two bananas – then virtually unknown and exotic luxuries – went under the hammer. The proceeds were sent to help the relief effort after the Battle of Stalingrad.

Life was pretty good for Tesco and for the Cohens. But every child born into a precarious financial environment knows that money can be lost faster than it is made. Jack's background, and his innate exuberance for the next deal, made it unlikely that he would slow down and enjoy his success from a comfy chair at Chessington Avenue.

Chapter 3

Britain's Counter Revolution: Was Self-service Jack's Genius Moment?

'You had a counter at the front and the customer would bring in and put on the counter what they wanted and you added up by remembering the prices. By today's standards the Finchley shop was rough, rough, rough.'

Eddie Clark, former regional managing director[1]

'Whilst during 1949 we successfully maintained our turnover, I regret our profits margin decreased . . . Steps have been taken.'

Jack Cohen[2]

It was the housewives of St Albans who were the unwitting guinea pigs for Jack's next experiment. He travelled to America and – though he had seen supermarkets on a pre-war visit – this time he was really struck with their potential. The American chains, such as Safeway, Food Fare, Atlantic & Pacific, had light, bright, spacious aisles stocked with attractively packaged groceries. Customers piled goods into trolleys then trundled to and through the checkout. About half of American food retailers were self-service, Jack was told, but they had around 80 per cent of grocery sales. He became determined to see what this system could do for English customers.

It so happened that at the moment he was checking out American shops, Jack's own stores were struggling to turn profit under the weight of higher costs, including wage bills and rising commodity prices. Those could not be passed on to consumers in an age of austerity. In turning to self-service, however, Jack came up with a solution that now seems obvious but at the time was not. Later, he would happily allow people to credit him with bringing the concept of the self-service supermarket from the United States back to Britain. Strictly speaking, there was already a Self-Service Development Association in England, set up after the war by two Co-operative Society retailers, but it was Jack who saw the possibilities and actually got on with making the idea a reality.

He chose St Albans as a test-bed. Redford Fisher, the manager at St Peter's Street, opened the shop in October 1947 with wall shelving, a central island and a National Cash Register near the door. The till began to ring at a satisfying rate with illuminating immediacy. Takings went from £350 to £600 a week within a fortnight, settling back at an average £500.

One of the reasons that self-service would not have been the obvious way forward in the late forties was purely social: prevailing wisdom was that customers would shun any shop so ill-mannered as to leave basket-filling to its clientele. It did seem that the middle-classes balked a bit, despite the initial success, and that may be why self-service at the St Albans shop lasted only about a year. There was also an issue with pilfering. However, it was enough to show Jack that he was on to something. The St Albans store was converted to self-service once more in 1949 and this time it lasted.

Dame Shirley Porter says her father never sat still. She recalls the tie pins he had made: 'YCDBSOYA: you can't do business sitting on your arse. He used to give them to prime ministers, anybody and everybody. He would not have got on in politics because he couldn't keep his mouth closed: he would say what he felt and be difficult. He could really lose his temper. He would be very sorry about it afterwards. If he had any politics at all, it was YCDBSOYA. He believed in people and hard work. He believed in doing things for yourself and he was very, very family-minded.'[3]

Jack hired his family – trusting them above all others – but he took his temper out on them. In 1946 he had persuaded his son-in-law, Irene's husband Hyman Kreitman, to join the company, but bullied him publicly and often. Perhaps Jack was worth putting up with: Hyman was one of the four founding directors when Tesco went to the City in 1947 to raise funds for expansion, and therefore he benefitted significantly from a material standpoint.

Tesco's offer document to prospective shareholders sets out what the business looked like as it went public. There were 110 stores, grouped under the control of four inspectors who answered to Thomas Freake, by then director of retail operations. The business had fixed assets of £120,000. Jack was the majority shareholder by a hefty margin, with 922,910 shares. But by the second AGM – at the Angel Road headquarters on 1 September 1950 – Freake had left. Possibly he was disenchanted with his standing in relation to the family. Possibly, not being family, he did not have to tolerate Jack's temper. Tesco's Annual Report puts it like this: 'On the 16th June 1950 Mr T. E. Freake . . . tendered his resignation as a Director from all Companies in the group, on the grounds, as he alleged, that decisions with which he was in disagreement had been made without reference to him and he has instituted proceedings for damages for breach of contract.' In other words, Freake and Cohen had had an almighty row, the details of which have never emerged but which took nearly two years to settle out of court.

The bigger bombshell that year – and possibly not unrelated – was that Tesco's profits had dropped off a cliff. The financial vital statistics and directors' update were conveyed on eight unassuming pages of typescript in the Annual Report. Trading profits were £76,750 against £113,597 in 1948.

Jack was apologetic: 'Whilst during 1949 we successfully maintained our turnover, I regret our profits margin decreased. This was due to the incidence of rising costs of commodities, increased wages and higher overheads, the full impact of which could not be passed on to the consumer. This we experienced in common with our competitors.'

Tesco's setback was a sign of changing consumer tastes in Britain. Jack noted a 'serious decline' in demand for imported foods, 'of which we had large stocks', and increased demand for 'proprietary commodities'. He cleared slow stock, incurring losses. 'Steps have been taken,' he stated.

Although Jack was wealthy, it was not through ramping up his salary. His fortunes were inextricably linked to those of the business. The Annual Reports show that the directors' remuneration barely altered for years. Jack owned a lot of Tesco stock. When the company prospered, he would benefit along with his shareholders; when it struggled, he would feel it at once.

Self-service was the rabbit in his soft, felt hat. 'Your Board is continually endeavouring to improve the nature and widen the scope of the business. Therefore in October 1949, one of our shops [St Albans] was converted into a self-service unit with the object of indicating to the Board the possibilities of this type of trading. The experiment proved successful in that it provided us with an increase in turnover at a very small increase in operating costs. It is our intention to pursue this policy when opportune.'

Tesco's shops in the post-war years certainly had a long way to go. Ronald 'Eddie' Clark joined Tesco not long after the company went public and remembers that the standard of the stores varied widely, from adequate to poor. There was little in the way of training and managers were left to their own devices, Thomas Freake's inspectors notwithstanding.

Clark was one of the early recruits to the post-war business. Like tens of thousands of British working-class people at that time, his family consumed nothing but absolute essentials, living from week to week on a poor income. Born in May 1925, he was the sixth of the eight children of Frank and Elizabeth Clark, both of whom had been raised in Liverpool orphanages. They moved south, to the terraced streets of Bow in the East End, when Frank followed his job with Kemp's Biscuits. Five years later the family moved to a council house in Burnt Oak, near Edgware. Upstairs it had an indoor bathroom, which to them was unqualified luxury, although four of the brothers still at home had to share one tiny bedroom, two sisters another and the parents the third. But Clark remembers his childhood fondly: the annual holiday – a day-return coach trip to go paddling in Southend; spending his pocket money ha'pennies at the sort of tiny sweetshop found on most street corners in Bow – 'you could buy anything you liked so long as you shared any sweets you bought with Mum'; listening to his brother play the piano in the front parlour; or playing solo whist with his father and siblings. Hearing him talk of what we would consider real privation, there are no echoes of Monty Python's 'Four Yorkshiremen' sketch. It's just the way things were for the Clarks and for most ordinary British families.

The main Sunday meal was eaten in shifts, with the elder children, who went to work, getting first choice of the food. 'We used to have what they couldn't eat. There was not a lot of meat. My brother said: "Guess who's buying it?" I said: "You wait until I go to work. I'll have a pork chop all of my own." We had sprouts, cauliflower and leeks. They were cheap. Pudding invariably was rice pudding or custard or treacle tart. It was water at the table. We never had squash or that type of drink. The Corona man would come once a week. He delivered on the Saturday morning and you would have that on Saturday and Sunday afternoon. We used to get a glass each and you would look along to see if the measure was the same as everybody else's. Mum and Dad would always have less than ours. Sometimes there would be apples or pears, "scrumped" by the children from garden trees – the only type of dishonesty tolerated at home.

'If you had dinner at home, it was chips and peas. Just that. It was better eating at school than at home because Mum couldn't afford it. We had bread and margarine at tea. It wasn't frugal to us in those days. It's only as you grow older you see. It was quite common in those days.

'Children didn't wear socks. Sandals were worn through winter with no socks. Mum spent five hours a day on washing. It is almost impossible to believe that you do your job and then go home and look after eight children. Our house was very clean. Our shoes had to be very clean. You were taught at a young age to tie your shoe laces and clean your shoes with Cherry Blossom.'[4]

Clark says his upbringing made him determined to build a better life for himself. 'I got my first job because there was a notice in the window saying "Boy wanted". I left school on the Friday and started Monday week. That was the longest time I've ever been unemployed.'[5]

The Second World War meant that Clark joined up in 1942, opting for the navy because even the few stories his father shared about his time in the trenches in 1914–18 were enough to put him off the army. Clark liked the navy with its routines and says he saw parts of the world that otherwise would have been unknown to a working-class Londoner of his era. In particular, his time in America exposed him to a bright world of consumer luxury and social well-being. Engaged to an American girl from a well-to-do family, he encountered napkins and coffee cups for the first time. He met people who owned horses. He decided to go to college to 'improve himself' and to stay in America. Then Mary, his fiancée, was killed in a riding accident. Clark returned to England with his American dream shattered, but also aware of a more consumer-focused society than most British people would have been able to comprehend.

His first post-war job was selling insurance policies door to door for the Provident Association. It enabled him to put down the deposit on a home at Palmers Green in North London and he recalls the beginnings of the surge in home-ownership. 'At that time the Provident Association of London did a policy for thirty or thirty-five years and after three years of holding the policy you could borrow the rest of the money – 80 per cent or more of it – at a fixed rate of 4.5 per cent. That's what people did. It was a good scheme. First of all I sold them knocking on doors. You looked for an older property and looked for two or three bells. Usually the best one was the top one. The bottom one was often the owner. You had a very small salary and commission.

'I had to go to college before I got the insurance job and [while I was there] I had to get a job where I could get flexi-time. I became a London bus driver. At college I was being trained in man management. I spoke like a Cockney: that wasn't appreciated by the big companies. "Firty free farsand fevvers" and "gertcha" and "naaaah" never went down very well. I felt very, very awkward. They said I needed to get rid of that. Go to college, work hard and speak a bit different. One night a week, a Friday night, I used to go to voice-training classes run by a lady. She'd say "It's not 'nar', Ronald, which is what I was called then, it's 'nowww'. Open your mouth, dear."

'I'd been doing it for about six or seven weeks. I went home to my father. I'll never forget it. I said "Good afternoon, Dad". Well you used to say "Artnoon". Never the name or "good". You'll never believe it, but he started to do the same. By the time he died he didn't speak like a Cockney.'[6]

Clark believed that to move up in the insurance company he would have to leave London for offices in the north of England. He wanted to stay in the capital, so looked around for another job and it was then that he saw an advert for Tesco. 'I said to myself come hard times people always want food.'

Now in his eighties, Clark lives not far from his old home at Burnt Oak geographically, but miles away in terms of lifestyle. Tesco became his route to wealth and prosperity and his appreciation of that fact cemented his loyalty to the company. Clark never made the main Board himself, but he managed future Board directors when they themselves were new to Tesco, including Philip Clarke and David Potts. He is one of the few Tesco people who can recall in vivid detail how the shops developed over the decades and became what they are today. By nature he was fiercely loyal to those who ran the company and would become a close ally of future boss Ian MacLaurin: he was known as 'Ian MacLaurin's enforcer'. He is one of the managers whose personalities shaped the company from the level below the Board downwards.

The group that Clark joined in the early 1950s was a mish-mash of stores – some of them trading under Tesco's fascia and some trading under whatever name they had had when Jack Cohen bought and bolted them on to his growing estate – such as Courts Food Stores of London's Bayswater. The first shop in which Clark worked was at Kenton, North-west London. 'It was counter-service and was run by a cheery Yorkshireman. A smile a mile wide. I was there about six months learning how to bone and cut bacon. The butter came in a big box and you had to get it out and cut it and pat it. You become very good at cutting a pound and a half pound of butter. He taught you how to cut it into twenty-four blocks of butter weighing two pound. I enjoyed doing it. The staff canteen was an upturned dustbin in the warehouse. There were no chairs. Your tea break was just that: a cup of tea.

'After three months a guy came in – George Matthews. He was the inspector. He was a wonderful man. He was big, clumsy, a laugh. He came from Lancashire. He did have this very good chuckle. He wasn't brilliantly educated and he spoke worse than I did. He said, "Listen to me, we want a manager for our store in Whetstone." I said, "I didn't know we had a Tesco there." He said, "We don't, it is a Burnards." My heart sank into my boots. That store had a roll-top front, a counter one side and a counter the other. The smell when I opened up was like old boots. It had a stone floor. It was mucky. A girl came in and said, "What you doing here?" I said, "I'm your new manager." There were two girls and two fellas, including me. It was a store Sir John had bought. He must have had a funny whim. The turnover wasn't great but it went up a bit.'[7]

In fact, Burnards was not so much bought on a whim but as a valuable fillip to Tesco's recovering profits. On 22 June 1955, the Tesco Board approved the purchase of the whole business, paying Charles Berzin £175,000 for its nineteen stores. They were cut-price retailers who adapted quickly to the relaxing of wartime fixed pricing and were now taking more money than the entire Tesco group. Arthur Thrush, later to train Ian MacLaurin, arrived as part of the package, along with another future influence in Tesco, Fred Turner. Eddie Clark remembers Thrush, whose professional obsession was the ratio of profit to wages in every shop. 'Arthur Thrush had a laugh that was infectious even when the wage percent was not 4.5 per cent, although it was a powerful dream of his to keep the wage percent at 4.5 per cent. He used to give some of the lads such a wigging sometimes [but] he was a very happy fellow. He was not a university man or an academic, but he was nice and he knew what made people tick and if you have that knowledge you have a lot to beat. Later on, he could have you in his office and the phone would go and he'd have an earpiece so you could listen as well. When he finished the call he would say, "That is how I would like all of us to be on the phone: polite and gentle." He used to say that you could be being taped at the other end and you could be saying things that you would regret if they became known.'[8]

Clark did well at Whetstone and was installed as manager at the Finchley store, just up the high road from the Cohen family home. Not much better than a market stall, it was the sort of general store springing up in many suburbs. Clark remembers: 'It was a single-fronted store with a plate-glass window which was taken out and a shutter came down instead. You had a counter at the front and the customer would bring in and put on the counter what they wanted and you added up by remembering the prices. By today's standards the Finchley shop was rough, rough, rough. At the time we'd be below Fine Fare and then there was Victor Value before Tesco bought it out. We were on a par with Victor Value, which we thought was a bit ropey.'[9]

This was decades before the introduction of marketing departments, so it was the manager's job to display and promote the goods. Groceries were arranged on shelves on the left-hand side as a customer walked in, with dairy products at the back. Goods such as polishes and cleaning fluid would be down the right-hand side of the shop and the floor was covered with linoleum.

'We had a display of eggs, as I wanted to sell a lot. We ordered forty cases instead of twenty. This guy came down from the head office and said, "The rep says you've ordered double. I hope you've got permission from head office because even Victor Value doesn't sell that amount." We got this display and a chicken called Ernie: "*These two together give us health and vitality.*" We sold them – the chicken and the egg. I've used that a lot. There was something to look at and laugh about.'[10]

According to Clark, there was very little coherency throughout the

Tesco group: 'There were 95 managing directors and 55 owners. Managers had the right to do almost anything they wanted to do and I really couldn't understand it. Reps used to call. The Peek Freans' rep would say: "You've sold out of petit beurre, I'll order you six since you sold three." I used to say: "No I'll have four. If everybody doubled their order I'd have no room in the warehouse."

'I invented what you'd call the stock-order sales card. If the stock was six and you've still got five then you'd write "nil" in the order column. George Matthews [the store inspector] cottoned on to it and he said this is good. In the end it was printed in head office and came out from head office. It seemed to me you didn't order ten if you'd sold one, but it was in the rep's interest to sell you ten more because he'd be on a small wage and commission. What happened in Finchley was the stock holding went down. If we were taking £500 a week, stock on hand was something like £3,000. All that money invested in stock. I reduced it down to two weeks. On some lines it was a week and a half. I could cross it off completely. I had that right as the manager. If the rep came in with a new line I could buy it. You had carte blanche. I used to say to George this is all wrong. I used to say, "I'm John Cohen, I'm you and I'm my manager. It can't be right."'[11]

Jack had responded to his customers' aspirations when he moved from market stalls to basic shops. Now he allowed his son-in-law Hyman Kreitman to convince him to install glass windows instead of the kind of roll-down shutters that Eddie Clark found at Finchley and the early 1950s saw a steady conversion to the new look, as well as to self-service shops. The 1950 Annual Report recorded that twenty 'units' had the new look by the end of that year. By the end of May 1951, thirty-five had been converted 'to this type of trading which,' opined Jack, 'is proving satisfactory'. This was despite the disconcerting truth that one of the impacts of self-service was an increase in shoplifting. Jack, however, was relatively philosophical: just as he tolerated store managers cutting deals provided that they made money for him, he accepted that pilfering was a side-effect of self-service because the growth in profits far outweighed the losses.

Part of the haphazard approach that Clark observed must be attributed to Jack's personal style. His piecemeal purchasing made it almost impossible to keep track of what was being sold. The answer was to delegate.

Edgar Ralph Collar, managing director of Mores Stores (another London-based multiple grocer) was identified as the man for the job. He came to Tesco House one day in October 1950, passing the disgruntled and departing director Thomas Freake, who was standing on the doorstep waiting for a lift home because he had just resigned and had handed in his car keys. Whether or not they spoke, or whether Collar, the cautious accountant, had other reasons for resisting, it took nine months for Jack to woo him. At last, in June 1951, he joined the Board. He introduced branch accounts and suddenly a clearer picture of profits, stock results and something euphemistically known as 'leakage' emerged.

By 1953, Queen Elizabeth's coronation year, Tesco was describing itself as more than simply Tesco Stores. It was now 'Tesco Stores Multiple & Wholesale Grocers & Provision Merchants'. Although profits were still not yet back to 1948 levels, the business was in sound shape: assets were robust (with the vast majority held as freehold property) and the board had been assiduously paying down debt. Jack remained gloomy about rising costs and falling demand for his trusty tinned goods from abroad, but the lifting of rationing – for most goods in 1953, but not totally until 1954 – greatly encouraged him.

Jack was also driving hard: sixty-three of his shops had by now been converted to self-service, he was opening new stores all the time (two years later, four-fifths of the estate was self-service) and he was also on the look-out for acquisition – that year, for instance, he paid £6,533 for Durbin's Stores at Ealing. His confidence was growing and in his 1953 chairman's address he offered shareholders a taste of what was to come: 'I now look forward to the freedom of supplies of all commodities and welcome competition, which I feel must come, as it is my opinion that this is essential in order to give value and a first-class service to the public. This group of companies was built up successfully in the pre-war days of acute competition by giving the best possible value for money, and it is our aim to continue this policy.'

Tesco's core strategy, then, was not for changing. British shoppers, though, were.

Chapter 4

Gadgets and Groceries:
Living Like the Other Half

'The Food Industry has become the most competitive trade in the country. Food and allied items are being offered to the housewife at prices well below anything that has been put before her in Post-War years ... In Peckham, where Tesco began in such a small way some thirty years ago, there stands today a modern supermarket.'

Sir Jack Cohen, July 1959[1]

'The fifties were wonderful years. There was plenty of work and plenty of enjoyment. People were happy. People by then had started to earn money because there was so much work about that you could have two or three jobs.'

Beryl Hinde, former Tesco shop assistant[2]

As a summary of the state of the British nation a decade after the Second World War, Harold Macmillan's July 1957 observation that 'most of our people have never had it so good' remains hard to beat. 'Go around the country,' he urged the Tory faithful of Bedford, 'go to the industrial towns, go to the farms and you will see a state of prosperity such as we have never had in my lifetime – nor indeed in the history of this country.'

If one measure of good times is that housewives have a tempting array of new gadgets and groceries within their grasp, if happiness is a Hoover, then many households were indeed contemplating easier, more colourful lives. For people who had experienced the Depression, war and rationing, this was an incredible change in fortune. Before the 1950s, large numbers of ordinary British families had regarded even bedsheets as a luxury and sleeping in your coat nothing much to remark upon. Now technological advances provided shiny, exciting, new products, and they also created jobs. Unemployment was below 2 per cent, while the male average weekly wage had almost doubled during the decade, outstripping retail price rises. Car-ownership doubled, and women such as Beryl Hinde from Enfield, later to join Tesco's butcher's department at the Cheshunt store, were rushing to join the workforce and fill factory jobs in the sunrise industries.

The Hinde family was, geographically and economically, typical of those people beginning to shop in stores such as Jack's as British living standards and choices rapidly improved. Born at home in Enfield in July 1933, fewer than 6 miles up the A10 from where Jack was then living, Beryl had a more typically English home life than little Irene and Shirley Cohen and her story emphasizes how greatly British lives were transformed after the Second World War. It is a poignant and intrinsically interesting account told in a matter-of-fact manner that belies how extraordinary the changes she describes really were.

Beryl Hinde was one of nine children, the daughter of a gun-maker who himself had been one of eighteen children. 'Most men in Enfield either worked on the land in greenhouses or in the Royal Small Arms. It was the main industry in Enfield. Enfield was countrified when I was young. You got dressed up on a Sunday and you just walked and met people like that. After the war and the Americans had been here they started bringing in the dance halls, but before that it was just pictures and walking. My dad first of all worked in the greenhouses in Cheshunt, but when the war started he got a job in the Small Arms. He couldn't read and write until my mum taught him. He made one of the first ever Bren guns and he was quite proud of that. They were all individually made in those days.

'Because of the bombing, we had to be evacuated. I went first with my two elder brothers to Hitchin [Hertfordshire] and we were there for two years, then we came back home. Then I was sent off with the younger children to Southport [Lancashire]. It took three days to get there. My younger brother was eighteen months and I was eight and I was his mother. I had to look after him.

'Nobody wanted four children. My mum had told us we had got to stay together. In the end it was knocking on doors. They had to take you if they had a spare room. My two brothers went off into their home and then I took the youngest one with me. He was still a baby and was wetting the bed. They used to smack him, so I smacked them. We were put into a home for naughty children and that's where we spent the next four years. We had a dormitory. We were fed, clothed and then sent out. It was a hotel on the front at Southport, the posh end of Blackpool. Our saving was that the Americans were there and they were very good to us. We were sent out after breakfast to walk the streets. One day we found my other two brothers. They went to school and they were looked after in a family home.

'Much of that part of my life has been wiped out of my memory. Mum said she used to send us parcels but we never received them. We didn't really get any contact. You were just in limbo land. You had your label on you telling people where you lived. It was a nothing time. It was always cold and it was always raining. We lived like urchins really. It was life, wasn't it? I don't think it made us any worse.

'I was busy looking after a little boy who thought I was his mum. It was very difficult when we came back. There was no schooling because the schools had been bombed. We went through another year without any education.

'After the war, when things got back together again, it was a different life. Our home was very warm but it was very, very basic. You couldn't get anything. You didn't have sheets on the bed. You just had a blanket and probably Dad's army overcoat. You always seemed to be cold in the bedrooms. We always had a fire downstairs. We had to go with a barrow to the railway station to pick up the coal. My dad had three allotments and he worked them. We always had vegetables. Anything that grew in the ground my dad would grow, and one row of chrysanthemums for my mum.

'The lights came on and it was a new life. You could walk about and be happy and see all your friends. The streets were lit up, the shops were lit up, dance halls were lit. It had been so dark for so many years and we were lit up again. Everybody just came alive. Wonderful times.'[3]

'My father wasn't earning very much in those days. Probably about £3 with all his overtime. The rent was 12 [shillings] and 6 [pence] a week. The rest of the money was spent on food and clothing all of us.

'We didn't have a lot, but we played and we were happy. We went to Epping Forest. Dad would send us off with a loaf of bread and a bottle of water and you'd spend the whole day there and he would come and get us. It never got dark because you had double summer time then. I think my mum worked in a tin factory. It was just a source of getting money. I had to stay at school until I was fifteen because they put the school-leaving age up. You had to take domestic science or office practice, but you didn't learn a lot.

'Most schools had been bombed, so you went to someone's house. I was head girl in the end. When you went to work there were a few children who had been to school and they did the office work, but most people worked in factories or in shops.

'I left school in 1948 and went to work. The fifties were wonderful years. There was plenty of work and plenty of enjoyment. People were happy. People by then had started to earn money because there was so much work about that you could have two or three jobs. I had two jobs. I've always liked going to work. I worked in a factory in the day and in a canteen at night.

'You couldn't afford to buy much because although there were clothes around then they were very expensive. We used to curl our hair up in iron curlers, which left your hair rusty. Everybody had curls. You wore sweatshirts because of the American influence in the pictures. You wore skirts with lots of layers of lace because they bounced when you did the dancing. The boys were very smart in their Teddy boy clothes. It was an era of clothes. Everybody dressed up and wanted to look good. I had the pickle, the beauty spot that we made with blacking. We used to blacken our eyebrows by putting a stick up the chimney. We had sugar water in our hair to be like a lacquer. We had lots of tricks. We used to mix cocoa with flour to have powder on our faces. It used to go on the boys' shirts when you danced with them.'[4]

Hinde's first job at a chocolate factory brought her freedom and money, though a portion of what she earned went straight into her family's kitty. 'In those days you gave up the bulk of your money to your parents. That was part of life. If you earned £1.10.0 [£1.50] you gave your mum £1.5.0 [£1.25] so you had 5 shillings [25p] for yourself. Most children gave up most of their money to their parents for their keep.'[5]

Beryl recalls that everybody was in the same boat and helped each other. Money was never discussed outside the home, and produce from the allotment was shared around.

For the first time, ordinary British people had money in their pockets and a growing range of products was being manufactured. Retailers had to respond.

'The social life of the country has undergone profound changes,' Tesco's Board noted in 1959. 'There has been a levelling-up of incomes that has altered the whole pattern of shopping, while the structure and layout of shop premises, the methods of merchandising and display, the techniques of warehousing and packaging have been continuously developed and improved.' Tesco had grown, they explained, by 'keeping abreast of these changes' and 'in some cases pioneering them'. They predicted: 'The next decade will see even more rapid changes, and imaginative, flexible planning will be needed to anticipate every new trend'.[6]

Tesco went to town, by its usual unexciting standards, on the Annual Report for that year. It was a production of glossy loveliness compared to the usual eight or so pages of close typescript. Money

was found for a glossy cover featuring pencil-drawn, modern buildings adjacent to neat lawns. Just visible are the corrugated-iron roofs
of the warehouse behind it. This complex was to be the new Tesco
headquarters, at Cheshunt, further up the Lea Valley from Angel
Road. Limousines are sketched outside the new building, giving an
impression of purring engines as they await important passengers.

Jack liked a bit of luxury – he once owned a racehorse called Tesco
Boy, and he liked to put on his white-tie get-up to take Cissie
dancing at the Trocadero. He sounded, however, an almost
apologetic note to shareholders for taking a moment to be pleased.

'This year we present the Annual Report and Accounts in a rather
more elaborate form than in previous years,' he explained in a foreword. 'The first part of the report reviews the great advance which
the Company has made since its formation, and the front cover
shows an artist's view of the new headquarters building, which with
the most modern food warehouse in the world is now nearing com-
pletion at Cheshunt. We believe that these achievements of the past
and present are sound auguries of our future progress.'

For the first time, there is a photograph of Jack. He has the look
of a Hollywood-movie Prohibition-era detective from the Chicago
police force (South Side). Hyman Kreitman, by then joint managing
director with Jack, is also pictured. He looks like a nice, supporting
actor in an Ealing Studios classic. Tesco was trying very hard to move
with the times.

'Forty years ago Mr. J. E. Cohen started the business that was to
become Tesco,' the review announced. 'Thirty years ago there were
half-a-dozen small shops in the London area. Today there are 150
Tesco Stores in the South of England. For Tesco, life begins at forty
. . . [but] numbers alone do not measure the progress of an organization which is built to serve the public, and Tesco has never
hesitated to close a small uneconomical shop in one location in
order to open a better store in another where the customers need it.
In Peckham, where Tesco began in such a small way some thirty
years ago, there stands today a modern supermarket.'[7]

The emphasis was on quick self-service, to reflect 'the modern trend in retail grocery practice, but trends do not stop. It is the task of Tesco's planners to anticipate not only the demands of the public in 1960 but to foresee the pattern of shopping in the years beyond.'

That included being prepared for another 'startling development': Britain's inclusion in a 'Free Trade Area of Western Europe'.[8] If that happened, customers would have more choice than ever as a greater variety of goods would be affordable and accessible; retailers would need to be positioned to take immediate advantage of such a change.

Tesco's Board stuck its neck out and made some predictions. They are worth noting because they stand the test of hindsight:

1. Supermarket development would continue and demand for self-service would increase. Packaging would continue to improve.
2. 'The habits of the shopping public are not easily predictable for long periods. Some goods will always be better served by sales staff, and the balance between self-service and counter-service must be carefully held to conform with the changing taste of shoppers'.
3. New towns would grow.
4. There would be congestion in the high streets of old ones.
5. Car-ownership would continue to spread – and so would the availability of parking spaces.
6. There would be an increase in the number of working house-wives 'who need the convenience of local stores and comfortable shopping conditions.'
7. All of the above change from district to district.

Ordinary people's aspirations were running high by the end of the fifties. They felt that opportunities were there for the taking and sensed they could have what 'their betters' enjoyed: sound schooling, decent healthcare and good jobs. These people were exactly the kind of shoppers Jack's team could serve best. Tesco's image, though, had barely changed since he was trading off a market barrow.

Chapter 5

A Successful Shambles: British Shopping before Health and Safety

'Retailing has changed so much: what we used to get up to in those days was mind blowing by today's standards. Horrific. But then we went through it. It was our experience and know-how that has created the great Tesco today ... There was no quality control. There were no refrigeration deadlines. It was a very basic industry in those days. We're talking the early sixties and things have changed dramatically over the years. We were at the bottom end of the market.'

Lord MacLaurin, chairman, 1985–97[1]

Ian MacLaurin – now Lord MacLaurin of Knebworth – was the very first Tesco trainee, but he was not a typical Tesco recruit. His mother would certainly never have shopped there; nor would her friends. Supermarkets were simply not 'the thing' in certain quarters, let alone packets-and-tins discounters. There was a link, though: the MacLaurins knew Edgar Collar's family long before Collar became Tesco's finance director. They all used to holiday at Whitstable on the Kent coast, where Collar's family had a department store on the high street. Ian was only a little older than the Collar girls, Ann and Barbara. The bucket-and-spade play-dates matured: in their teens, Ann, by then at St Paul's Girls School in London, would come to watch Ian play cricket or football at his school, Malvern. Sometimes they would go to choral concerts. They were married in 1959, the year that Ian joined Tesco.

Ian's father-in-law to be – pointedly, as it turned out – did not arrange an introduction to Jack; that happened by chance. He had only just completed two years' National Service at the air-force base at Wilmslow, Cheshire ('most of it playing soccer and cricket'), and had taken a job as a washing-machine salesman for a firm owned by the father of another Malvernian. 'I met Jack Cohen at a cricket match for Old Malvernians in Eastbourne. We were staying at the Grand Hotel. Dick Beatty was the manager and he loved cricket. We were dressed for dinner. Jack was in the bar and he was quite taken by these guys in dinner jackets. He bought us all drinks and he gave us all cards. He said, "If any of you guys want jobs come and see me." In September I phoned him. I went up to Cheshunt and he showed me round the warehouse and talked to me about the business. He asked if I wanted a job. I said not really. He asked me what I was earning and I said £900 a year. He said, "If you join me I'll pay you £900, but I'll pay it for six months and if you like me and I like you then I'll make it £1,000 a year and I'll give you a company car." In 1959, £1,000 a year was your first goal. I took it. I went home to my mum and my dad and I remember saying to my mother: "I'm going to join Tesco," and she looked down her nose and said, "I haven't spent all this money on your education for you to join a company like that".'[2]

MacLaurin's parents had aspirations. That they were rearing a retailer would simply not have occurred to them. Ian's mother came from a large family in the Woolwich area of south-east London. His father, Arthur, was a hockey-playing engineer and they met through their shared interest in sport. In 1935 the newly-weds bought one of the houses being built around Esher in Surrey and with it the lifestyle of the English upper-middle class. Number 101, Claygate Lane, Hinchley Wood had four bedrooms, a bathroom and an upstairs lavatory. The large garden backed on to the Surbiton golf course (soon to be ploughed up and farmed for wheat by land girls during the Second World War). Ian was born over the county border at Blackheath because his far-sighted father wanted to guarantee his eligibility to play cricket for Kent.

MacLaurin's memories give a glimpse of the living standards of a small portion of English society on the eve of the Second World War.

'Hinchley Wood was upper-middle class. Esher was very upper class. Oxshott too. They had lots of big houses and lots of big grounds. The chap right next door was a retired army officer; the chap the other side worked for Shell. That sort of ilk – professional people. I was not aware of class as a child, except in those days people looked up to politicians, and the Royal Family was sacrosanct. We sat rigid every Christmas listening to the King's speech.

'It was very Christian. Mother was an enrolling member for Mothers' Union. I was a young chorister – part of the choir that opened Guildford cathedral. People were very churchy then. There was a strong feeling of belonging and getting involved. I didn't come into contact with anybody who was not Christian. Most of our circle went to church. At school, my prep school, every day started with prayers.'[3]

When war broke out, Arthur continued his daily commute to London throughout the Blitz. Ian can remember seeing the bombers heading for the capital and watching aerial dogfights in the Surrey skies. The family's nights were often spent in the air-raid shelter.

'I remember the doodlebugs, wretched things. The engine would cut out, then nothing – [then] a terrific explosion and you knew somebody else had been killed along the line and my mother would say, "Please God let it land in an empty field." One did land nearby and it blew our windows out. There was this tremendous relief that we had won after everything that people had been through.

'Mother shopped a couple of times a week. All the trades were there: two grocers, a baker, a butcher. All the skills were there in the little square of the shopping area in Hinchley Wood. She bought what you could get. Provisions weren't flowing fast and furious. I remember a shopkeeper saying he had a nice little bit of lamb or beef – it was a bit of a treat.

'It was a good childhood. That was life. Everybody had the same so there was no great discussion about it. Breakfast and supper were the big meals of the day and it would be full of home-made stuff in those days. Breakfast was always a cereal and then toast. Sunday was the big meal of the week: after church we always came back and had a special meal.

'There was no drink around. Wine was certainly not available widely. Sherry was drunk by most people as an aperitif. Gin and whisky were not high on the agenda. Fruit and custard was the pudding. There was not huge availability of anything. My mum always did the cooking, my father did the washing-up and I did the drying-up. The evening meal was at half past seven or eight o'clock when he got home and we ate in the kitchen except Sunday lunch, which was in the dining room. You had roast-whatever-the-butcher-had. I always had water to drink, and then latterly orange juice became available. Cocoa and Horlicks were the two big drinks at that time. It was Bourneville Cocoa and tea was Typhoo in our house. Coffee was not a strong drink in volume terms at that time. Topside or sirloin would have been considered a real luxury and if you were really lucky you got a chicken – that was serious luxury – and then the vegetables to go with it. They were virtually all from the UK. You only got exotic fruits, way after the war, at Christmas time. Tangerines came in from Spain just before Christmas and the oranges came from South Africa after Christmas.

'I remember going down for the last time with coupons for my sweets and the lady saying, "You won't need these any more, Ian," but as soon as they went off ration there weren't any in the shops. It had been peppermint toffees during the war. Before ice cream became widely available you had frozen blocks of fruit juice. It was quite an interesting childhood and, compared with now, pretty frugal.'[4]

MacLaurin's mother was determined that he should attend private school, so he was sent to Shrewsbury House prep school at Ditton Hill, Surbiton. He captained the soccer, rugby and cricket teams, but still managed to stay in the top three of the form because his father bought him a new Dinky toy car every time he excelled in a test. From there MacLaurin was sent to Malvern. 'I was a lazy little so-and-so. In those days if you were a good sportsman everything else paled into insignificance.'[5]

When he left Malvern in 1956 the tall, captain-of-every-sport MacLaurin looked set fair for a career commuting from Surrey to the City, or as a schoolmaster with a useful sideline in leading match-winning teams (his mother's dream). That he went on to take a punt on Tesco instead was surprising. His mother was appalled. 'My parents made considerable sacrifices for me to have that education. I had a very, very good start in life.'[6]

Nevertheless, parental concerns were pushed aside and MacLaurin accepted Jack's offer and went up to Cheshunt to meet Arthur Thrush, who was to mentor the company's first management trainee. MacLaurin says, 'He was a fantastic man. I was put under Arthur and my father-in-law to be, Edgar Collar. He was not pleased that I joined Tesco because there was a lot of disruption within the [Cohen] family, rows and so on, and he was in the middle of it all in a very senior position.'[7]

Friends in high places Ian may have had, but his first job was in the warehouse behind the headquarters at Cheshunt and his recollections give us a picture of Tesco at the start of the 1960s – including some rather dubious stunts pulled by store managers.

'I started loading vans in the Tesco warehouse, which was then one of the most modern in Europe. The warehouse was very busy, with all the goods coming in one end and out the other. It was huge. There were forklift trucks rushing around everywhere. You could only pick from the level. You had the order from the stores – [say] it would be two cases of Libby's peaches – so you hoiked those out, then went round the warehouse and got two cases of Persil and you took them out to the lorry and put the pallet on rollers, rolled them into the lorries and stacked them. It was very hard work and still is.

'Hyman Kreitman was the brains behind it. He was very technically minded. He was the one who thought through the designs for the supermarkets and going into various departments. He was a very quiet, very intelligent, very nice man and a totally different type of man to Jack, who was rumbustious.

'Then Arthur put me around the stores. Epsom was one of my first. I learnt how to bone a side of bacon and then I moved to Staines to the butchery department and broke down sides of beef and pork and lamb. My first store as a manager was Neasden. It was very, very small. All the canned and packet stuff came from the Tesco warehouse and all the rest from outside suppliers. They were tiny stores. Everything had to be marked by hand. All the tickets you had to mark yourself. We had red striping down the shelves and yellow stickers. We weren't allowed any short stocks so we had something called "buncing".'[8]

Buncing could be a matter of accepting, say, an extra free packet of biscuits from the sales rep and using it to balance stock (or taking it home to the wife). Or the manager would price it up a shade and – for this was before electronic tills, let alone barcoding – then use the extra money to balance the books. It was a widespread and generally quietly accepted practice in retail and it went on for decades. Buncing was not the only unsavoury norm.

'We could add anything,' recalls MacLaurin. 'Up to a shilling we added a halfpenny, from a shilling to 2 shillings it was a penny and anything over 2 shillings you could get what you wanted. Your stock was taken every ten weeks and you should at least break even. It is unbelievable when you think about it now.

'We didn't have any refrigeration at the back of the store, but there was a small lavatory for the boys and the girls. We used to stock the cream, butter, margarine and perishable things in the lavatory. In the summer, what refrigeration we did have would break down and the customer would say, "Manager, can you get me some butter from the back, please?" and you used to go into the lavatory and cut the butter from the packs and give it to the customer. It's mind-blowing now just to think that that happened.'[9]

During this time, Tesco was expanding rapidly. The company moved into the Midlands and the north-west, servicing the stores from distribution centres at Wilmslow in Cheshire, and Liverpool, which had come with the Irwins chain in 1960, along with James (Jim) Grundy, whom Jack installed to run Tesco North. There were additional stores in Hampshire, Surrey, Kent and Middlesex, as well as a new one at Burnt Oak. The 1962 Annual Report notes this last store with some pride as being 'of particular note' as it replaced Tesco's original store, opened there thirty years ago.

By now Tesco was beginning to acquire a bit of glamour of a sort. MacLaurin recalls that the new headquarters – like its predecessor, called Tesco House – was just two buildings standing on Delamare Road by the Tesco-owned Railway Nurseries, which grew cucumbers, tomatoes and lettuces. Cheshunt was almost completely rural then, which meant that Delamare Road was not subject to the usual highway restrictions, which Colin Chapman, maker of high-performance Lotus sports cars, found handy.

'Tesco House was a brick building emblazoned in red on blue tiles. It was a 1950s post-war building: nothing exciting at all. There was a boardroom right in the middle over the front doors. We used to park our cars along the front next to Leslie Porter's Bentley: LP4000 [Porter had married Shirley Cohen in 1949].

'There was just the Colin Chapman motor factory right opposite us and he used to race his motor cars up the road. There was just countryside. It was sponsored, I think, by the local council and we almost certainly got a grant for coming here. There were chairs for people to wait to see the buyers. Jack was always pretty aggressive in his buying. All the buyers went down the left-hand side of the building, next to Daisy Hyams' office, which was next to the boardroom. Jack's office smelt of cigar smoke and he had a very big desk. It was very nicely done, with a big table and leather chairs.'[10]

While in the 1962 Annual Report, Jack, Hyman, Leslie, Arthur and Ian's father-in-law, Edgar, were reporting the eleventh consecutive rise in annual profits – (£1.4 million, pre-tax) – MacLaurin was slogging hard at a supermarket on the Broadway in Muswell Hill. His experience would have been fairly typical of a Tesco store manager at that time, though his results marked him out as one to watch.

'It was really quite small. It had a very, very small road up to the back door. All the goods had to be manhandled down a roller. We had a very, very tiny warehouse. We had one loo, a very small staffroom, four checkouts, a little provision counter and our shelves were so thin we could only get two or three tins deep at a time. It was Christmas 1962 and we were trading very, very well and I had a wonderful assistant manager, Mick Rosario, whose girlfriend was also working in the store. Mick and I didn't go home for the whole of that week. We slept in the warehouse and were filling the store up through the night and trying to deal with deliveries through the day. I asked my wife to come down and work the tills because we were so short-staffed it was ridiculous, and at the end of the week we were absolutely exhausted.

'I had the money all over the staffroom table because there was no cash office. We closed at five o'clock on Christmas Eve. The police came in as we were having a drink and said we're happy for you to have a drink here but if I were you I'd lock the front doors. We had taken £10,000 and we were the first store to do that. Immediately after Christmas I had a visit from Jack Cohen. He said: "I never thought we'd take £10,000." I was very proud of that. I got promoted from Muswell Hill to run a group of stores, about fourteen or fifteen. Colchester was one and Chelmsford was another and they were our two big stores in the country, taking a lot of money. Colchester was the first to take £50,000 when I was inspector.'[11]

The Muswell Hill store at which MacLaurin broke the £10,000 record was nothing grand. It was typical of a Tesco store at that time – about as big as a Metro would be today – and sold general groceries, from bread and beans to soap powder and cereal. Muswell Hill was an affluent area over all, but Ian recalls that the middle-class shoppers went elsewhere. The housewife who could afford it would have passed MacLaurin's shop on the Broadway and headed to Sainsbury, which, along with Marks & Spencer, was the doyenne of the grocery trade. It was social classes B, C and D who patronized his shop.

'We were pretty cheap in those days. Jack Cohen was a very good retailer. Every year he used to go off to South Africa and buy amazing packets of guavas and apricots and peaches and so on. There was a funny story about the gambas, which were sent out to all the stores.

45

We looked at the tin and there was a beautiful label, a dark blue label with something red, like a plum, so we put it in the fruit section and marked it up. Then we got a lot of complaints from customers because they bought them as a plum but it was actually a seeded pepper and they had had their Sunday plum pies with it. That didn't go down too well.'[12]

Nor did Jack's thirst for a great deal stop at exotic produce, which few in 1960s England had ever encountered. The fabulous aspect of tinned produce was that it took an awful lot to damage it.

'A cargo ship from Denmark went down on Goodwin Sands,' MacLaurin recalls. 'It was full of cans of Flying Bird cream: Jack bought the whole lot as a distressed line and he sent them out to the stores with a case of Duraglit because all the tins were rusty, so before we could put them on sale we had to take the rust and salt-water off and patch the labels up as best we could and sell all this distressed stock for tuppence-ha'penny. There was no quality control. There were no refrigeration deadlines. It was a very basic industry in those days. We're talking the early sixties and things have changed dramatically over the years. We were at the bottom end of the market. The business was just like that in those days.'[13]

Although official late-night trading was unheard of, and Sunday trading undreamt of, Tesco's managers and staff worked long, anti-social hours and the tasks were physically demanding. Stores opened from 8.30 a.m. to 5.30 p.m. most days, with a half-day closing on Thursday, and remained open a little later than 5.30 on Fridays. But managers and some staff worked much longer hours to get their shops ready for the next day's business.

'I was working huge hours right through my Tesco career, to the detriment of my family, no doubt about it. I had a wonderful wife who was the rock at home while I ploughed away and built my career at Tesco. I wasn't out of the ordinary. Everybody worked jolly hard.'[14]

Tesco's pay rates were competitive, with managers earning up to £2,000 a year, plus an annual bonus – not much less than Board directors – but staff turnover generally was very high.

'There was no staff discount. You came to work and got paid every week. There were no other perks at all. We didn't look after our staff at all well and the staff turnover right through the sixties and seventies was about 180 per cent. People didn't stick because the work was so hard. It was an emerging company that didn't have the kind of management that thought too much about the staff. In those days the staff were a necessary evil. You had to have them but there was no loving or caring for them.

'The unions were quite strong. In latter days we have worked closely with the unions and changed the structure and the bonuses and everything for the staff, [as well as] training the staff. In those days we didn't train anybody. It was training on the shop floor by the manager, as I did at Muswell Hill. "What do I have to do manager?" "You see those goods? You have to put them on the shelves and do it as fast as you can." It was a bit of a Fred Karno outfit[15], a bit of a shambles, really, but it was a successful shambles, and we came out of it.'[16]

Wages were raised significantly in the late fifties and the sixties, some of those increases as a result of equal pay laws (the majority of the Tesco workforce in stores was female). Ian's recollections are not unique among Tesco people. For those with the stamina to slog physically, this was the era when the foundations of future careers were being laid down. Men without the education that Ian had enjoyed were joining a company that, at that time, they never imagined would outlive, and even surpass, the grand retail names they knew.

Kevin Doherty was one of them. He was not quite fourteen when he started as a Saturday boy at the Tesco-owned store in Walthamstow High Street; at the time of writing, he is still employed as a business coach at Tesco. Doherty's 'in' to the company was his brother Eric, who already had a job at the store. 'They called it casual labour then. You made about 12 shillings – about 60p – that was a lot of money then. I enjoyed working there from day one. I really felt I could deliver. I always wanted to make the shelves look good. I liked the environment, the hustle and bustle, the speed of it and the customers.

'I took a full-time job there when I was fifteen, on 5 April 1961. I carried on until I was about sixteen and a half. I earned a lot of money signwriting. It was self-taught. I used to do all the prices for the store. One of the area directors came in and said they were really good. They offered me a job on the new store-opening team. I'd never been away from home in my life and suddenly I was up in Leicester and Wolverhampton. I was on that for probably eight or nine months, and then they put me back [as an assistant store manager] into Essex Road [Islington].

'I was great at filling the store up and presentation skills. But when it came to the books I hadn't got a clue. They moved me to Chapel Market [Islington] and then I was a store manager at eighteen. My first stock result was a disaster. I was about 3 per cent down. I realized I was making the store look good but I hadn't got the skills to do the books. I worked very hard and never had another bad stock result.'[17]

Chapel Market was not all bad for Doherty. He met his wife there. 'Hilary was fifteen. I was seventeen and I was an assistant manager at the Chapel Market store. I gave her a job as a checkout operator. Best day's work I ever did. That's how I got to know her.'[18]

Doherty's story illustrates how Jack's company created social mobility. He was born in Walthamstow on 5 April 1946, one of nine children of an Irish immigrant father and Walthamstow-born mother who had converted to Catholicism in order to marry. The church was part of growing up, even providing second-hand clothes. Doherty's mother worked in a toy factory and managed what money there was. His father had a series of jobs – chauffeur and lorry driver at the Beautility Furniture Factory, Edmonton, and also worked weekend shifts as a security guard to supplement his wage. Doherty remembers lots of money rows and living in fear that his parents would split, even though the family was close-knit; his grandparents lived in the house next door. The children played in Waltham Forest at weekends, their numbers dwindling as the older ones found Saturday jobs.

He was top of his class at the local Catholic primary school, St Mary's, but failed the 11-plus and went to the nearest Catholic

School, St George's in Shernhall Street. The family had moved by this time, to a longed-for modern council house in Winns Avenue with three bedrooms, an inside bathroom and lavatory, two good-sized rooms and a kitchen. Doherty devoted his energies to making pocket money, not least because he was spending his school lunch money on cigarettes.

'I was thirteen and a half when I started working at the shop in Walthamstow High Street.[19] My first job was filling shelves. You went up three flights of stairs to get three boxes. You had a felt pen to write the price of every single item. Then fill up the shelf. Then back up. Price changes happened on a Saturday. It was the most boring job in the world just keeping focused on it. If you changed Heinz baby foods there were [50–60] different varieties. Say they were 6½d, they would go up to 7d. I'd sit there with a Brillo pad scraping the [prices] off for hours and hours then have to go through every can and put 7d on every one of them. A whole half a day for 3/6d.

'You worked in a pair of jeans at first. Then a white shirt, a black bow-tie and then a huge, white overall. We had slanted mirrors so you could look to see if customers were [shoplifting] goods. We kept sugar in a cupboard at the back and I had to stand on top of it watching these mirrors. I'd say, "Security, tinned fish section please" [down the tannoy system]. By the end of the day, so much of the sugar would have been sold that I'd be hanging on to the mirrors. Shoplifters were a combination: there were some surprising people who looked very smart – they probably didn't need to steal. They took a tin of salmon or butter, Oxo, tins of canned meat. Oxo was expensive in those days: twelve would be 5d. It was more about was it easy to steal – would it go in your bag or pocket? They'd have the shopping basket and their own bag. The hope was if you called security on the tannoy they would dump it. Some managers, if it was a little old lady, would give her a good telling off and leave it at that.

'A lot of people shopped in Tesco. It was seen in those days as a cheap store, the quality wasn't particularly good and it didn't sell good branded products. Sainsbury's was seen as the affluent, premium retailer.

'I knew Jack Cohen. I met him lots of times. When I was working in [Chatsworth Road, Clapton, as a young store manager] he came in and the store manager introduced me to him. I had given my notice in. I had been working long hours for God knows how many weeks overtime and never got paid for it. Jack Cohen said, "Mr Doherty – why are you leaving?" I said, "I'm really upset. I've worked all these long hours and I've not been paid." He said, "How much do we owe you then?" I said, "A hundred pounds." I guessed. He said, "A hundred pounds? How much tax would you pay on that?" I said, "Twenty pounds." He said, "So we owe you eighty." He said, "Take it out the till. We can't lose this man."

'I felt like I'd won the lottery. I had four or five weeks' wages. He was a great guy. He had great instincts: very sharp, a real trader. He could spot a deal a mile away. He was very fast, very astute. He made decisions quickly. He was very streetwise and very tough.

'By Chapel Market there was a wallpaper shop, pub, clothing shop, lots of stalls, a bit like *EastEnders*. Watch stalls, fruit stalls, quite a few stalls selling yam yams for African customers. Record stalls. It was quite a short and busy market. [Chapel Market remains a busy street with a similar range of small shops and market stalls today.] We had a few products – brown rice, black-eyed beans, split peas – that we learned [about] over the years. We'd watch what the stall-holders were selling and then we'd recruit local people who understood what the customers wanted.

'I remember looking in some of the butchers' windows on the way to work and the butcher would have a cigarette in their mouth. They'd cough their heart out and there'd be ash all over the meat so they'd brush it off. That was how it was in the sixties. I used to have a manager years ago with an ashtray on the side of the meat counter. Eventually trading standards stopped all that, but it used to be a way of life.'[20]

Doherty's future wife and fellow Chapel Market employee, Hilary, lived around the corner in the City Road on one floor of a three-floor house. The couple saved for a house of their own in order to marry and were earning enough to secure a mortgage on a £3,500 home in Chingford Road, Walthamstow.

'The mortgage was £25 a month and my father said it was a mill-stone around my neck. I said the world is changing and you've got to do things differently. My father bought us a bed and a table. We had a lot of second-hand furniture. I was twenty-one. I had to include overtime and all sorts of things to get to the salary [where] they would lend me the money. I was probably earning about [£1,500] or [£1,800] a year.'[21]

Tesco in the early sixties was only just getting going and there were many other store groups of the same size at this stage, plenty of them headed by men not dissimilar to Jack Cohen. Their response to consumers' developing awareness of what was available and afford-able – from fresh fruit to fridges – as well as their practical innovations would determine which of them would thrive and which would be absorbed by their rivals.

Chapter 6

The Best for Less from the Housewives' Friend: Tesco's Battle of the Brands

'The opening of the Tesco supermarket and discount store at Leicester created a sensation in the national, financial and trade press and in newspapers and magazines throughout this country and the world.'

Tesco Annual Report, 1962

Lee Circle in Leicester today is in that bit of urban no-man's-land that is neither the centre nor the outskirts of a city. Jack described it as 'off-town-centre'. In December 1960 it found its fifteen minutes of fame as the place chosen for the latest British retail experiment: a supermarket and non-food discount store combined. Tesco's Board boasted in the Annual Report covering 1961/62 of unprecedented public fascination with the future of shopping: 'The unusual design of the building with its multi-storey car park on top, its enormous size and Tesco's declared policy of attacking Resale Price Maintenance in non-food lines made the occasion unique', they reported.

Among Tesco's VIPs at the Lee Circle opening was Jack's daughter, Shirley Porter. She recalls, 'The crew worked all night long to get it looking good. I wore, to show our merchandise was good, a Tesco raincoat and boots. You cannot imagine the excitement in

Leicester. The goods just flew out. That was the beginnings of it.'[1] Opening day was theatrical, not least because comedian Sid James appeared to do the opening honours. Queues of shoppers waited to rush in the moment the doors were thrown open, eyes fixed on the dayglo posters suspended above the shelves, cabinets and tables for the best offers. The directors there, including Ian MacLaurin, stood at the checkouts helping to pack bags – and of course Jack was ready with some trader banter.

Leicester, bang in the middle of England, brought together two of Jack's ideas of the moment: tackling the manufacturers' remaining grip on price rigidity – Resale Price Maintenance (RPM); and bringing his customers a vastly wider range of goods than his smaller supermarkets and self-service food formats could muster.

To Jack's way of thinking, powerful companies were perpetrating an outrage against the citizen. Resale Price Maintenance – a law by which manufacturers set a minimum price at which retailers could sell their product – was two years older than he was, having been set up in 1896 by the Proprietary Articles of Trade Association. The manufacturers' legal right to set and enforce prices set them on a collision course with retailers who, like Jack, wanted to offer customers lower prices on branded goods. Supporters of RPM claimed that they had to be able to make sure they fixed prices in order to be able to cover their costs and operated a 'Stop List', blacklisting traders who flouted the rules. They argued that cutting their profits would threaten the fragile fabric of the nation's economic health.

The issue came to a head around the time that Tesco opened the store at Lee Circle. The Restrictive Trade Practices Act of 1956 had banned suppliers from acting together to fix prices but allowed them to do so if they acted independently. Suppliers took out eighty injunctions against retailers between 1956 and 1962, though not all were upheld, as retailers used dodges such as fake clearance sales to get around the fixed prices.

Jack faced a choice. He could play the game, work the dodges and have the branded goods, or he could tackle the big suppliers head-on. He went for the head-on approach. Using Lee Circle, Tesco's first general discount store, he 'declared war' on Resale Price Maintenance (RSP). His decision sparked legal action by British Xylonite, which made BexBissell carpet shampoo. Although Jack was forced to restore the shampoo's 'list' price, Tesco put 'sorry' signs up in the shop windows, explaining that customers had to pay 67/6 (67 shillings and sixpence) against the 36 shillings that Tesco's buyers paid. Tesco had wanted to sell at 47/6, the posters explained, meaning a saving of £1 for the customer. The profit margins the producers were protecting looked stark when splashed in big, bold print in shop windows. Tesco also offered customers 2lb bags of Tate & Lyle granulated sugar for a knock-down one shilling by way of consolation.

Ladies' fashion was next. Tesco put Gor-Ray skirts on sale at Lee Circle for 75 shillings rather than the 84-shilling list price: the manufacturer retaliated by allowing the other retailers they supplied to undercut Tesco by 6 shillings, promising them it would reimburse them after Tesco caved in.

Further unilateral action by Tesco led to fresh court action by manufacturers. Kayser Bondor, a maker of tights and underwear, sought a High Court injunction after Tesco's Home 'n' Wear team (headed by Shirley's husband, Leslie Porter) cut the price of branded nylons and knickers. Tesco was sourcing the underwear indirectly through a wholesaler with links to one of its subsidiaries. Kayser Bondor's managing director defended RPM as something that protected the consumer: 'for unless one has constant prices, the goods must deteriorate because the price must go below the economic level.'

Jack had to admit defeat on the tights. Tesco tried to use a technicality on the invoice to get around the fixed price and this went down poorly with Justice Cross, who said this was not honourable (whatever he thought of the price-fixing). Kayser Bondor hung on to its right to fix prices back then; nowadays its former factory at Baldock, Hertfordshire, is a Tesco Extra.

In the 1962 Annual Report, Tesco's Board continued to make its case to the public: 'The inflated profit margins taken by many other retailers can be drastically reduced for the benefit of the shopping public by Tesco's methods of bulk buying, streamlined distribution and quick turnover, while ensuring continued profitability in trading.'

Jack put it pithily in his statement for the report: 'We [at Tesco] have received a great deal of publicity in the National Press in our fight against Resale Price Maintenance, and are confident that we have the sympathy of the general public on our side. We have been referred to as the "Housewives' Friend". It is very gratifying for us, and it is our constant endeavour to live up to it'. He eagerly awaited, he added, the outcome of a Board of Trade inquiry into Resale Price Maintenance.

The government was broadly in the same place as Tesco. Harold Wilson, as president of the Board of Trade in 1949, had proposed abolishing all forms of price-fixing in a White Paper, but before anything could happen the Labour administration was voted out. The 1956 Restrictive Trades Practices Act having stopped short, Edward 'The Grocer' Heath, then at the Board of Trade, published a Bill to abolish RPM outright in January 1964, which received Royal Assent in June of that year. Heath was unable to finish the job, but the new Labour government, under Harold Wilson, ratified it and it became law in January 1965.

Jack was delighted. In the Annual Report for 1965 he described how 'The group was the first to take advantage of the new freedom offered by the abolition of Resale Price Maintenance' and cut prices on wines, beers and razorblades to an 'enthusiastic response from the public'. Tesco then went ahead and cut confectionery prices, but had to abandon the ploy to wait for manufacturers, including Cadbury, to bring their cases for exemption from the ban to court; it was another two years before the confectionery companies suffered a High Court defeat. The final hurdle, cigarettes, remained in place until 1968, but Tesco was confident enough in the widespread support for its cause to go ahead and cut prices ahead of this.

The RPM battle had an unexpected side-effect. In February 1965, Distillers, makers of whisky, abandoned a legal action in the light of the new law. This meant that whisky could be sold at prices that Tesco's customers might be able to afford. Jack already had a handful of shops with licences to sell alcohol and now he applied for many more. This would involve another battle with established interests.

Jack tasked the company secretary, Laurie Don, with acquiring licences. He had to go through the Brewster sessions in which justices of the peace, sitting in magistrates courts, authorized liquor licences. Jack himself stood in the witness box to argue his case on more than one occasion. Eventually, Tesco found a brewer who would support an application: the promise of significant sales through the growing network of shops must have appealed. In 1966, Tesco had eight licences. A decade later, 378 stores were able to sell beers, wines and spirits.

The battle typified Jack's approach of kicking on doors until they opened. Sometimes, however, this had to be supplemented by less direct action to bring 'the best for less' to customers. Reluctance by some brand manufacturers to let go of RPM, for example, accelerated another trend: own-brand lines. Leslie Porter and Daisy Hyams looked for alternatives to pricey national brands while the row dragged on. Tesco introduced non-food goods – such as men's shirts – under the label 'Delamare' and expanded the Golden Ring tinned food range in order to give customers products at much lower prices. Jack thanked his manufacturer partners for their growing appreciation of the need to promote their products in the stores and for their cooperation over such things as improved packaging to make their goods appealing to customers.

He was about to take Tesco into new territory.

Chapter 7

The 'Widening Front' and Stamp-collecting: Keeping Up with Rising Living Standards

'We were in advance of the other companies because we came in ahead of them and we had somebody who knew something about it.'

Dame Shirley Porter[1]

'Green Shield was very successful for us ... In the sixties, goods were becoming slightly more plentiful, people were feeling better about themselves, new homes were being built and you could save a few books of stamps and get yourself a steam iron or something basic for the house.'

Lord MacLaurin[2]

Tesco was outgrowing its position as a simple grocer. Its social superiors such as Fortnum & Mason and Harrods had sold all kinds of consumer goods for years. Now Tesco decided that what could be done for the well-heeled could be done for the masses and began to focus more seriously on its non-food ranges. Leicester's Lee Circle was one of the first stores to display the results. Non-food meant everything from pans to aquarium fish and frocks, though clothing was not an obvious choice for a grocer.

It is possible that Jack's decision to diversify in this direction had a lot to do with his tendency to keep Tesco in the family. His son-in-law, Leslie Porter, was in the textile business; Jack wanted him in the

Tesco business, like his other son-in-law, Irene's husband Hyman Kreitman. Moving into clothing when Tesco did may have been a useful hook for Jack to pull Leslie in.

Leslie and Shirley had married in 1949, but, possibly having seen how things were for Hyman, Leslie was determined to marry the girl not the company and he held out for another ten years before joining Jack's team as a part-time consultant. He became a full-time member of the Board in 1960. Two years later, Tesco was firmly on the non-food road, which it described as 'the Widening Front'.

Dame Shirley Porter recalls that her husband was very happy in his own business, which was partly why he resisted attempts to get him to join Tesco during the fifties. There was also the stormy relationship Jack had with Hyman and Irene. 'We didn't get involved in any of the disagreements which inevitably take place in a family firm, as it was then. Then one day Leslie happened to have in the back of the car some tea towels and he said to my father, "Why don't you sell something other than food?" Nobody was the least bit excited about it. In those days they didn't have any interest in anything that wasn't food. We had a competition later on to find a name and it was called Home 'n' Wear. The tea towels went out and they all cried out for more and that was the beginning, and finally Daddy and my brother-in-law convinced Leslie to come in and he was in charge of Home 'n' Wear. We were in advance of the other companies because we came in ahead of them and we had somebody who knew something about it. [Leslie's] firm was J. Porter and Sons in Old Street. They supplied the Co-op as well as Tesco.

'"Jack the Nagger" just went on and on until we joined. He trusted [Leslie]. Hyman was a very, very good thinker, an organizer, his strength was that he was thinking ahead. It was due to him that it became much more professional. He was more of a private man than Leslie. They complemented each other. Leslie was an extrovert . . . he was much more one of the boys. Hyman was a different type of person but they got on very well. I was the younger sister so Hyman and my sister were the bosses.

'Hyman came round to ask Leslie to join and help him. My father was a very dominant man. He came from a background where to get what you wanted and to build up a business you had to impose your will. You had to be very, very tough and work very, very hard. He knew what he wanted and he would fight for it. That was difficult for Hyman because that wasn't his background. Leslie was different. He was able to handle that.'[3]

Dame Shirley describes her late husband as a man who worked hard, who loved life's luxuries and a good game of golf. Like her father he had the ability to create a rapport with people from all walks of life, and he had Jack's toughness. His story illustrates the journey that many Jewish immigrants from Eastern Europe embarked upon when they arrived in Britain in the twentieth century.

Sir Leslie Porter was born Leslie Pasamount on 10 July 1920. He grew up in Finsbury Park, 'the youngest, the baby, the much-loved blue-eyed boy'. His parents were both Jewish-Lithuanian immigrants, though his mother was 'very anglicized and well-spoken', and his father died 'at a youngish age' with diabetes. Porter's father was in the millinery trade, but, after leaving Holloway County School, Porter became a mechanic. He worked at Owens, the up-market car dealer in Park Lane, where he sold Rolls-Royce cars before joining the army at seventeen. His Second World War was spent in North Africa, Crete and Italy and he finished the war as a quartermaster sergeant. One of his proudest moments was returning to the Park Lane garage in later years to buy a white Bentley from Sam Owen, recalls Dame Shirley Porter.

Straight after the war, Porter and his brother, Phillip, took over their father's business, renamed J. Porter Textiles, and they lived in a flat in St John's Wood. The business became Harrow Stores, later bought by Tesco. He met Shirley, ten years his junior, through friends when she sold him tickets for a charity event on a boat. She recalls that they met again at a wedding. 'I was at my best friend's wedding and at a table wishing I was somewhere else. Leslie caught my look and he came over and asked me to dance. He was about my height.' They had a short courtship. 'I've got a side of me that enjoys down-to-earth things, and that surprised him.'[4]

Jack's reliance on family and friends was always strong. Two of his most trusted directors died at the start of the sixties and this coincided with – or perhaps was partly the reason for – a turning point in Tesco's journey. Fred Turner, who had joined Jack as a store manager in 1933, died in April 1961. Two years later Edgar Collar, Ian MacLaurin's father-in-law, died after suffering a heart attack during a game of golf not far from the Cheshunt headquarters. MacLaurin says of Edgar: 'He formalized the business. Everybody I have spoken to has said if it hadn't been for him the business would have gone all over the place. Edgar got Jack under control. He died just as we were about to announce our first million pounds profit.'[5]

Despite the profits peak, MacLaurin recalls 'it was a very tough time for the business'. There was much change to absorb. In 1961 Jack had bought the Liverpool-based store group, Irwin Stores, which had greatly increased Tesco's presence in the north-west of England. Throughout the country, Tesco's shops were busily converting to the self-service model. The company was growing so quickly that one of the biggest threats it faced was a collective collapse from exhaustion.

MacLaurin, by this point running a group of stores in the south-east that included Colchester and Chelmsford, the two most profitable shops in the company, turned his attention to recruiting and promoting. Among those he took on at this time were David Malpas, Eddie Clark, Colin Goodfellow, Brian Williams, Michael Darnell and John Gildersleeve. They joined a business still regarded as a store for blue-collar workers and the unemployed, but Gildersleeve was part of the team that would slowly upgrade Tesco's image.

Like Eddie Clark and MacLaurin, Gildersleeve was attracted to Tesco by its potential. He recalls, 'I started at Shell, my father's employer. I worked out it was dead men's shoes. It was like the Civil Service. I bought a London evening paper and there was an ad for Tesco trainee managers. Tesco had been a really successful share [stock]. I took an interest in these things that rich people did. It was a new industry relatively. I made the phone call and went for an interview with a chap called MacLaurin at the Greenford Tesco. The manager was abusive because my arriving meant his boss was coming and his boss was probably going to give him a hard time. He [Ian] said, "Yes, you can start with us, and how much do you think you should be paid?" It was £600 a year, £12 a week.

'I figured Tesco was a meritocracy where I would get rewarded if I was good enough. Shell was full of people in suits. And I got lucky. My first manager was hopeless – I filled shelves and swept floors and was disenchanted and felt I wasn't learning anything. His boss was an inspector called Alan Gray. I went to him and said, "I'm supposed to be a trainee manager and all I do is menial tasks that other people don't have time to do." Alan Gray said, "Don't worry, we've got a plan." The plan was to remove the manager.

'I got a new boss. He'd been in the industry for ever. He knew every wrinkle – some of which weren't entirely legal. I learned a huge amount about how to duck, dive and survive. He made me an assistant manager – I didn't know anything: butter was yellow, cheese was orange and meat was red. He could deliver. I hung on his shirt-tails.

'Then the business was desperate for people, so I was given a shop to manage. I wouldn't have got a shop at another time. It was at Walton-on-Thames. I was living in Tooting. I didn't have a car. Today an HR department would say have you got a car, or we'll move you, or here's a timetable. So I had to walk a mile to Wimbledon, get a train, then change for Walton-on-Thames – the shop was three miles from the town centre. The railway was meant to get people from the suburbs into London. I was going the other way. I managed to get a lift on a building contractor's truck – the journey took an hour and a half. For £36 a week.'[6]

Not that he wasn't used to hard work.

Born in 1944 in South London at the Clapham Hospital for Women, the son of a Scottish regular soldier and his Northern Irish wife, Gildersleeve says: 'I come from what people would call a humble background. My father, being a serving soldier, didn't really come back to us until I was eleven and off to grammar school, by which point I had established my life and he was a bit surplus.

'My mother knew that education was the only way her children were going to change their lives. My brother and sister were brighter, but I was the eldest. My mother would sit me down for an hour every day in the winter and insist I did my reading with her. I went to an LCC school in South London – forty kids in my class and I was the only one who passed the 11-plus and that was because of my mother. She ingrained certain values in me. And not having a father once I was seventeen [John's father died of a heart-attack aged forty-eight] probably changed life a bit as well. Working hard, doing your best, not complaining, accepting life has ups and downs.'[7]

The family was church-going and Conservative, regarding anything left of centre as 'communist' and Gildersleeve says he has, broadly speaking, seen no reason to take a different view. He was, however, one of that first generation of British children to reap the benefits of the Welfare State, combined with full employment and no major war to fight. 'Our home was part of a modest, terraced house, in which the kitchen was also the bathroom (the bath in the kitchen was put in some time after we moved in). I shared a room with my brother and my sister had her own bedroom. When my grandparents arrived [from Ireland], my sister moved in with our parents and her room went to the grandparents. By the time they arrived I was at school or out playing. I wasn't in the house that often.

'We went to a counter-service grocery store. Sweet rationing didn't come off until I was nine or ten. It's why I've got such a sweet tooth now. I can remember the day sweet rationing came off. I came back from primary school and it was on the radio and my mother gave me a thruppenny bit and I ran to the corner shop and they had completely sold out because it had been on the radio at nine in the morning and the locusts had been in. The corner shop was the community centre: it sold tobacco, confectionery and newspapers and was run and owned by a family who were the richest people I knew because they owned a business and made profits. You went there whenever you could afford to. It was a nice place to go, you got things that indulged you there. And they were nice people.'[8]

Gildersleeve did a newspaper round every morning and every evening as well as Sunday mornings. 'I made my bike when I was twelve from bits: there was no prospect of anybody buying one for me.'

His description of food at home might resonate with many who grew up in Britain's cities or towns after the war.

'It was mince on a Monday because the Sunday joint wouldn't all have been eaten. We had a big iron mincer. There was a lot of stodge in the diet because potatoes were popular. It was cheap, stomach-filling food. Fruit didn't really figure because it was seasonal, so we'd get some apples in September and October when English apples were available. You didn't get strawberries or bananas – strawberries were for rich people and bananas were limited by war. Carrots, onions, swedes, Brussels sprouts, cabbage – none of which I now like. I was never hungry. When you are a child you don't care about food so long as you aren't hungry. I didn't eat in a restaurant until I was twenty.'[9]

He says the area he grew up in – Balham and Kennington – became more violent in later years. 'I became aware of our social inadequacies when I went to grammar school. Five per cent of the population was allowed to pass. By some miracle I had done well in the exam and I was allowed to choose any school in London. Because I was this amazing choirboy they decided I should go to St Paul's choir school. I passed the entrance exam. I had to have a singing test but had the most dreadful cold the day of the test. My father was in awe of St Paul's – he was a working-class soldier; I was terrified because I was eleven. Neither of us had told them I had a cold [and I didn't get in]. My second choice was Battersea Grammar, which had been a public school until 1948 and then Direct Grant. I had to go for an interview [which was successful]. My father was dumb-struck. The other boys had more than one blazer and didn't wear the same shirt two days in a row. It just made me ambitious.'[10]

Five decades after he was born there, John was involved in

purchasing for Tesco the by then defunct Clapham Hospital for Women: it is now the store opposite South Clapham tube station.

Soon after Gildersleeve arrived, Tesco's stores, already over-stretched as a result of acquisitions of other stores, surged forward again after launching Green Shield Stamps in 1963. It very nearly didn't happen, though.

Trading stamps were an American import. Highly favoured by more advanced US consumers, retailers were wondering whether British shoppers would embrace the idea of collecting tokens to redeem them. Jack Cohen thought the stamps were 'a menace', or so he said to a journalist in 1963. It seems that his colleagues on the Board agreed; or at least, they agreed provided that no other retailer caved in and started issuing trading stamps. Hyman Kreitman – who had retired but had only just been persuaded to return as vice-chairman after finance director Edgar Collar's death in June 1963 – was authorized to execute a smart *volte face* if necessary. He decided that, if it came to it, Tesco would work with Green Shield Stamps, the only operator based in the UK.

Over the next few months, retailers began a strange sort of dance around the issue, which included secret meetings between various store groups and the demand from a Labour MP, John Stonehouse, (who was then also president of the London Co-operative Society) for a Board of Trade Inquiry, which Edward Heath declared unnecessary.

Three retailers (Garfield Weston, Fortnum & Mason and Fine Fare) decided to partner US pink stamps operator Sperry & Hutchinson from the end of November 1963. They announced this in the summer, sparking turmoil in the retail trade. Jack was later to recall that it was only when he read the story in the *Financial Times* that he really woke up to the situation. But Pricerite (ironically a company Jack had helped establish in 1930) beat the other retailers to the wire, issuing Green Shield Stamps on 14 October, despite its owner Michael Kaye's public denouncements of trading stamps. Hyman Kreitman made his move. In a matter of weeks, Tesco was ready to launch Green Shield Stamps and did so, one week behind Pricerite but ahead of the others, with all the theatrics that Jack and the directors could muster.

Lord MacLaurin describes the launch at the shop in Coventry Road, Small Heath, Birmingham: 'We all went up there for this amazing opening. There were all the Green Shield posters and stamps and the Green Shield girls were everywhere giving out stamps. It was hugely successful. It started to transform our business, much to the annoyance of Sainsbury and Marks & Spencer.

'Sainsbury's were very much against going into stamps. They thought it wasn't ethical trading. They said people don't want to collect them. They were proved wrong. Green Shield was very successful for us. The country was emerging from the war and in the sixties, goods were becoming slightly more plentiful, people were feeling better about themselves, new homes were being built and you could save a few books of stamps and get yourself a steam iron or something basic for the house.'[11]

Customers queued to get into Tesco at Small Heath for the launch, with reports of housewives fainting, presumably overcome by the excitement or crush rather than the presence of comedian Tommy Trinder. The list of giveaways to boost the promotion and help attract customers into the shop offers a glimpse of what appealed to the sixties housewife. Tesco gave away bread rolls with each pack of four frankfurters, free mint sauce with cuts of lamb and sets of saucepans for £5 for the first hundred through the door. Fine Fare countered with an offer on chicken. Pearks cut the price of detergent. *The Times* reported: 'This unlovely highway is now the Alamein of the trading stamp war.'[12]

Eddie Clark was running the store in Penn Street, Bristol, at the time the trials were going on and he was desperate to get the stamps to help him rescue the troubled shop. 'I used to write SUS – send us stamps – SUS on the back of the weekly sheet recording takings. Why were stamps popular? They were new in this country and they were worthwhile. If you spent £10, you got the stamps and the book was worth about £5. The average housewife could fill it up by the end of the month, especially when you had double Green Shield days.'[13]

Lord Sainsbury led an alliance of retailers that included International, BHS, United Dairies, Boots, Marks & Spencer and WHSmith to resist further stamp-operator incursion. The alliance argued that the stamps should carry their true face value and be converted into cash, presumably aware that, as Jack had stated earlier in the year, the stamps represented a 2 per cent levy on profits and would cost participating companies dearly.

Brand manufacturers were also unhappy again. They said stamps were covert discounting and against Resale Price Maintenance, which, in 1963, was still being hotly fought over. Imperial Tobacco, Distillers and Cadbury were among the brand-makers who threatened to withdraw supplies if stamps were given on their products.

With his knack for a good bit of PR, Jack combined stamps with discounting, going back to his roots and choosing tea to ramp up the row: he slashed the price on quarter-pound packs of tea in half. It triggered a price war, pulling in detergent and sugar. Commentators tut-tutted. Jack said he was there to serve the customers and they seemed to want stamps.

In 1965, two years into the experiment, the Board agreed that trading stamps were 'no remedy for inefficient trading' but was 'satisfied that our correct use of this merchandising aid has proved beneficial to the Company'.[14]

Through his 'best for less' policy, his high-profile tussle to the death with Resale Price Maintenance and the new 'something for nothing' trading stamps, Jack was now firmly established as the housewives' friend.

Chapter 8

Growing Pains: Adapting to the Shopping Explosion

'In pursuit of the Group's avowed aim to establish a large supermarket in every major town in the country, the immediate areas of expansion are in South Wales, the South West of England and Yorkshire.'

Sir Jack Cohen, chairman, July 1965[1]

'I got the sense of here was a group of people who had a tiger by the tail: they were opening stores every week. They didn't have the people to manage or man them or the systems to support it but they knew they were on to a winner and they were living and breathing this business.'

David Malpas, former Tesco managing director[2]

Tesco's chart-topping growth in the 1960s made for internal stresses at every level of the business. The company delivered an increase in profits every year as it opened more stores and sold an increasingly broad range of products. Yet it had to absorb costs that were rising rapidly. It was also a struggle to find people made of manager material to run the shops, and there was an increasing split between the South and the North as the various store groups Jack bought were bolted on to his central company.

Fiefdoms grew up, from the autonomous store managers to the different divisions of the business, which by 1965 had mushroomed to eight separate retail entities and six other divisions: two wholesale, two packing, a catering and bakery division, and an agricultural nursery. There were ten executive and non-executive directors and twenty-eight additional directors, many of whom came along with the acquired businesses.

The Board intoned in its mid-decade report that 'the secret of supermarket trading is in streamlined headquarters' control, buying and distribution', but in reality Tesco was fragmented, as its race for expansion created imbalance. There were, for example, two head-quarters: one at Cheshunt for the South and one at Winsford, Cheshire, looking after the North and under the overall control of James 'Jim' Grundy, formerly of Irwin & Son. Tesco, however, was not such a big company then that it needed two head offices doing the same job, as people could see even at the time. 'I don't know the reason why they were divided,' reflects Eddie Clark. 'The Tesco hold-ings Board and the Board up there maybe needed different empires. It was like Arsenal and Tottenham Hotspur.'[3]

At Board level, there were the splits over Jack's takeover targets – in particular the Liverpool-based Irwin Stores in 1961. 'There had been an ad hoc acquisition of stores or groups of stores simply because they could be slotted into the wholesale business and were available,'[4] says David Malpas, one of a new wave of desperately needed recruits in 1966. He recalls an advert in the trade magazine, the *Grocer*, and thought that Tesco was a 'shady, Johnny-come-lately outfit'. He applied mostly because he had decided to leave his depart-ment-store job, was coming to London for an interview with a voluntary group and in the spirit of the era thought he would do the Tesco interview and receive two lots of travel expenses. 'They wanted people badly. So I applied, I arranged an interview on the same day at 136 King Street, Hammersmith, which was where Tesco directed its retail operations from. It was a store with an office above it.

'I met George Wood [then head of Tesco's retail operations]. It was a major thoroughfare and there was a terrific din. I couldn't hear too much of what he had to say. I got the sense of here was a group of people who had a tiger by the tail: they were opening stores every week. They didn't have the people to manage or man them or the systems to support it but they knew they were on to a winner and they were living and breathing this business. I joined as a trainee manager at Lee Circle, Leicester. It was a Back Door job, the most important, checking the goods in.'[5]

Other Tesco people describe Malpas as a 'thinker' and refer to his brightness, energy and humour. He was not a typical Tesco manager back in those days, but his story illustrates how much less British families had – or expected – and what the norm for schooling and hard work was.

He was born in 1939, the son of an aircraft technician who opted to avoid the family market-garden business in Barry, South Wales. Jack Malpas had a love of music and a talent for the church organ that enabled his (essentially poor) family to live in grace-and-favour church homes. Having survived scarlet fever and the bombs that fell on Barry docks, David Malpas moved to a farmhouse where life was very similar to that of the Gloucestershire village a couple of decades earlier described by Laurie Lee in *Cider with Rosie* – much the same array of privations, but also delights. 'I had fairly poor parents but it was idyllic, I suppose. We never really noticed rationing. I remember people being a bit jealous when we were able to have a chicken or something.'[6]

The church where Jack Malpas played the organ provided a house in Tibberton, which had a cellar that flooded to 6 inches. Rainwater was collected for washing and there was no electricity until David was fourteen or fifteen. He churned butter, snared rabbits (to supplement rationed meat) and waited for the bread man to cycle past in the evening. His father, who rode 18 miles a day to work (at the Gloucester Aircraft Company), would ride a further few every evening with two buckets to collect drinking water after the family found a dead cat at the bottom of their own well.

Money was tight, but Jack and Nancy Malpas decided the local school was not for David, who recalls his first spelling mistake ('bocks' for 'box') earning him a smack from the teacher. Off he went to Gloucester Cathedral's King's School. There was no money for boarding school, but Malpas sat for Monmouth School anyway to practise for the 11-plus that nobody expected him to pass. He won a scholarship and in this way received a similar education to that of Ian MacLaurin. 'If you could survive a minor public school in the 1950s then you could survive anything,' was his opinion. 'It was survival of the fittest at school. I failed to get the A-levels to go to a university. Partly it was because that was the year that National Service ended'[7] [thus dramatically increasing the competition for the university places available]. After a year out teaching at a Surrey prep school – where he 'became the French master, who had disappeared overnight' – he was accepted by Liverpool University. He graduated without much idea of what he wanted to do. 'I had very little understanding of what business was by the time I went to look for a job at twenty-three. I couldn't have told you the difference between industry and commerce. Nobody would have been able to in those days.'[8]

He had, however, had some experience of serving customers thanks to a holiday job on Barry Island when he was fourteen, working in an ice-cream parlour owned by a branch of the Forte Hotel family. 'It was very hard work and enormous fun. I worked 8.30 a.m. to 10 p.m., seven days a week, but it was lots and lots of money for a fourteen-year-old. I loved it. Serving people, interacting with customers, guessing what that customer is going to ask for, if they were happy or sad, where they came from. I was always doomed to become a retailer. My employer is still a friend of ours and is now in his early seventies.

'It turned out Lewis's [a department store group, though not the same as the John Lewis Partnership] had a graduate management-training scheme which was absolutely brilliant. We were taught in a classroom and had to pass exams. I still use the calculations. After three years I became a sales manager in charge of a few departments and people.

'Department stores were just about past their zenith. [The Lewis store in] Birmingham was two stores separated by the Minories over about 250–350 thousand square feet and on eight storeys, then a basement and sub-basement. The staff were treated well.

'I don't know whether people realize how much things have

changed since the days when people did something like a stock take and counted the number of pencils, worked out how much stock might be needed because it might be a school holiday, then ordered it, checked it and priced it. Nowadays not only will a computer register a pencil has been sold but it will work out how many will be needed because it knows it is a school holiday. Then it is ordered, distributed and arrives on a roll cage in the order in which it should appear on the shelves.'[9]

He must have been glad to get to work, even though it meant catching a bus before it got light. He was living in a bedsit in Kings Heath [Birmingham] where the inside of the windows became covered in ice and frosted over in winter.

'We had a good deal of fun because it is a fairly repetitive job. I hope I was fair but firm. I think I was reasonably clever in terms of spotting fraud or security issues.'[10] He had a good trainer: Sergeant Bouncer, a former policeman, was head of security when Malpas was the store manager. 'A shoplifter got caught and when he was brought into the office, he collapsed. Sergeant Bouncer walked in off his lunch and said "Fred, get up", and he did.'[11]

The experiences were many and varied and stood Malpas in good stead. 'I learned that you shouldn't buy unless you are properly trained. Good buyers have no pride. A bad buyer will always have his pride appealed to by a salesman.'

'When I left Lewis and joined Tesco I was astonished to find that Lewis was making twice as much on bread – Tesco got a 12.5 per cent discount and Lewis got a 25 per cent.'[12]

Although he enjoyed working for Lewis, 'I was terribly bored. [There was] so little to do I decided to go and look for [another] job. I loved the business but it was grossly over-manned and over-managed.'

Malpas describes Tesco as being very downmarket when he joined in 1966. This was true of supermarkets in general; they were regarded as beyond the pale by his department-store colleagues. 'At Lewis we thought they were all right, but it was very much "My dear, you wouldn't want to do your shopping there." In those days it was all cut cases and boxes and cut price and that was it: no quality, no service, no nothing. At Lewis, the directors perceived supermarkets as a bit of an irritant but not really anything to worry about because *people are always going to come to us aren't they?*'[13]

The Tesco of the late sixties, then, was not glamorous and Malpas paints a colourful picture. 'Tesco was very different. The training was more by threat than anything else, but you just got on with it. My first store was tiny – it was 3,500 square feet. The warehouse was 600 square feet – "warehouse" is too distinguished a word for it. It was at Oatby outside Leicester and it took £6,000 a week in sales.

'There was not much in the way of refrigeration. There was one refrigerated multi-level cabinet of 20 or 30 feet. The rest would be shelves of groceries. Things people buy now were not available then: paper kitchen towels were a province of the elite rich who had money to burn. Bath products? There weren't any. You could have bought a packet of bath salts perhaps somewhere, but not in a supermarket. There would be crisps and snacks. There was no market at all in bottled water.

'On the other hand a terribly important, arguably the most important, part of the store was canned fruit. We would sell at least four sizes of cans of sliced peaches in syrup. Halves, sliced, in syrup, then in juice. There was a great big family size you don't see these days at all. The shop, going back to 1967, would have looked the way an old-fashioned supermarket looks today with a very basic, very restricted range. Fresh fruit and vegetables? It's embarrassing. There was a fruit and veg packing firm, Bellevale packers, which Tesco owned. It was not an upmarket operation. When I was at Lewis we gave Bellevale a trial but the quality was so bad they didn't last a fortnight. There was no concept of trying to get anything of quality: it was simply buy what you could for the cheapest price and sell it for what you could get.'[14]

Malpas's recollection of the structure was that the original Tesco team – Jack Cohen and Daisy Hyams in particular – almost viewed the stores as 'an unfortunate but necessary adjunct to the important business of running a wholesale business'. Ian MacLaurin recalls his father-in-law, Edgar, telling a story to a journalist, *Grocer* editor Tony de Angeli, about 'losing' cables from Jack on his travels in South Africa that requested £80,000 to buy a vast consignment of tinned fruit.

Tesco was evolving and expanding so quickly that it seemed decisions were made before the full consequences could be appreciated, let alone planned for. Stores such as the Bull Ring at Birmingham were 'bought on a whim from Fine Fare', according to Malpas, and were totally unsuited to the needs of modern supermarkets and their customers. Modern stores needed to be on one level, not several, with good access for customers and also goods coming in. The older stores on high streets were configured for a time when shoppers bought small amounts of groceries regularly, rather than a weekly shop.

Malpas was promoted to be an inspector and then was brought south from the Midlands, to London.

Like Irwins, Victor Value was another northern chain of stores. It was owned by a family of Cohens, not related to Jack but running shops pretty similar to his. They had bought two businesses outside the North – Swettenham's of the Midlands and then Anthony Jackson Food Fare in the London area, which was controlled by one of Jack's nephews, Sidney Ingram (Jack had helped set him up in business in the early thirties, supplying goods to his store). Alex Cohen offered the whole lot to Jack, and the Tesco Board eventually authorized a bid of £8.5 million. It was a brave move, and a big bite to chew on: the acquisition added 217 stores to Tesco – a third of its estate again. There were now 834 stores and turnover was £200 million.

Harry Quinlan was the twenty-six-year-old manager of Victor Value's shop in Hough Lane, Leyland, when the takeover went through on 18 June 1968. He did not think much of the Tesco over the road: 'It had had thirteen managers in one year. I thought, that can't be good.'

His memories suggest that, as Victor Value teetered, its old owners kept their staff in the dark. 'At Victor Value we were using

S&H pink stamps as a trading gimmick and Tesco used Green Shield, the stronger and more recognized stamp. We were summoned to a meeting in London on a Sunday to be told we would continue with these stamps and within a week we had stopped using them, so we had to remove all reference to pink stamps. We adopted a new pricing policy, which probably turned out to be a wrong policy, but nevertheless we traded on and for the first time my sales were less than we had been achieving. For the first time I saw Tesco claw back sales from me in my personal battle with them.'[15]

Quinlan had no idea of what was coming. 'I went for a summer holiday down south. We never took a newspaper on holiday. I returned at the end of two weeks. I was cutting the grass at the front of the house. My next-door neighbour said, "How is it working for Tesco?" I said, "I don't work for Tesco, I work for Victor Value. I thought you knew that?" He said, "No you don't, you work for Tesco."

'Tesco had taken over Victor Value in that two-week period. I went into work quite early that morning and the staff were all asking questions. Tesco took over Victor Value and most of the higher management, as happens in all takeovers, was dismissed. The one thing they needed just as much as ever was the store management because they were the fighting troops. I made it clear to the staff I didn't have concerns for them, they would be all right, but I had some concerns for myself.

I met one of the new management. It was pointed out that my store would receive some money to do a refit quite quickly. They would convert the Tesco store over the road, an older building, to Home 'n' Wear, which was clothing at the time. The result was that I was to be the store manager. The Tesco manager from the store opposite was to be my assistant. He declined because he thought it should be the other way round.

'It certainly was a shock with the takeover but, supermarkets being supermarkets, most of the operations were similar. Having stopped using pink stamps we had green stamps instead. We had a few months of trading and, because they were going to convert my store, it became very good again.'[16]

Though never a Board director, Quinlan was to become one of Tesco's senior managers and ran a large number of stores during transformational periods for the company. He worked directly for Philip Clarke ('a human dynamo with an amazing facility for recalling people's names') and got to know MacLaurin after Quinlan turned down a new Tesco role in the mistaken belief that because he was asked, he had a choice. Quinlan ran a team that established the supply system that made barcode-scanning possible and survived several 'reorganizations', which he puts down to having had a reputation for being able to manage people.

Born in 1942, Quinlan was raised in Crossens, near Southport. His grandfather was a butcher and his father was an RAF mechanic. He was not academic and when he left school he took a job working eighty hours a week in a farm-produce shop. His ambition was to earn £1,000 a year, 'the same as professional people.

'My wife Joan, who wasn't my wife then, saw an advert. We had local small shops near us. I had never heard of Victor Value. She had organized an interview for me for the Friday evening. I didn't really know what the job entailed other than it was for a trainee manager. The assistant manager, Mr Jones, interviewed me. He asked me whether I was prepared to work hard. I had to phone the next morning and was told I had the job. I told my boss I was going to leave. He thought it was a wrong move. He said, "Do you know what you are going into? What are supermarkets? What do they do?"'[17]

On the shop floor Quinlan encountered the low morale that many in the North were suffering as the Tesco and Victor Value stores were crunched together. 'We turned the store the other way around. We were going to work longer hours and that was understandable. The refit went on for four weeks. I had accrued about forty hours of extra time and so had a few of my managers. I put in this request for the overtime for myself and for the others who had been involved. Some of us had worked until 2 a.m. At that time I was told that management did not get paid overtime. I said I appreciated that, but I [had been] told different.

'I said: "Why haven't you got the guts to sack me? You're going to get rid of me eventually. I've seen over the road the conniving ways that you work. Where would you like me to leave the keys? You need to send another manager. I think you are underhand. You lie. You scheme. I have worked hard, so have the other people. The store is up and running. It has never not opened on time."

'I phoned Joan and said I could be out of work in an hour and a half's time and be home. She said, "You have to decide what you want to do."

'I received a call to say we would be paid. But I did think, is that what they are going to be like? We were not in pensions at that time. They were there as optional. I worked for seven years before joining the pension because I always had that feeling that your job wasn't safe. Something might happen that might suddenly change your life. That is how I felt at the time.'[18]

Although Quinlan stayed for another three decades and was responsible for several major initiatives, his experience bears out the memories of people like Ian MacLaurin, David Malpas and John Gildersleeve, all of whom recall that often people were not treated well.

Tesco was charging ahead. The old ways were fast becoming obsolete and managers who wanted to hold on to their old privileges and practices were, by and large, going to sink. Harry tells several stories of 'bloodlettings', when managers would be called out of the blue early in the morning and fired. Others would be waiting outside offices believing they were about to be fired only to find out that their roles had been expanded, or they had been picked out for promotion beyond their wildest imaginings. Either way, those days would be fear-filled.

As it happened, the culling was not just at Quinlan's level. Regardless of the need for managers with experience, Tesco was changing to survive.

Chapter 9

The Fight for Control: Battling through Difficult Years

'Leslie walked into Jim Grundy's office and said I'm sorry to tell you that you are retiring due to ill-health.'

Lord MacLaurin[1]

'Although Sir John has relinquished his office of Joint Chairman he has not retired. He attends the office daily and participates in our policy discussions, playing an active part in the Company's affairs.'

Hyman Kreitman[2]

Jack celebrated his seventieth birthday in 1969 with a grand party at London's Dorchester hotel, still a favourite with retail royalty more than half a century later. Television presenter and disc jockey Alan Freeman arrived at the party to tell him 'This is Your Life'. Now a household name, Jack had recently been knighted in Prime Minister Harold Wilson's New Years Honours list.

Dame Shirley Porter recalls the impact the knighthood had on her father. 'I remember he just had a look on his face the day he had the letter. He couldn't keep a secret. You couldn't tell him a secret – it would be out the next day. He was amazed that I guessed. We all kept terribly quiet. It was a most exciting thing for him. When my father got his knighthood he was thrilled out of his life. You were allowed to take two people. I was sat in the gallery and as my father came in they were playing "If I Were a Rich Man" [from *Fiddler on the Roof*]. It was quite an amazing ceremony. It was one of the greatest times for him.

'It was wonderful. To come from nothing to something. You can't actually feel the same if you haven't done it yourself. People are for ever seeking satisfaction and success and a lot of people don't feel good about themselves because they are not sure if they could have done it on their own, but if you have done it by yourself you are sure.'[3]

Sir Jack Cohen now also boasted a coat of arms with a cod Latin motto: '*Mercatores Coenascent*', which he translated as 'May the traders be convivial together'. In the light of the rows over Resale Price Maintenance and trading stamps, somebody had a nice sense of irony as well as a knack for punning. Classical scholars would disagree; but, like John F. Kennedy's '*Ich bin ein Berliner*', the power of the phrase is in the sentiment rather than its literal meaning.

Half a century after he began with a barrow in Hackney, Jack was a business legend. Tesco's profits had risen from £4 on day one to more than £10 million in the year to February 1969. He employed 21,220 people in around 600 stores and had already bought out a number of his rivals. Expansion had been spectacular.

But had Jack bitten off more than he could chew?

Tesco's executive management – by now a massive beast numbering about 70 people and made up of the Board (11), directors (27) and executive directors (29) – needed attention. The family's shareholding outweighed everybody else's – a physical sign of the Cohen influence. Somehow – records do not explain – external consultants were invited in. A team from management consultants McKinsey arrived in 1969 and by March 1970 had delivered their report, recommending significant pruning and further centralization of Tesco functions.

There were immediate results: Jack Cohen was to be retired and Tesco's North/South divide was to be obliterated. Easier said than done, on both counts.

David Malpas summarizes the situation: 'There were two separate businesses: Tesco North and South. The stores were the only part that was pretty much the same. The systems and controls were substantially different. There were separate profit centres. These were usually brought together with a mix of instinct and violence in the mid-seventies, largely by Ian MacLaurin. Leslie Porter had decided the two businesses had to be brought together. He breezily told us, "Mr Grundy (the chairman and chief executive) has just retired." That was a fairly typical way of making a management change at that point.'[4]

MacLaurin was the managing director responsible for the stores in the South. He recalls driving Leslie Porter to Winsford to speak to Jim Grundy, Ian's northern counterpart. The northern stores had been struggling to keep up with the growth and profits in the South.

'The Board said would I go and take over the North. I remember this classic drive – taking Arthur Thrush and Leslie Porter to the Winsford head office. Leslie summarily dismissed Jim Grundy that morning. He said right, Ian MacLaurin is in charge. I drove them back to Wilmslow station. I was left with a hostile northern management who didn't take too kindly to this southerner coming up and running their business. The first day I went down to the canteen and nobody would sit with me; I sat by myself with the others looking at me sideways. We brought a team up: David Malpas, Mike Darnell, Eddie Clark, John Venner. We took over the North and put the whole lot into one. We got that right after a period of time. The North had lost touch with the business. Asda was doing very well. We weren't very well run. The calibre of management wasn't as good as the calibre in the South. Southern guys went up there and put their professionalism up there. That gave opportunities for other bright people in the South.

'We didn't get most of them on side – we removed most of them. It had to be done over a period of time. It was hard for the people up from the South because they were away from their families. They made huge personal sacrifices for the company. There was a hotel just off the M6. You would stagger in and have dinner together at 10 p.m. It was a Posthouse, quite near Stoke. I see it nowadays and think oh my goodness me, I used to spend hours there. It was awful really: like any hotel, okay for a night but night after night . . . I used to do 60,000 miles a year. I had a new car every year because you just burnt them out. That went on for two or three years.'[5]

The semi-feudal managerial style in the North was at play in the South, too; it was just that change began closer to Cheshunt than it did to Winsford. The Board, prompted by the McKinsey report, decided to speed it up, as Eddie Clark recalls.

'After being number two to Ian MacLaurin for a few years I knew where the limitations were for me. But one day I was invited to see Hyman Kreitman, who was the chairman. He was a gentleman who would rather say four words than five. A nice, kind man. He closed the door. He said, "Mr Clark I want you to do me a favour. We have a store making a great loss when I personally think it should be making a jolly good profit. This store is in Yorkshire, Wakefield." I closed my eyes and thought oh no, not another Bristol [an earlier tough 'foreign' posting for Londoner Eddie].

'He said, "What I would like you to do is go there and only report to me. I want you to take the store over and do exactly whatever you think you need to do." I asked to think about it. He said, "No, if you don't want to I'll accept that, but I think you will want the challenge." I stood up and shook his hand and said, "When would you like me to start?" He said, "Tomorrow."

'It was a fair-sized store with a small car park usually occupied by people shopping elsewhere. The store was in a terrible state. This isn't a criticism of Tesco North, but it was in a state because of the company's policy of their promotions up there. When I walked in the first thing I saw on the left-hand side was a huge stack of Vim scouring powder. The next thing I saw was a big stack of sponges. I walked round the store and every opportunity for point of sale, and instead of being something a family would like it was to do with high-profit stuff.

'And one end, believe it or not, had Dulux paint. I thought God almighty. I scrapped all that. Instead of Vim we had Tesco own-label baked beans, which was a good-quality bean. Then we had things like jellies and consumable foods. The greengrocery – it's a shame to call it that, it was so bad – manager wouldn't conform so he left. We promoted a young lady in store to be in charge. Her father used to own a greengrocery store in town. Surprise, surprise, hers was a lot better. She took over and she inspected the greengrocery when it came in, which was not done before. She only signed for what she got. There was some doubt before whether we got less than we signed for. We went from there. The butcher was the same. It was not well done . . . Everything was half-hearted. Shoulders were dropping.

'We changed it around. There was no point in putting large cuts of meat out in Wakefield on Monday, Tuesday or Wednesday because nobody had any money by then. We did different cuts for different days. Big sacks of potatoes weren't needed Monday, Tuesday, Wednesday – 5lb bags were big enough. The greengrocery deliveries had come from a local supplier – he was up in arms. I said no, Tesco pays the bill and we only want the best. If the apples are going out of season, we don't want them. We'll import them. The bread supplier was the same. They would come in the early morning and deliver what they wanted. There was doubt in my mind that we were getting what we were signing for.

'Sales started to increase. Then we decided multi-training would be better – you don't need to be a specialist to operate a till or fill a shelf up.

'It was magic. Everybody was going home happy. We'd keep staff instead of losing them. The wage bill went up. Mr Kreitman came every Wednesday and he said it was a transformation and that the store looked bright and alive.

'After about nine weeks Mr Kreitman came in with a big smile – "You won't believe it, we made a profit last month – it's never been done." At the end he decided to give the store back to Tesco North. Three years ago [2002] we had a Christmas card from Mr Kreitman and it said, "Eddie, the next time you are in London pop in and see me, I'd love to have a chat." I didn't and then he died and I was very upset I had not been to see him. It would have been difficult to have small talk because he wasn't interested. "Vot is, is." Like my dad.

He was a nice, nice guy. A charming man with a charming wife.'[6]

David Malpas also recalls the big move north. 'In 1971 I was rusticated, dispatched from the London area up to Yorkshire to take charge of a group of branches based in Harrogate. In Cheshunt they thought it was Harrowgate.'[7] This was not a reference to William the Conqueror's 'Harrowing of the North', an ultra-violent suppression, but for some it felt pretty brutal.

Malpas, by then in charge of a group of inspectors, spent eighteen months in the North. Harry Quinlan, who had survived the post-Victor Value rationalization, remembers that Malpas 'dealt' with the regional managing-director level during one round of sackings. He says, 'It was about bringing stability and control to the company. There were five or six directors in the North and another number in the South and they had quite a lot of autonomy and what they did in every instance wasn't good for the company. They would do deals. That didn't help with the buying function. The profit coming from the North wasn't as good as that coming from the South, nor was the turnover.

'We had at that time a new company being set up called Asda who were operating in very old but very large converted mills that Lancashire had plenty of. The range and prices they were selling at made it very hard to compete against them. They also had lots of car-parking space. Tesco had none. A lot of changes were taking place. I started in this new role [controlling a large group of stores] and found it quite difficult.

'Today Tesco are fantastic about training people generally, and even for higher management train them extremely well for the new job, but in those early days they didn't. On the Saturday night I was in charge of one store. On the Monday morning I was in charge of fifteen stores. Nobody said it would be different on Monday. What you tried to do initially was work harder, quicker.

'You didn't have meetings together. You didn't learn from each other. You learned from your experience and mistakes and hoped they weren't too big or that serious enough that you could be fired. There were instances with store managers and executives of pilfering from the company. It was quite common in the early days to catch managers who were removing stock from the company and they were caught and prosecuted. It did happen to some executives.

'As with any company that is growing, changes occur. The move bringing North and South together brought about some good changes. We very quickly learned from the benefits and different style that Ian MacLaurin brought from what this chap Grundy had delivered, and the removal of these barons of old, the choice of the old directors, brought stability. New people came who had better ideas. They were more focused on the business. They were still not into the people aspect, and staff turnover was not good in those early times and wasn't for quite a while. But the regrouping was very good.

'As with everything Tesco had done, it worked better but you had to go through that phase of heartache and concern for yourself and your colleagues. You thought thank heavens I'm okay and the restructuring was put into place.'[8]

There was simply no mention at all of Jim Grundy in the 1971 Annual Report. The waters closed over him, along with the North/South divide.

Jack Cohen's dominance needed different handling. No management consultancy, not even McKinsey, would try to boot him out altogether. In December 1969 the Board had met to consider Jack's role and replaced him as chairman with his elder son-in-law, Hyman Kreitman. Jack was appointed Life President, with responsibility for public relations. Some might have felt this to be a logical progression, possibly even a relief for a seventy-year-old who might like to slow down a bit and enjoy his achievements. Jack does not seem to have thought so.

Ian MacLaurin recalls, 'He was difficult. The sadness for me was he was such a great guy but he was still hanging around the business as the business was moving on. You can't do that. Towards the end when he wasn't very well he was pretty disruptive in the business. He used to come into our offices and tell us we were all idiots. We'd have some differences of opinion. He'd always come into my office though at the end of the day and say, "Well goodnight Ian, tomorrow is another day."

'McKinsey came in. Jack was made president. Hyman was chairman and had an office in Grosvenor Street somewhere and worked from there [rather than coming into Tesco House]. In the end he just had enough. Jack made it hell for him. That rubbed off on us in the business. We knew the chairman wasn't coming in and wasn't getting on with Jack. Leslie [Porter] was totally different, rumbustious, and he would give the old man as good as he got.'[9]

It must have been hard for Hyman Kreitman's friends to listen to him being screamed at. In his years as chairman, before he handed over to his brother-in-law, Leslie, he seems to have tried to make it work. In the 1971 Annual Review he announced, 'I am happy to inform you that although Sir John has relinquished his office of Joint Chairman he has not retired. He attends the office daily and participates in our policy discussions, playing an active part in the Company's affairs.' It is hard not to imagine the gritted teeth, given the accounts of the boardroom during this era.

Few would argue with Jack's results and, in his family life, he may have been charming. He was brusque rather than a bully towards less senior staff. However, at Tesco House in Delamare Road he seems to have ridden roughshod over his directors' sensibilities.

By the mid-1970s, David Malpas had returned from the North and was spending a lot more time at Cheshunt, managing store operations. He recalls that 'Jack Cohen's role was to attend Board meetings and come to offices on other occasions but not really to contribute much except some rather wild and antagonistic things.'[10]

After Kreitman stepped down in 1973 ('because he couldn't stand the old man badgering him the whole time,' says MacLaurin), Jack rowed with Leslie instead.

'On one occasion,' Malpas recalls, 'there was literally a stand-up row between Jack Cohen and Leslie Porter. The Board minutes after that said, "Sir John Cohen joined the meeting and offered words of advice and encouragement." That was very nicely put. I think in today's parlance he was pretty much out of it.

'Leslie Porter was not an incisive chairman. He looked for consensus. He was a jolly fellow in the best sense. He had no pretensions to be a great strategic thinker but he did introduce one or two matters, like telling me to get on and set up a proper research unit to develop sites.'[11]

MacLaurin says that Porter, a 'very engaging wheeler-dealer' who, like Jack, was 'in the big cigar game', was very supportive of the upcoming Tesco leadership and 'allowed us to get on and run the business'.

For all the internal restructuring, Tesco was entering unfamiliar territory. Its glorious run of rising profits was about to hit the buffers against a backdrop of economic chaos and spiralling costs. And, simply put, it was not living up to its best-for-less promise.

David Malpas believes that the problem was baked into the business because there was tension between the wholesale, buying side and the store side. 'Buyers bought stock into warehouses and distributed to stores roughly on the basis of what stores had ordered and partly by what buyers needed to push through the system, which was called allocating.

'The profit centre was the wholesale arm. The buyers bought and warehouses distributed and stores were charged a cost price and the selling price for the goods they sold. Half the profit – nearly all of it by the end – was reserved to the wholesale division by a mechanism called the over-riding discount.

'As the company got larger, stores were authorized to buy from a large range – too large – on top of allocations from head office. They were grossly over-stocking and the stores were full of things people didn't want to buy and short of things people did want to buy. It was never corrected until we took control in 1980 and changed the business around, so stores bought what people wanted to buy rather than the things we wanted to sell.

'It's difficult to explain now just how much of an earthquake this was for the business. It had been brought up in the wholesale tradition.'[12]

With Kreitman and Porter at the head and MacLaurin (newly appointed to the main Board in 1970) directing the daily operations, Tesco tried to modernize, but the early 1970s were not an easy time to be running a business, especially for a retailer. Wage inflation was spiralling and retailers were the last link in the chain, picking up a piece of every manufacturer's or supplier's increased costs. Tesco's own wage bill increased by £1.5 million in 1970–71, partly because the Multiple Grocers Association made awards to bring about equality in male/female pay. High levels of competition among food retailers meant the costs had to be absorbed. Kreitman pointed to a National Board for Prices and Incomes report as confirmation that Tesco had not passed costs on to customers.

Decimalization, which came into effect in 1971, was another distraction, costing the company £500,000 in training and new equipment (with 62.5 per cent of that charged against profits). At the same time, union strength was formidable: a dock strike in the summer of 1970 disrupted supplies, particularly of clothing lines, while the power workers' strike coincided with the critical Christmas trading period that year, leaving 'supermarkets in darkness for long periods, restricting shopping and putting stores at security risk. Housewives in the North and the Midlands – regions especially badly hit by strikes and job cuts – were finding it difficult already, said Kreitman, without having the rise in food prices to contend with as well.

It is interesting that Tesco first flagged up 'possible entry to Europe as a logical extension of future expansion' in the Annual Report for 1971. It was premature: this was a business that didn't open a store in Scotland (Greenock), never mind outside the UK, until that year. The move to Scotland seems to have been the result of a joint venture struck in the same spirit as some of Jack Cohen's earlier slightly whimsical purchases, but it did indicate that Tesco was finding conditions in its traditional home market very challenging.

Tesco now wanted to move to bigger sites, but town planners were not wild about the proposals. 'We are not acquiring any supermarket sites of less than 20,000 square feet, with car parking,' explained Kreitman in the report. Tesco was not the first food retailer to spot that customers were changing: Asda had already moved in that direction and French company Carrefour had a hypermarket in Wales. However, Tesco's reading of consumer trends back in its 1959 Annual Report was turning out to be spot on. The Board believed that the hypermarket – a smaller concept then than it is today – would answer most of those needs, including car parking, shopping in comfort, a larger range of goods priced more cheaply because of economies of scale and relieving high-street congestion.

Tesco was doing its best to woo planners. At Yiewsley in the London borough of Hillingdon, for example, it built a 'new modern church' as part of the package, and in Liverpool it developed a number of shop units for other retailers and built a cinema. It also employed architects to make the shops fit: a picture from the period shows the store at Leamington Spa, which was 19,000 square feet of reproduction Regency in a Georgian terrace. Where the buildings were modern, such as at Reading, so was the new Tesco store. Tesco was hampered slightly in some cases: as Jack (then in charge of public relations) observed, many of the sites Tesco wanted to develop were on scrubland where any 'landscaping' had been created by the wind or by fly-tippers.

To some, even wasteland was preferable to a Tesco. The president-elect of the Royal Town Planning Institute, Ewart Parkinson, opined: 'Many Councils regard Tesco as something of a retail cowboy, and while Sainsbury and Marks are always welcome if they are looking for anchor retailers, Tesco is rarely considered.' He added that councils took exception to 'visual pollution of their high streets resulting from Tesco's abrasive trading style'.[13]

Tesco approached the Secretary of State for the Environment, Peter Walker, to make its case and to try to gain clarity on the government's planning policy, which a series of reports and papers (some Labour sponsored, some Conservative sponsored) had not solidified. Politicians proclaimed themselves against 'runaway devel-opment' but, without any factual definition of 'runaway' the debate continued to be largely subjective.

Tesco failed to gain permission for any new supermarkets in 1971–72, though there was plenty of investment and innovation in existing stores: off-licences and in-store bakeries increased and some stand-alone Home 'n' Wear and furniture shops opened. Meanwhile, the programme to close down smaller stores went ahead. Come 1973 – the year the oil shock undermined the global economy – businesses were contending with government restrictions on prices (through the Prices and Incomes Act) and on dividends (through the Counter-Inflation Programme), as well as the introduction of Value Added Tax, which triggered an artificial boost in trade ahead of its imposition as well as increasing prices.

This year was also Tesco's twenty-fifth anniversary year. In 1948 the company had a turnover of £1.3 million, made profits of £71,000 and had on average 60,000 customers each week. By 1973 the turnover was £360 million, pre-tax profits were £21.7 million and 6 million shoppers visited Tesco stores each week.

Nationally, inflation was running at 10.6 per cent and Britain's balance of payments deficit was 4 per cent of GNP. Counter-inflation measures persisted.

In 1972/73 Tesco opened 250,000 square feet of new space and closed thirty-four smaller stores. In the 1973 Annual Report Kreitman acknowledged: 'There can be relatively few towns where we can say we are represented with all the space we require, especially bearing in mind the many groups of merchandise we are able to offer our customers.'

That year, Hyman Kreitman stepped down as chairman and handed control to his brother-in-law, Leslie Porter. Porter appointed MacLaurin and Laurie Leigh joint managing directors. Porter's first chairman's review, in the 1974 Annual Report, is a list of the woes besetting Tesco, describing the past twelve months as 'a year that has been exceptionally full of incident'.

In Cheshunt staff had transferred over the road to New Tesco

House (still the company headquarters today), celebrating the move with a new computer, the company's third. Home 'n' Wear, meanwhile, had moved to Milton Keynes. Staffing was a major issue in an era of full employment and in the report Porter thanked the likes of Eddie Clark and David Malpas implicitly when he noted the burdens placed on executives: 'For many, due to circumstances beyond their control, travelling to and from their places of work and on company business was for some a miserable experience.'

Was there, even, a note of envy in his formal 'thank you' to Kreitman for his service during the twenty-eight years to September 1973? 'One can understand his wish to enjoy some of the benefits of private life which most are able to enjoy as a matter of course, but which are denied to a great degree to those at the top carrying the complexity of burdens of modern business.'

The idea of a venture in France was being pursued (David Behar, the property expert on the Board, was the inspiration through his interest in a development there, meaning that he and his son and fellow Board member, Robin, had to stay out of discussions). Meanwhile, back home, in the spring of 1974, Tesco had experimented with customer banking facilities in four stores, but had not progressed the trial.

There had been a disastrous acquisition (Square Meals) from Brooke Bond Liebig, which had to be smartly reversed with the help of the courts when Tesco decided not only did the business model stink (customers bought freezers and got vouchers for frozen food) but so did the deal: none of the stores had the correct retail planning permission. Tesco got its money back but was still out of pocket as a result of costs incurred.

On top of this, supply lines were still being damaged by waves of industrial action. The miners had gone on strike in 1972 over pay; long after they returned to work, the impact on industry of their action meant shortages of all kinds of manufactured goods.

Internally, Leslie Porter was contending with his father-in-law Jack's helpful interventions, or, as he put it, 'It is pleasing to tell you that our Founder and Life President, Sir John Cohen, still comes to the office every day and gives us his wise counsel.' Again, it is hard not to imagine the sound of teeth being ground, let alone gritted, for by now the new leaders were beginning to feel that Tesco needed radical change.

Porter also pleaded for urgent reappraisal of planning policy, arguing again that superstores would bring costs, and therefore prices, down. In an era of runaway inflation, every month's delay on a building project threatened the budget. 'Profit in the current climate has become a "nasty" word, and it is indeed unfortunate that the more efficient the company is in containing its operating costs, and selling goods at highly competitive prices, the more it appears to be penalized. Let there be no misunderstanding – we need profits! We need them to expand our business, we need them to invest to create further efficiencies and savings in order to maintain our competitive position in the market place'.

The following year, 1974, Tesco's profits fell for the first time in a quarter of a century.

Chapter 10

The View from the Shop Floor: What Was Going Wrong

'Customers in those days were no different than they are today. If your counter looks rubbish they will walk past it and go somewhere else.'

Joe Doody, former store manager[1]

Ian MacLaurin's elevation to joint managing director and Leslie Porter's to chairman coincided with the dip in Tesco's profits, though turnover had hit a record £500 million. Put simply, more Tesco stores were selling more goods but doing so less efficiently. If there were problems at management level, there were clearly also serious issues on the shop floor. People who were there recall a rough, tough and scam-ridden culture that may provide at least part of the answer to what was going wrong.

David Potts joined Tesco in 1973 straight from a Manchester secondary modern. He remembers that Tesco's reputation was so poor that he wanted to keep the fact that he worked there a secret. Quite a reflection from a man who would become a Board director running thousands of shops.

'I left school on the Friday and there was a sign in the window of the Tesco store in Ashton shopping precinct asking for a general assistant. I started on the Monday. I came out with £9.99 for forty hours' work and sold cooked meat behind the provisions counter.

'My three friends scootled off to the local factory that made pills and got jobs there, but I didn't fancy working in a factory. In those days people hardly dared go into a supermarket let alone work in one. Tesco was considered down at heel and a place not to be seen dead in. People had been brought up going to the smaller, more traditional grocers' stores. Supermarkets were Johnny-come-lately sort of things. Tesco was brash and garish and giving out Green Shield Stamps. Staff had to wear green and white.

'I was acutely embarrassed to tell my friends I was working there. I remember saying to my mates about the meat-prep room upstairs and one assumed I meant a laboratory. I didn't change his view because I thought it made the job sound more interesting.'[2]

David Potts was born 'on a Monday, washing day' in 1958, the youngest of two children, in Ashton-under-Lyne, Manchester. His father was working class with a white-collar, managerial job and the family was comfortably off with their own home and a car. Family life for David and his sister was what it would have been for thousands of other British children then. They walked to school on their own from an early age, and he was happy provided that he was playing football, whether thirty-a-side with a lump of coal in the playground or one against one on the full-length pitch at the local park until it got too dark to see. His mum cooked staples like cauliflower cheese, meat pie, fish fingers or egg flip for tea and his dad got back from work at around the children's bedtime, or even later.

Their life changed drastically when David's mother, suffering with an illness that these days might have been diagnosed and managed, took her own life. David was not taken to the funeral and his mother's death was not spoken of. His father suffered a heart attack soon afterwards. From being comfortable and secure, the Potts children, aged nine and six, were no longer typical. The household income fell drastically when David's father left his managerial job and began teaching engineering.

'It was a small place so [my mother's death] was in the papers and in the school and some people react kindly and some don't.

I had to have a day or two off and then I had to go in. I went from life being pretty cosy to wondering where my next pair of shoes was coming from. But it made me go and work at fourteen, and it has made me get on in Tesco. People who experience those things can only grieve, but likely things will come out of it that are positive. It's part of life. It's part of my history and part of what makes me determined.

'I joke about the shoes, but there was a spell when I had to wear my grandma's shoes and the clothes I wore were not right. There was me, in the second year, with my grandma's zip-up boots on and short pants. The main thing was it makes you strong. I realized I could earn money from selling newspapers and I did as much as I could. I loved selling them on the street corners during the weeks when everybody went to Blackpool and the shops put the papers on the corner.

'I got a job at a local shop through Auntie Margaret – eight until one o'clock on a Saturday for 7/6, which is about 37½p. You could buy sweets; you couldn't go and buy a suit or a pair of shoes but you could buy things. I did that from fourteen years old, selling over the counter. I knew every product, and eventually I'd come in and do it myself. I asked for some more money when I was doing it on my own and at the end of the day she gave me 12 shillings – I thought she'd got it wrong – but I had to do a delivery too. I used to boil the beetroot and cut the lettuce. It was a single shop front with boxes of apples and potatoes. Customers would stand outside and pick what they wanted then they'd come in and queue and have a pound of potatoes, or a lettuce, and I'd wrap it up. That's how I can add up very quickly. The till had big buttons that made a hell of a racket when it opened. It was all cash. In the back there was a little room where you could have a cup of tea and there was a smell of apples and oranges. Manchester was blessed with Ashton Moss: the soil was rich and black and grew every kind of vegetable and salad there.

'My dad did the shopping in Ashton market – it was a big building full of stalls, full of character and characters. He also used a little grocer's store in Ashton that smelt like tea and coffee and ham and delivered quite a lot, though he used it a lot less when he had less money. The way they displayed products was very good – big counters, and racks on the wall. It had lots of character. You were probably stiffed on the prices because I remember supermarkets coming along and thinking, "That's a lot cheaper than where my dad is getting his groceries." The market felt like it was for everybody, whereas the shop felt quite posh and I used to feel a bit embarrassed going in there. You were a bit more anonymous in the big market: people would travel for many miles to go there. I go back still to keep my eye on it.'[3]

David failed the O-levels he took. 'I was useless at school, but I've not been useless at work. That has probably influenced how I've approached work.' His aunt Margaret had set him off down a road in retail that transformed his life, leading him to the very top of a globally successful grocer. He discovered he had a talent for making food look so good that people wanted to buy it and he loved the produce itself, especially its seasonality.

'You have to sell things so they look proud to be in the case they are in – I used to show grapefruit with newspaper underneath them, or cut one in half so people could see it was juicy and a different colour to the skin. People buy with their eyes. If you have a sack of potatoes you take the tape off the top and roll some of it back and you show more than one sack. You can make anything look different and exciting to people. I learned by doing it. You've got time between customers. You fill the water up in the watercress or take a leaf off the lettuce to make it look greener and fresher.

'When I was selling tomatoes I would make it just over a pound [weight] to the ones who could afford it and just on the pound for those who couldn't. I knew all the customers very well.

'I just knew I could sell products – I could put a newspaper through a letter box and make it land right, I could make my stack of papers look really good.

'I was a provisions-counter assistant at Tesco at fifteen – a general assistant. I was immediately at home because of my selling skills. I could make the counter sing and dance.

'I used to fill the shelves on the Thursday evening – it was a rough-and-ready small supermarket, goods were piled on the floor. You used a small knife to cut the packaging, put the tins of peaches out and people piled in to buy them. It was garish light, small aisles and a limited number of products and four or five checkouts. You would have got much more personal service from people who had worked in that corner shop for years, as well as an aroma of coffee, cheese and authentic food and people queuing to be served over counters, though the range would be much more limited and the prices much higher. The higher-quality products would have been in the little shop. The supermarket was regarded as new, innovative, saving money. You would go to Marks & Spencer if you found a tenner or wanted a treat. Supermarkets were for people making pennies count in the main. It was pile it high and sell it cheap.'[4]

Potts's memories of shop management shed light on why super-markets were regarded the way they were – and suggest a reason for at least some of the financial inconsistencies.

'The manager was a hard taskmaster, constantly smoking a cigar with his glasses on his head. One measure of him was his stock result, which is the measure of what is thrown away or stolen. He spent a lot of time putting the prices up of products in order to have a good stock result. He used to stand for hours near the lift using white spirit to erase the price ticket and put another on. He managed to get a fridge to blow up in order to over-declare how much stock had been in it.'[5]

Having worked the stores himself, Ian MacLaurin knew about all the stunts – the buncing and the deals with sales reps – that were commonplace in retail back then. But he and David Malpas also knew the workload and the strains that Tesco had piled on to people unready for the challenge. Malpas recalls, 'A typical store manager would be in his twenties and either a tradesman, like a butcher or baker, or someone who had just been able to work harder and faster than anybody else. There was a certain amount of guidance to help him with wages and so on, but much of it was left to him to cope with, including ordering the stock from warehouses and suppliers.

Much of the first day and a half of the week was taken up with sales representatives. Records had to be kept and account taken of goods on special price promotion that week. There was staff recruitment, welfare and discipline. You had to pretty much learn while you were on the job. There was a breed of managers who had to be self-confident, self-sufficient and unabashed by unknown territory where rules, regulations and systems were concerned, because there weren't very many.'[6]

Joe Doody fitted the bill. He started at Tesco on a small shop's meat counter and his story illustrates the social mobility that Britain's newly emerging supermarket sector could provide.

Joe was born in February 1948 to an Irish farmer from Athy, County Kildare. He says that electricity in people's homes was unusual, while indoor lavatories were almost unheard of. He describes an early life aimed at getting out into the wider world. By the age of nineteen, he was working for an Irish supermarket, Five Star. Dublin's attractions faded quickly, however: country boys, such as he was, were treated as second-class citizens by the city boys, so in 1970 he and two friends joined the steady stream of compatriots who took the ferry at Dun Laoghaire for Liverpool and boarded the train for Euston Station, London.

'We followed Crawley O'Connor from Five Star. We called him up and he said he had a job. He was an area manager at Tesco.

'We arrived in Euston Station at six in the morning on 11 March 1970, got to the store at midday and we were working by one o'clock. We didn't know that much about Tesco but we had heard there were big opportunities for people who were prepared to graft. There was also the attraction of England.

'You got £4 or £5 in your hand for working the afternoon. Everyone worked five and a half days a week and the store always closed for a half-day. We got overtime on a Sunday. We were a "hit squad": we'd work hard and get done what they wanted done – it might be re-laying a warehouse or a store having a refit.'[7]

Joe and his friends arrived in London when IRA activity in mainland Britain was in a particularly violent phase, and being Irish marked them out for attention. On one occasion they wound up in a cell at Bromley police station until Crawley O'Connor came to get them out; Joe remembers sleeping well and enjoying the breakfast there. 'For weeks and weeks there were jibes about "We've got the bombers here." In general, people were all right. Many people made us very welcome. We were just over twenty, young lads, so the girls used to talk to us all the time.

'The manager treated us with respect and never made fun of us being Irish: there are Irish jokes you can laugh at and there are jokes that are insulting, and he would never do that and he would stop other people doing it. He would praise us to his boss. If he asked us to do a job in the warehouse on a Wednesday afternoon after the shop shut, you would just do it.'

Joe soon progressed to the butcher's department, working for a man whose strong Cockney accent made him as much of a foreigner in West Wickham, Kent, as Joe felt. They barely understood a word each other said for a while, but Joe says they enjoyed a couple of pints in the pub at lunchtime and had a laugh when they were at work.

In West Wickham, he remembers, 'There were the sorts of houses you used to think it would be nice to have, and then you work hard over the years and you end up with one of those, but I never could have imagined it back then.'[8] The town's Tesco was a high-street store, not as small as some and quite modern for its day, with a car park. In terms of reputation, however, it wasn't the first choice for the kinds of people who lived in West Wickham.

'Customers in those days were no different than they are today,' says Joe. 'If your counter looks rubbish they will walk past it and go somewhere else. We were cheap and didn't have the best quality of gear and we were sitting in the middle of West Wickham. Just down the road there was a Sainsbury and Sainsbury had a far better name than us. Most people had cars as well, because it was a wealthy area. They travelled to Sainsbury and got far better quality than we had. Our butcher, though, could set up a display like you've never seen and take loads of money.

'In those days Sainsbury wouldn't take on a person who had worked for Tesco because of the bad training. Nowadays they'd poach you tomorrow if they got half a chance. A lot of it [then] was what they call experiential learning – you learn as you go along. You would get better if you were really interested.

'Sainsbury were the enemy. You hated it if they opened up near you because the customers loved them.

'You could sell the best all day every day but your biggest job was to make the cheapest cuts attractive. Women then knew how to take any joint and make it look fantastic. Cafés used to come and buy our bacon, which I loved: they would take the cheaper cuts like collar bacon if they were good slices with proper thickness. As long as you always had what they wanted they would come back to you.'[9]

Not that they always had what customers wanted. Joe describes a chaotic ordering system, running out of best-selling lines and having to take what head office sent rather than what he knew he could sell. He also recalls the 'wheeling and dealing' that went on between store managers and sales reps from brand manufacturers like Heinz and Persil, which went direct to stores rather than through the head office. 'There were reps queuing outside the store manager's door. They'd come every week. He only liked to see the reps himself because there was wheeling and dealing. "I'll order fifty cases if I can have a calculator for my wife", that sort of thing. So much of it went on it was ridiculous.'[10]

The old ways meant that the second most important man in the store after the manager was the Back Door man. Says Doody, 'He had to be trustworthy because of all the fiddling that went on. He had to be good at checking or he would be turned over by the suppliers. Everybody was trying to do everybody, which was horrible. The Back Door man might be on a fiddle with the driver, who would deliver ten and charge for twenty and the Back Door man would give him a receipt and see him later. It was so open to abuse. I don't think the company realized how much of it was going on.

'There was collusion on checkouts: the cashier's friend would come through the till and it would not all get rung up. You cannot do that now with scanning. You can spot if somebody is not scanning something.

'Sometimes you could look at a trolley of stock and think, it sounds horrible, but I don't think that customer can afford that. Nobody just throws the most expensive products into their trolley: people are shrewd shoppers. If they went to the checkout and didn't try to push it out of the door, you'd think it odd: £150 at the checkout when people were earning £20 a week was odd. You started to get a sense about those things.'[11]

Joe had a fairly straightforward way of dealing with the people who walked out of the door without paying. 'I used to have so many rows with shoplifters – especially the male ones who always want to fight with you outside the store. You get the funny ones who want to argue with you and start laughing, and it depends whether they are on drugs or drunk. You'd have to go down the police station for three or four hours, then you'd have to go to court and the first time you have to do that it is nerve wracking going up to read out your statement.'[12]

A few years into the business, Joe was managing a store at Peckham, then a tough area in South London where unemployment was high. 'We had this girl who came in with her mum and she was known as a shoplifter but we hadn't been able to prove it. The mother was off down one aisle, the daughter was down another, bunging all this stuff into her bag. When they left the store I stopped them and took them back into the office. The daughter emptied out her bag and she had all this red salmon, which in those days was so expensive. The mother said, "Can I just talk to you outside the office?" She said, "If you're willing to let her go, I'll get her to look after you for a couple of weeks." I thought what does she mean? She said: "You're a man, she's a woman, I'll get her to look after you." I couldn't believe what I was hearing. We called the police and I told him and he said she was on the game and her mother was the pimp. I felt awful for the daughter. What chance did that kid have?'[13]

It took a certain strength of character to manage shops in areas like Peckham, and Joe Doody had been earning himself a name for being able to handle the stress ever since his first manager's job, at Plumstead, South-east London. Having experienced the 'hire' part of 'hire/fire' culture himself, he saw the 'fire' bit for the first time: a manager who could not look after his store, keeping stock and staff secure, would find himself out of a job fairly fast. Doody recalls, 'I worked for a fellow called Bruce Foreman, who was the area manager for our group at the time, as assistant manager at Bexleyheath. I was called to Plumstead store to meet Bruce, and I went there thinking I had done something wrong. I had ordered fifty cases of Campbell Soup and got a bottle of whisky just before that, so I thought maybe that was it.

'He sent me to the office to wait for him. He sounded iffy. I sat waiting for three quarters of an hour. He came in and said, "Do you know how to cash up, put it altogether and add it all up?" I said yes. I hadn't a clue but I wasn't going to say "no" to this man. He said, "Go downstairs, cash up this store and take it over." I said, "As manager?" He said yes. There was no conversation about money. He had just thrown the manager out of the store. Three bad stocks or whatever it was. That was how it was then.'[14]

Store managers needed to be tough, or at least as tough as their customers. 'I was asked to go to Paddington by security because the manager had been beaten up and he didn't want to go back,' Doody relates. 'I said this is going to cost you, plus it was going over the river. They got me another £30 a week to go there. I took over on the Monday. On the Friday night I had a couple of really good lads and I was going to buy them a pint. There was this big bloke by the counter and Mick Devaney, one of my lads, said, "That's your man who beat up the manager and put him in hospital for three weeks." He pulled all the stalls out for the market traders in the morning. He was a big strong ox of a man. I walked to the bar. "Can I buy you a pint?" I said. "I'm the new manager at Tesco. You've given me a great opportunity to take over this store." I bought him a pint. Every morning I got the wave from him.

'One time I got into trouble with two shoplifters. Stupidly I went out on my own – of course they wanted to fight. I was getting licked, I couldn't hold them, and he came over and got them by the neck. He was good as gold to me for the two years I was there.'[15]

In his first week at Paddington, Joe stopped enough shoplifters for word to get around that his store was not worth the trouble.

Around this time, Joe met his wife. He was passing a school hall on the way home and heard the strains of Irish music across the playground; he went in, looked past the nuns and priests, and lit upon the young, Irish trainee nurse sipping a cup of tea. Joe and Phyllis saw their mutual love of dancing as a good omen, married and they went on to have five children.

Luckily for Joe, he had discovered that he could use his sound reputation at Tesco to ensure he earned decent money, pushing up the salary every time he was sent to another tough store. His supermarket career enabled him to afford the sort of home he had looked on as the stuff of dreams when he started out at West Wickham. He stuck with his career as a store manager right up to his retirement in 2008, by which time he was managing one of Tesco's largest stores in Beverley, Humberside. 'Tesco have been good to me, so I am loyal to them: it is strange how it gets in your blood. As far as I am concerned this is not just Tesco the big company, it is *my* company. I am part of it. I am one of the cogs in the wheel and I love it. I'm never happy until I am taking more than the company expects me to take.'[16]

David Potts also transformed his lifestyle. At Tesco he was widely admired as one of the best examples of how hard work and ability, plus opportunity to get on, could create significant social mobility. Former colleague John Gildersleeve puts it this way: 'Every store manager knows and respects David. Tesco is a meritocracy and they can see if David Potts can get to the top they may also have the opportunity. He cares about his people. If there's a performance issue David will tackle it, but it's not the first place he looks. He has rescued a few people over the years others would have considered to be basket cases. People consider him inspirational.'[17]

Potts and Doody began their careers at a critical time for Tesco:

business as usual, with its fear factor and blind eye where cheating was concerned, had to stop. That could be achieved only if the people at the top led Tesco in a new direction.

Chapter 11

Operation Checkout: the Campaign that Saved Tesco

'He came into my office – this old man, this wonderful old man with his worn-out face – and he got hold of my lapels and he shook me and he said, "It's all your bloody idea and if it fails you know what's going to happen to you", and I said, "Guvnor, I know what's going to happen to me."'

Lord MacLaurin[1]

'All of a sudden Jack Cohen stumbles up on the stage. Everybody thought it was part of the agenda. Looking round this room he said, "I don't believe in this, but if you don't all get up off your arses and roll your sleeves up we're all going to be out of the window, cars and all."'

Kevin Doherty[2]

After the 1974 fall in profits, Tesco's new leaders – headed by Ian MacLaurin with Leslie Porter right behind him – spent a couple of years taking a good look at the business before deciding on radical surgery.

'Towards the end of the 1970s, the appeal of Green Shield was going and the amber lights were flashing about the future of the company and we really had to have a good, good think about what we were going to do,' MacLaurin says. 'Jack created a fantastic business but it started to fail in the 1970s; we had to do something dramatic to revive it. We launched Operation Checkout. We had a vision: we wanted to be the best and we knew how we were going to get there by developing superstores and out-of-town stores.

'If we hadn't changed it in '77 we'd have gone out of business. We'd have been taken over. Customers didn't want Green Shield Stamps. We just had to move.'[3]

The causes for the dip, as set out by the company, were many and included government restrictions on business and regulations such as the new Price Code; increased charges by public authorities, utilities and the Post Office. It was difficult accessing stock caught up in the chaos after industrial disputes at the ports. Then there was the wages bill (in one year it rose by £11 million on static staff numbers of around 39,000 people). And a further problem was what Tesco called 'foot draggers' in national and local planning departments.

To begin with, Tesco looked for routes around the obstacles. It increased the portion of textiles made in Britain to counter any more supply blockages at the docks and any cost increases related to sterling's falling value abroad. Own-brand ranges expanded generally. Lager, newly popular in Britain, was added to the own-label offer in 1976 and the Tesco-owned De Georges wine range was relaunched. Despite planning headaches, the first hypermarket opened in February 1976 at Irlam, Manchester, with selling space of 76,000 square feet plus a petrol station and a tyre bay for quick fixes. Tesco was training staff to watch their power usage and was looking for ways to cut the energy bills through more efficient equipment and practices, but it still needed to do something drastic about itself and its fundamental offer to customers.

Operation Checkout was a do-or-die attempt to achieve this. The old guard was not allowed to stand in the way. To get back on track would mean jettisoning some aspects of the company that had achieved talisman-like status.

Ian MacLaurin and David Malpas had formed what MacLaurin terms a 'magical liaison'. Malpas was the junior of the two in terms of age and service at Tesco, but their backgrounds were not dissimilar, both having attended public schools. Malpas's family was less well-to-do, and he had taken a degree before heading into retailing, but the pair saw eye to eye. They characterize themselves as the communicator and team leader – MacLaurin – and the thinker – Malpas. Others who recall their leadership agree. For what it is worth, though, Malpas's turn of phrase and style of telling a story are as natural as MacLaurin's; the main difference is that Malpas appears more impatient to finish and get on with the next task.

MacLaurin needed the right people in place to help him drive through change. Malpas was to be one of these people and in 1976 he was promoted to run all of Tesco's retail operations. He recalls, 'This was somewhat to the discomfiture of those in the business longer. One of the best things about Tesco is that sometimes you find yourself promoted over the head of your boss and sometimes you find your subordinates promoted over you. You don't mind and you accept it and you get on with it. One of the magical things about Tesco is people's sense of ownership of the business and so they don't really mind.'[4]

With Malpas and his other allies, such as Eddie Clark, in place, MacLaurin set about unpicking the Tesco Board's reliance on Green Shield Stamps. 'By 1976, when customers had to save an awful lot of stamps to get anything worthwhile at all, the stamps began to lose their appeal. It was quite clear we were spending quite a lot of money on Green Shield and customers didn't want them: they were giving the stamps back to the cashiers. In 1976 Green Shield's bill to us was £20 million. We weren't competitive. The profits were going down. We quite clearly had to do something about it.

'We test-marketed coming out [of stamps] in four or five stores in the Midlands that were Tesco but not branded Tesco [they used the name Adsega, from an earlier store acquisition]. It was quite clear to us that Green Shield was a spent force. When Leslie Porter wrote to Green Shield and said we'll be withdrawing they said you can't – there is six months or a year's notice. They hadn't read their side of the contract. Leslie was quite right. We pulled the plug. Green Shield went to International Stores after us and that was fatal for them.'[5]

David Malpas recalls the negotiations. The two teams met at a motel on the Borehamwood turn-off of the A1, roughly halfway between Green Shield's headquarters in Station Road, Edgware, and Tesco's head office in Cheshunt.

'[Negotiations] were not very good humoured, as the Green Shield people wouldn't accept the fact that there was any need to contemplate change,' Malpas remembers. 'The Green Shield people were presenting a new vision starting from the assumption that we were continuing. We all pretty much knew that we wouldn't be. So that was slightly odd. They still had some difficulty believing it because it was a big step for us. All our competitors had been saying for years that the only reason that Tesco was enjoying any kind of success was they had Green Shield and we had half come to believe that ourselves, so getting rid of them represented a considerable risk.

'At the beginning I would have been on the side of a compromise – a discount in large stores, stamps in smaller stores. But I got to a place where it was one way or the other.'[6]

Research by the marketing men from London-based advertising agency McCann Erickson confirmed what those working in the stores – and reading the customer complaints in head office – already knew: fewer than 5 per cent of the people polled would be upset if the stamps disappeared and more than 5 per cent said it was the stamps that put them off ever shopping at Tesco. Green Shield Stamps, once a reason to queue and even faint at Tesco, had become a total turn-off. The ad men had spoken: shake off the low-rent image and do something about prices that had grown flabby.

The battle on the Board split down predictable family lines. Ian MacLaurin had support from George Wood, Francis Krejsa (the property director), Donald Harris (the IT and systems director) and Ralph Temple (the finance director). The vote came down to a letter from an absentee, David Behar, by then a non-executive director who had passed Tesco's property baton to Francis Krejsa.

MacLaurin describes the fight: 'There was one vote in it. Jack Cohen was on the Board still and the family wanted to stay. David Behar was ill in the south of France – he wrote back and said, "You're right – I can't stand the sticky little things." The first vote was five-five. Jack Cohen said, "You've got the casting vote" to Leslie

Porter – but I had David Behar's letter and said, "No, it's six-five."

'The family stuck together. All those who were close to the business and were out in the stores could see. One vote from a sick man in France gave us the opportunity to reposition Tesco. You've got to be a bit lucky in life.

'He [Jack] was furious. He'd never lost a vote. The old man sat there with his eyes shut but he was listening to everything, sharp as ever. He wanted the vote taken again, twice, but in the end we came out by one vote. My office was just around the corner from the boardroom and his office was about twenty yards down the corridor and I'll never forget he came into my office – this old man, this wonderful old man with his worn-out face – and he got hold of my lapels and he shook me and he said, "It's all your bloody idea and if it fails you know what's going to happen to you", and I said, "Guvnor I know what's going to happen to me."

'He had wanted to do a deal – he wanted to get half-price stamps with Richard Tompkins. He was a great trader. But the economy, everything, was moving on. It would have been crazy for us to stay in stamps. It would have been the death of the company.'[7]

Once the decision had been made, MacLaurin set about devising the exit strategy. 'I took a team of people to the States to look at companies that had been through stamps and out. Mike O'Connor was then president of Food Marketing Industries of America – I phoned him and asked for advice and help. He arranged for us to visit Pathmark in New York, Stop & Shop in Boston and something in Washington. We put the programme together and it was a great, great success and [Jack] was absolutely thrilled and at the end of the day of course it was all his idea, which was absolutely fine. We were ten days in the States studying what they did. We came back and with our advertising agency launched Operation Checkout in June 1977, over the Queen's Jubilee.'[8]

It was a complete coincidence that the Green Shield contract should expire on 7 June, which was precisely the weekend earmarked for Jubilee celebrations, but the timing was a PR dream.

It fell to Malpas to give staff the news. Leaks were a genuine worry, even in an era when instantaneous mass communication would have been viewed as far-fetched on an episode of *Star Trek*. The risk was that Tesco's entire campaign, built on teaser adverts and mystery, might collapse. A national roadshow was the answer: Malpas and MacLaurin covered 12,000 miles between them to brief the store managers.

The first meeting was with Tesco's most senior managers at the company Country Club near Cheshunt. Kevin Doherty was at the meeting and recalls, 'It was all kept close to people's chests. There must have been 500 executives. David Malpas stood up and talked about the rationale. There was a lot of concern in the room. Most people were against it as they were worried about the impact on the business. He said we had to take a leap. All of a sudden Jack Cohen stumbles up on the stage. Everybody thought it was part of the agenda. Looking round this room he said, "I don't believe in this, but if you don't all get up off your arses and roll your sleeves up we're all going to be out of the window, cars and all." They had to lead him off the stage.'[9]

Like the meeting, everything had to be done with what Malpas describes as 'a considerable degree of secrecy'. This is his 'insider' account of the way it panned out.

'We didn't let on to the business. We ran a secret trial in a village in the Potteries. It seems a trivial thing now, but it was very exciting. Those of us who were convinced it was the right thing to do anyway weren't concerned too much about whether it was successful or not. We found reasons why it was more successful than it had been. It was the biggest decision we, or possibly any other retailer, had made at that point. So we had to make a big, headline-grabbing fuss.

'The discount of stamps meant there had been an obvious temptation to let the price creep up. So the Tesco price minus the discount was higher than the Asda or Sainsbury price. We were becoming uncompetitive. We had to make our prices much, much more attractive than everybody else's. We burned a lot of midnight oil while we tried "what if" scenarios without the benefit of computers.

We wanted to give a discount of 4 per cent. That was an enormous amount to cut our gross margin, far more than the company's net margin would have been, and had we taken no more money we would have been bankrupt fairly quickly.

'We had to get the right level to generate enough extra turnover to pay for the discount. There was a lot of hard work put in by buyers and others to secure better prices. Having arrived at what we thought was the right level, we had to produce new price lists in secret, with the selling prices in Cheshunt all ready to be issued overnight. In the end, for the people who took the decision, it was pretty simple. We weren't going to have Green Shield Stamps and we were going to cut prices viciously, and we were gambling on achieving a sufficient level of turnover to pay for the new discounts.

'We had to have a marketing campaign. We had on board McCann Erickson. They devised the Operation Checkout idea and much of the gimmickry that went with it: the whitewashed windows, the open secret. We bought a lot of advertising. At that time it was innovative, teaser advertising.

'We closed on Saturday, whitewashed the windows to make out it was an even bigger secret but one that everybody knew everything about, then re-opened on Tuesday with no Green Shield Stamps and an array of very low prices – oddly enough, returning pretty much to the Jack Cohen roots of cut-price groceries. Up to that time weekly takings were about £11.5 million. I was doing the sums and I think it was about £14 million we had to take to make the thing worthwhile. I remember thinking I don't know if we'll do that. It seems tiny now.

'A day or two before we launched, Ian and I had a little discussion in my corner of the office. We mulled over £11.5 million and £14 million and we said in the end well, we'll see what happens, but if we don't we know two people who won't be here next week. It was betting the company.

'On opening morning I decided to go to Newton Abbot, which I thought was just about the typical branch: sizeable, bit in the doldrums in recent years. If it was going to work there it would work anywhere. Well before opening time, I was pleased to see a good long queue so I knew we'd be all right.'[10]

Jack's right-hand woman, Daisy Hyams, whose team ran millions of shopping lists based on some 16,000 products through the computers that Tesco had had the foresight to invest in, was named Woman of the Month by the BBC: Operation Checkout was viewed as a triumph over national inflation. It had taken little more than one month to execute.

'We got headlines in all the papers, lots of cartoons and comment,' Malpas recalls. 'We immediately got ourselves into trouble because we couldn't get enough goods into the stores. We didn't have enough people to serve them.'[11]

Kevin Doherty decided to spend the Tuesday at the [Enfield Wash] store, in Tesco's historic heartland. 'The weekend was the Jubilee weekend: a lot of people didn't want to work on the Sunday. We whitewashed all the windows and when we opened up on the Tuesday we had prices like you couldn't imagine. The stores got the prices just in time to change the labels. They were unbelievable prices. They were delivered by hand; they couldn't be posted because we had to keep it secret. It was 30 or 40 per cent off prices – unbelievable prices that the competition couldn't cope with. It was an incredible risk for Tesco.

'We were cutting our margins by 6 or 7 per cent, serious stuff, on the gamble that we would increase our market share. It was an incredible risk, a real gamble. Sales went up 40 per cent overnight. It was unbelievable. We couldn't cope. People were flocking into our stores. It was from that stage when the company started to see some serious change in strategy. Bigger stores, clear plans, clear standards in every store and our reputation started to improve. But we still had an image problem: we were trying to lose twenty or thirty years of poor image.'[12]

Mike Walastyan was managing one of Tesco's biggest stores, in Reading. The decision to ditch stamps meant hours of extra work – Brillo-ing off old prices and repricing every item by hand. Shelves were cleaned, new shelf-edge labels and advertising stuck up. But the weekend shifts saw the results immediately as, for the first time in years, customers queued to get in when they finally opened up. 'It was exactly the right thing to do. People were motivated more by price than by little stamps.

'Customers were waiting outside the stores from the early morning. We had mainly working-class customers but some middle-class customers even then. The service was not as good as it could have been [because] we were not expecting the success we had.'[13]

From coffee to pet food, products were shooting out of the shops at rates increased by between 50–90 per cent. Lorries were running twice as many deliveries from the depots as they were pre-Checkout, but even so Tesco was facing a retailer's basic nightmare: empty shelves.

'Operation Checkout was an overwhelming success, but it was overwhelming for distribution, which I was in at the time,' says Victor Weeks, one of Tesco's computer pioneers. The computer-generated picking lists and warehouses were out of sync. Weeks recalls an executive-level explosion directed at his boss, Donald Harris. 'Ian MacLaurin was enraged. He had one of the much later versions of the picking list. The warehouses couldn't cope with the big increase in orders. Ian was waving this document around in the room; he stood up and tore the document into little pieces and threw them into the air. I can't remember the words he was using but he was basically saying if we carry on like this we won't get any goods into the stores. Donald Harris tried to grab the showering litter of paper, trying to get all the bits because he knew somebody was going to have to get them all and stick them together again. It was a serious meeting – we couldn't cope with the success.

'It was a surge for distribution and for the company in all areas. We were not in total control of our own area. The buyers were having to redirect a lot of goods to the shops, bypassing the Tesco warehouses because they were saturated. Our productivity rose tremendously but it still couldn't cope.

'It was traumatic. It wasn't a blame culture, but there were various factions. The retail management hierarchy would say distribution is letting us down. They are not getting the goods to us in time.'[14]

One of the main reasons that they were ill-prepared was the commercial desire for secrecy in the run-up to the big launch. Departments had been given only little bits of information on a strict need-to-know basis.

'Two or three weeks before, we were told that something big was going to happen,' Weeks explains. 'I knew a bit more than most people but I didn't know what was happening on the retail side other than that the shops would be closed for a day after the Bank Holiday and what was happening externally. I'm unclear as to whether I knew Green Shield Stamps were being withdrawn until a day or two before. To say it was successful was the understatement of the decade. I was excited and proud that the company had done this and achieved a tremendous success. It upped Tesco's credibility, improved their standard in the City. It made competitors step back and take stock.

'Coinciding with Operation Checkout, Sainsbury, who were the leaders, had an industrial dispute. The one and only industrial dispute I can ever remember them having. So we got an extra load of customers from Sainsbury, some of whom never went back.'[15]

Long before Operation Checkout, Weeks had spotted that the proto-type computers could bring real benefits to retail. Having done well at school (Latymer Grammar, in Edmonton, North London), he left at fifteen because he wanted to 'be the breadwinner' after his father died of a heart attack. He had a delivery job at the Co-op ('more a mix of middle class and working class than Tesco, which was just working class') before the appeal of an office job at Cheshunt won him over. He started at Tesco on £4 a week, a pound or two less than he was earning as a Co-op delivery boy (with tips). He worked with Hollerith machines – early computers that collated orders using punch-hole technology.

The Tesco computer department was born in 1964 with the arrival of Donald Harris and the acquisition of the ICT 1300, which, although it occupied most of one room, made the existing Hollerith tabulating system look very antiquated. Tesco was among the very first retailers to invest in computers and Victor, with his programming experience, was a natural fit for the new department.

Weeks recalls how small Tesco's head office was. Everybody knew everybody else. Jack Cohen teased him for smoking when he did not look old enough. 'I got to know him quite well over the years,' says Weeks. 'To me he didn't have moods. He would like a chat and a joke with people when he felt like it as a form of escape. At other times, he could walk into the office and ask a few very serious questions about trading and expect whoever was on the receiving end to respond.

'Leading up to Christmas we'd have an evening in the boardroom and all the management could fit in. It was basically a Jewish organization and they didn't celebrate Christmas much, but we would have a few drinks. It was to a great extent a big family. Everyone knew each other. In the main they got on, although that wasn't always the case; it depended on how things were going with trade.'[16]

By the time of Operation Checkout, though, Tesco would have struggled to fit even just the Cheshunt staff in the boardroom, let alone the wider management. The Victor Value acquisition in 1968 had brought another computer system, Honeywell 200, and another office block (Dairy Glen House, Waltham Cross) to be absorbed. Then there was the move across Delamare Road to New Tesco House on 1 April 1973. Weeks's recollections portray a company very much on the outskirts, despite the new headquarters. Delamare Road, on the Lea Valley floodplain and close to a canal, would flood regularly, forcing staff to wade knee-deep to the train station. The teams were getting to grips with expansion, just as profits were under pressure.

Weeks's love of computers and systems matched Tesco's will to invest in new technology. His contribution to the *Tesco: An Oral History* archive provides a wealth of detail about IT innovation and his career at Tesco, including transformational technological change such as bar-code scanning. He eventually retired in January 2006.

*

Whatever the technical hiccoughs Weeks's team handled in 1977, Operation Checkout brought two million more shoppers through Tesco's doors.

'Our £14 million a week was easily exceeded and in turnover terms we didn't look back for a long time,' David Malpas records. 'We made price reductions across the board. We were among the first retailers to realize that the concept of KVIs – known value items – is actually daft. People remember the price of just about everything, even slow sellers like mango chutney.

'Some items were cut more than others – promotional items. They would have been the top-selling items. Sugar was easily the biggest-selling item, then bread, milk, butter, then Heinz beans, then the leading detergent brands. It was like any other promotion and the kind that still happens today.'[17]

Advertising agency McCann Erickson invested more than £1 million of Tesco's money in blanket advertising through the rest of June and store managers had to shut the doors on customers for safety.

For this campaign Sir Save-a-Lot, a fancy-dress knight who had graced many a Tesco store opening with a grand arrival on horse-back, was absent. Not that he had always been a great asset: on more than one occasion his trusty steed had slipped on highly polished shop floors and come a cropper against a carefully crafted pyramid of tin cans. Operation Checkout's marketing and advertising suggested that Tesco was moving into more sophisticated spheres.

Robin Gray, then a McCann Erickson advertising manager based at Cheshunt, remembers the campaign. 'We had a couple of double-page spreads in national and local newspapers. We were in 200 or 300 different papers across the country. All the ads were different because the stores had different opening hours. We had big stars and products in the adverts with big headlines of price cuts.

'We did two different commercials with different ranges of products on the conveyor belt with "check it out check it out check it out" coming up on the cash tills. We probably had three weeks before we launched to come up with the ideas and work behind closed doors on it. It was good fun.

'All the team who worked on it were given a certificate with a little gold medal on it. That was the beginning of having a strategy for advertising.

'All the £9 million we had spent on Green Shield Stamps was ploughed into low prices. People could not believe that they were going to save £5 on an average shop – that was a fortune in 1977. There were queues of people waiting to go into our stores. It was the right time: people wanted money in their pocket and not gifts for the home.

'It was the best decision Ian MacLaurin ever made dropping those stamps – they were a pain in the bum. It was the beginning of our success. It was the beginning of the last thirty years.'[18]

It may have been a noisy launch, but Tesco's competitors seemed to Malpas to be unmoved. 'From memory, they didn't react much. You usually try not to react to somebody else's promotion. Asda didn't do anything because they thought their prices were good enough anyway. Sainsbury was a bit lofty.'[19]

Industry figures from that time show that in fact the major supermarkets did lose share in the aftermath of Checkout. Tesco temporarily overtook Sainsbury and made the number two slot behind the Co-operative Group.

The campaign also triggered a supermarket price war. Malpas says that smaller stores lost out, though Tesco directors believed, then as now, that no shopkeeper doing a reasonable job had anything to fear. Soon after Operation Checkout was launched, Tesco's then-chairman, Leslie Porter, stated in the 1977 Annual Report: 'Our belief, often stated by officials of this company, that there will always be room for the efficient small independent retailer, is borne out in practice: the small shopkeeper in the catchment area of a superstore is affected least by its presence, and indeed is frequently assisted by the overspill of new business brought to the area by the attractions of a large store.'

Ian MacLaurin, meanwhile, was advocating 'jaw jaw not war war' with local planners. The debate about the high street, at least in relation to Tesco's impact, has gone on ever since, but the opposing arguments have barely altered.

*

Operation Checkout saved Tesco and put down the foundations underpinning its expansion. Sales were already significantly up on the previous year in the three months before the campaign, but Checkout increased sales by an additional 40 per cent. From Checkout to year-end in February 1978, turnover rose by 43 per cent. However, Tesco's margins took a bashing and Checkout cost an estimated £2 million of investment, which counted against profits. Meanwhile the stress on the warehouses and distribution system generally meant temporary cover had been bought – at a cost of £1 million.

Ultimately, Operation Checkout bought Tesco time, rekindled customer and staff enthusiasm and loosened the Cohen culture, but it had not resolved a host of underlying issues.

'We didn't really make any more profit,' Malpas acknowledges. Two years after Checkout, Tesco was ready for more radical change.

Chapter 12

High Street Wars: Moving Out of Town

'There can be no doubt that the price war will continue in Britain's High Street; we, for our part, have no intention of slackening our efforts and can fairly claim to have done more than Government in reducing the impact of inflation.'

Sir Leslie Porter[1]

'A family's weekly shop weighs over a hundredweight. And unless you want to shop every day, which people don't, how do you get a hundred-weight of groceries on to the bus or train to take home?'

David Malpas[2]

Sales soared and customers flocked to Tesco's new-look stores after Operation Checkout. The drive to find more sites was re-invigorated. Kevin Doherty, by then managing a sizeable group of stores, remembers opening up one new supermarket in Well Street, Hackney, in 1978.

For founder and Life President Sir Jack Cohen, the occasion struck a nostalgic nerve. Well Street was the site of Jack's first stall almost six decades previously, in 1919, and he wanted to attend the opening. Now in his eightieth year, he looked like a very old man and Kevin was not expecting what happened next.

Kevin recalls, 'I was twenty-seven and one of the first stores [in the large supermarket division] that I opened as a group controller was the store in Well Street. I got Jack's autobiography, *Pile It High, Sell It Cheap*. It has got this list of products he sold on his stall. I built a stall exactly the same as the one he had in those days and I got as many of the products as possible and put the prices on, as they would have been. I put it outside the store and I put a big banner right across the street with "Welcome Back Sir Jack". [We] invited the [BBC] down. It was Jack Cohen back to his birthplace. He had Daisy Hyams with him. He staggered across. He was quite old. Tears came into his eyes and he started flogging everything. Suddenly there were hundreds of old ladies [around Jack]. I thought, "Oh my God – my stock result, my inventory! I haven't even counted it." It was "Five for fifty pence! Four for fifty pence! Take the lot for thirty pence!" He was selling everything. These ladies were saying, "Jack, you're not as cheap as you used to be." He was saying, "What do you want – my jacket as well?" He took it off and threw it into the crowd. Incredible.

'All this finished and I was in the middle of the first gangway in the store and had quite a bad headache with all the stress of the last couple of days. The regional director introduced me [to Jack] as Kevin Doherty, the group controller. Jack got hold of my hand and said, "Hello, my boy. What a fantastic job we've done here today. I'm sure this is going to be a big success, this store – another success for Tesco."

'He said, "I want to give you something very special." He took 2/6d out of his pocket – half a crown. He put it in my hand and he said, "I want that to bring you the same wealth it brought me years ago when I left the army. This is what I started my business with." I felt really proud. I took it home [and] I said to my wife, Hilary, "Look at this coin – look at what Jack Cohen gave me. Look at this coin he came out of the army with." I told my father and all my relatives. I was showing them the coin and the photographs. The next Monday I was up at New Tesco House and I was walking along the corridor and there is a staff restaurant, and who was coming the other way but Jack Cohen. I said, "Hello, Mr Cohen." He said, "Hello, my boy. Which department do you work in?" He'd completely forgotten me! He was getting on.'[3]

Not, as Kevin discovered, that Jack Cohen had forgotten a bit of barrow-boy blarney. Kevin, in the gentlest fashion, had fallen for a little street-trader hustle. 'I was telling John Bird, the managing director, about a week later. He said, "I shouldn't worry about that, Kevin – he gives everybody one of those when he opens a store." That was the kind of guy he was. There was a lot of charisma about him.'[4]

Well Street was one of the last store openings that Jack attended. His daughter Dame Shirley Porter recalls how his health was failing, but how he still loved to live life and have fun. Her story about the last few months of Jack's life illustrates how far he had travelled, literally as well as metaphorically.

'He was very old, eighty, and we [were] in Florida in winter. He could hardly move, but I knew he wanted to [so] we went on the dance floor and danced. They [Jack and Cissie] were very much people who enjoyed life. There were always parties and fun and groups of people. For him it didn't matter from whence they came. He was absolutely amazed at where he'd got to and with whom he was mixing, and how come he was Sir John and the people that he was on first name terms with. He never lost that amazement at it all. I used to say, "I don't understand, Daddy. You've been mixing with these people for ages, you're enormously successful – why should you be in such awe?" But coming from where he came from he did not forget. England was certainly class-ridden. It meant a lot to him. He was excited, thrilled, amazed. Everybody knows that if you've made it yourself, you've done it yourself, you never have to question "Am I good enough?"'[5]

Back from Florida, in England in March 1979, the 'Old Man' died. Store stalwart Eddie Clark was one of the many Tesco people who attended the funeral and paid respects in a corner of a Palmers Green cemetery. Jack had resolved any differences with Ian MacLaurin, to whom he bequeathed £5,000. That year's Tesco Annual Report carried a memorial tribute to Jack and a simple statement in a black-bordered paragraph.

The company paused and then moved on, for there was much to do. Six decades after Jack stood at a market stall in Well Street, the business he founded reported annual turnover of £1.24 billion (up 26.2 per cent) and profits of £37.66 million (up 32 per cent).

'A year ago it was already clear that we were going to reap benefits from what was becoming widely known as the "High Street War",' Leslie Porter told shareholders. 'We have consolidated our position, having achieved all we set out to do. Tesco had now been completely re-positioned in the market place. Our aggressive pricing policy contributed towards a further two million shopping transactions per week.'[6]

The company reviews immediately after Operation Checkout highlight innovations and trials – including the Tesco Credit Card, the first till receipts and bar-coding systems, the first international move to Ireland and the launch of the staff pension scheme.

They do not tell the whole story.

Ian MacLaurin and David Malpas say that when they lifted their heads to look at the retail landscape after Operation Checkout in 1977, they realized that a fundamental problem remained: lots of Tesco was in the wrong place. Though about 250 shops had been closed in the previous five years, almost half the remaining 571 stores were tiny.

MacLaurin says, 'When we came out of Checkout in 1977, we had stores dotted around the high streets. Then we started to go out of town. Planners didn't think too much of Tesco in town, and when we said, "Okay, we want to go out of town", they said they didn't like that either.'[7]

Changes in society, in particular the number of women in the workplace, produced a shift to weekly shopping instead of traditional daily top-ups. Tesco's stores couldn't hold the ranges of increasingly varied produce that customers wanted and they were too far from parking spaces. As David Malpas puts it, 'A family's weekly shop weighs over a hundredweight. And unless you want to shop every day, which people don't, how do you get a hundredweight of groceries on to the bus or train to take home?

'Fundamentally, it was the customer who decided that stores were no longer suitable in town centres.'[8]

Malpas had been promoted from regional controller in the North to the director in charge of all retail and on 1 January 1979 he joined the main Board as managing director.

'We had larger and larger stores in the 1970s in city centres, sometimes built on four floors with two selling floors. There was no proper attention to how customers would use them or how the stores would be serviced. There was no concept of having a free flow. Hundreds of deliveries were made every week. Goods came up by lift or were thrown up and down stairs. A typical stock-holding in those days would have been about three and a half weeks, which is an enormous amount of stock for a supermarket to hold.

'It was obvious the customer wanted a store that was big enough to hold a very wide range of goods, was convenient to shop around, with plenty of available car parking on the flat that was properly related to the traffic system. They wanted a secure and comfortable environment. We wanted servicing arrangements that would be easy to manage.

'This was totally radical for Tesco. There were awful arguments with the property people, who weren't used to us taking them to a place and saying that's what we want. They were used to waiting for stuff in town centres to come in.'[9]

The head of the property division, Francis Krejsa, may have taken some convincing, but to MacLaurin and Malpas it all seemed to point in one direction – the edge of town.

As with many of Tesco's good ideas, somebody else had done it first. 'Asda were the first to do anything out of town,' acknowledges MacLaurin. 'They were very successful in the North, and we decided we would go out of town.'[10]

Two of the first Tesco superstores were at Basildon and Pitsea in Essex. Pitsea opened in July 1978 and Tesco described it as the 'prototype' for the 1980s supermarket. The 'clock-tower era' began:

stores were built with red-brick walls and sloping, tiled roofs topped off, for no apparent reason, with a clock tower.

Perhaps it was a sublime visual reference to the English ideal of town planning, as depicted in the still fondly remembered children's television series *Trumpton*; or perhaps the design chimed with the cultural climate of the day: Britain's idea of aspirational style in the eighties was epitomized in the TV show *Dallas* with its sprawling Ewing family ranch, Southfork. MacLaurin favours the *Dallas* explanation, but whatever the inspiration, David Malpas says that the then property director, Francis Krejsa, 'hated them, because clocks need maintenance'.

The new stores had everything that Tesco had to offer. In grocery, they displayed the new, improved range of fresh fruit, vegetables and meat that the food buyers were sourcing. Tesco's recently launched own-label wines were added to the shelves (by 1979, 390 of the 571 shops were licensed to sell alcohol). The full range of non-food, from T-shirts to television sets, cardigans to cameras (some of them well-known brands) could be displayed. There was an in-store bakery, one of sixty in the group, and a self-service restaurant (these last two the legacy of the acquisition of café chain Cadena). Somebody thought to suggest customer toilets, and so they were included too.

According to David Malpas, though, Sainsbury had set the standard. 'Sainsbury opened a large store in Coldham's Lane on the outskirts of Cambridge which had pretty much all of the attributes I am describing. Neither we nor they took any notice of the fact that it was very successful. They didn't bother to develop any more for many years. I, in particular, didn't see at the time that this was the prototype. Town centres were the wrong place. It was just too small a sales area for food. They were often on more than one trading floor and the car park would be grossly inconvenient or non-existent. We simply had to change it.'[11]

MacLaurin, then managing director, agreed that the need for change was acute. 'We couldn't cope with the volume of trade in a lot of the stores in town. The motor industry was changing. Many people had one car, a lot had two. It was easier to park out of town where there could be flat, free parking and there was a restaurant and loos. I don't think changing the location was a risk at all. It was a natural progression.

'We had a Site Research Unit that could tell us very, very accurately what sort of trade we would do in any particular location. They were never far out. If Dr Nick Penny and his team said you'll take £150,000 or £200,000 or half a million pounds, they were never far wrong.'[12]

The Site Research Unit was so highly regarded that it had an un-official licence to operate as it pleased. 'There was nobody there at 9.30 a.m., but they were still all there at after 8 p.m.,' recalls John Gildersleeve, then running a significant group of stores.[13]

'They brought their university culture with them. They behaved as if they were still at university. They were bright, interesting agents of change. That was one of the more significant things that under-pinned Tesco's success during the last twenty-five years. If you look at Tesco's stores and their performance, the research unit was one of the prime departments. Our businesses still use the data and skills developed by Nick Penny and Stuart Moore.

'We worked hard at the policies of store development. We wanted to be at the front of centres with flat, free car parks. Francis Krejsa was as able a property man as you'll ever come across, but his prejudice was for town centre. I spent quite a lot of time closing lots of little shops and trying to open new ones.'[14]

Tesco invested a lot of money opening new stores and the SRU work all but guaranteed great results. Ian MacLaurin describes how 'They looked first at population, then the A, B, C, D make-up, and then the ease of access – how good are the roads? – on the edge of the town so people don't have a huge long drive. When some of the traders started to close in the town centres a lot of people were dis-advantaged, especially the old people, so we ran free buses. We tried to look after the people who couldn't get to the Tesco store. We vis-ited planners, talked to them, showed them the plans. Once we had two or three up and running and they were very good – the new gen-eration. We could take planners around them to take photographs and so on. It was a Southfork ranch-type building. Some planners wanted a particular kind of store. We opened a store at Bristol which was very modern. There is one at Tetbury in Wiltshire, a very modern construction, which I personally think is appalling – but the council wanted it. Stow-on-the-Wold is very nice. It is done in Cotswold stone with a tiled roof, and Trowbridge is very pleasant-looking with a clock tower. We worked with the councils.

'At one stage we were trying to open one a week. We probably opened eighteen to twenty a year of the superstores on the edge of town.'[15]

Tesco's chairman, Leslie Porter, noted in the 1978 Annual Report that Tesco was getting planning permission where other supermarkets were not. There had been a policy change at the DoE, and Francis Krejsa's estates team was working hard at cooperating with local authorities. MacLaurin took pains to convince the DoE that not only were large stores providing price cuts of up to 10 per cent on groceries, but they were not pushing smaller traders out of business.

'We appealed most of the sites – going before an inspector to argue our case against the local authority or whoever it might be. When we first started to go out of town and were closing down pretty poor, pretty grotty stores in town centres there was a lot of resistance from shopkeepers or the council. The typical situation would be "There is a terrible Tesco in the middle of town. We don't want a bigger one of those out of town." But we did a lot of work on our buildings and they were attractive, with flat, free car parking – all the things customers wanted – and the resistance got less.'[16]

Planning discussions may have been different, but they do not seem to have become much easier: Tesco still had to allow a minimum of three years and sometimes up to six years between obtaining outline planning consent and sending in the construction teams. It was a pipeline through which stores moved exceedingly slowly. Being in the Tesco property department required foresight and patience.

Tesco was not the only retailer to have noticed the need to go where customers could reach you easily and competition was hot for the best spots, even if Leslie Porter was reassuring the shareholders that their company was ahead of the game.

The combination of lengthy planning, Asda's strength in the North and Sainsbury's still embedded lead position meant that Tesco was unable to grow as fast as it knew it could through new-build stores alone, and it continued to look out for groups to buy, such as the Cartier group of sixteen stores in Kent, which was acquired in 1980.

That was also the year that Tesco's first international move was consolidated with the creation of Tesco Stores Ireland. Tesco bought seven 3 Guys shops in the Republic in March 1979 and then opened six more. To pay for the deals, Tesco raised debt – a dramatic departure from its general practice and so requiring much explanation to shareholders.

But of all the changes, it was the decision to move away from cramped high streets to large shops in accessible locations that most people inside Tesco believe pushed the business ahead. The company had fifty-three stores of 25,000 square feet or more by 1980, ten times the number it had had in 1972. But it had shut more than 300 smaller units.

The plan was not to get out of the high street altogether, and there were many examples of where two Tescos co-existed well. Weston Favell, for instance, was built in 1974 and the shop 4 miles away at Northampton suffered no loss of trade at all. That was encouraging, so other town-centre stores were developed and improved even as out-of-town shops were planned. Nor was it the end of the two-storey shop, and Tesco installed its first 'merculator' system (the moving slope that can take trolleys) at the new Maidstone superstore in 1977.

Operation Checkout had galvanized Tesco's expansion: the increase in sales and profits underpinned Ian MacLaurin's next moves. Without it, Tesco would have been trying to expand, to borrow money and to sell innovation to shareholders in a difficult era for Britain. Unemployment was at record levels as Margaret Thatcher moved into 10 Downing Street, industrial relations were dreadful and the economy was weak. There was little prospect of fast recovery, as Leslie Porter noted in the 1979 Annual Report. Due to the government's commitment to a monetarist solution to the UK economy's problems of inflation and stagnation, businesses would face very high interest rates without the prospect of an increase in consumer spending on anything but food. VAT rises compounded the situation. Expanding into this kind of headwind took determination.

Chapter 13

Managing Better: Why People Began to Matter

'It used to be a joke that if you were at the bottom of the employment heap you ended up stacking a shelf or operating a checkout in a Tesco store. It was low productivity and low wages. Consequently it was not high-quality people. We determined to change that and make retail employment, not just at Tesco but in the retail sector as a whole, a better place to have a job.'

David Malpas[1]

'I thought, "I've made a terrible mistake here", and I spent the first year absolutely certain that I was going to leave this business. It was only through inertia that I didn't get around to leaving.'

Sir Terry Leahy[2]

John Gildersleeve – by then a regional managing director – remembers that the speed of Operation Checkout left people thrashing around in its wake: the old ways would no longer suffice.

'Operation Checkout in 1977 generated turnover but no profit, and exposed all sorts of vacuums in the business and called into question just how professional the business was and what skill sets were missing. Ian MacLaurin, who is a pretty extraordinary person and pretty excellent leader, had real insights and understanding of what his abilities were, and the first thing he did was to promote David Malpas. David was cerebral, bright and pretty idiosyncratic.

He was not out of the hard-nosed, 24/7 retailer mould that had previously made successful Tesco retailers.'[3]

The new Board, suspecting deep levels of dissatisfaction throughout the company, commissioned Tesco's first staff survey. 'Our people thought we were awful and arrogant,' remembers Ian MacLaurin. 'There wasn't one thing that was good about the bosses of the company. We had to have a good look at ourselves. There was a lot of fear factor. Now we have three generations of families working for us.'[4]

One of the young store managers who remembers the atmosphere at the time was Paul Nally. Nally arrived in England from Dublin in 1975. His was a farming background and the family had a grocery shop, but he had ambitions to emigrate to America and Birmingham was supposed to be a staging post. He took a job at Tesco to make some money for his new start: two years later he was managing a store in Roath Park, Cardiff, on Tesco's trainee scheme.

He remembers a particularly hard boss who 'took no prisoners'. 'It was a tough place to work. It was all about delivery and sales and controls on cost, particularly on wages. We didn't have the same principles about waste as we do now. One was judged on standards in the shop, the volume of sales, wage per cent (the cost of pay roll against sales), and then stock results (the difference between what we got charged and what we sold). If you had successive poor results then invariably you'd be looking for a new job. Two or three was not acceptable.

'We didn't have performance management as we do now, with documentary evidence and objectives. It was more brutal than that. "You're not right – you need to look elsewhere and do it quickly." A lot of the people I was training with are still around, though some didn't have the drive and push necessary and got out of management or didn't stay. You needed to be tough, and innovative in terms of displays of a fairly limited range. A lot was about driving sales. We had much more of a trading requirement for the managers than we do now. In those days you moved half the shop if you felt it was a good idea.'[5]

This fear factor had fermented nicely in a workplace atmosphere of 'two bad stock results and you're out'. A visit from a store inspector or, heaven forbid, a regional managing director sent grown men into a spin: northern store manager Harry Quinlan remembers his boss, telephone receiver clutched to his perspiring head, chain-smoking as he scribbled down instructions from his superior at head office.[6]

'We didn't want people staying up all night because a director was about to do a Royal Visit,' explains Malpas.

So Tesco began to look after its people in practical ways to demonstrate that they were valued. First, they increased pay. In November 1979, the average staff wage went up by 15 per cent and was lifted a further 8.5 per cent in April 1980. Then the pension scheme was improved and by 1980 there were 11,000 members, almost three times the 1977 number. Staff turnover slowed until it reached around 25 per cent.

It took vision to make those changes, recalls David Malpas, who credits a fellow Board director, Michael Darnell, as the 'inspiration' behind the reforms. 'He was the first of us to think in an original way about what we actually wanted from the stores in terms of their results and how they might be measured. He was the first to understand that, as senior managers, we had to treat people with the respect and consideration with which we would wish to be treated and he became known through the business for those traits.

'Working in a supermarket had always been a bad job. It wasn't somewhere where you would want your son or daughter to go and get a job at all. It used to be a joke that if you were at the bottom of the employment heap you ended up stacking a shelf or operating a checkout in a Tesco store. It was low productivity and low wages. Consequently it was not high-quality people. We determined to change that and make retail employment, not just at Tesco but also in the retail sector as a whole, a better place to have a job.

'Here again we'd had an example staring us in the face for years and years in Marks & Spencer, who looked after their people well and paid them well. We set about increasing the wages and working conditions of our staff, explaining it as best we could to our owners in the City [shareholders]. We reckoned that higher pay and higher-quality staff would lead to a higher-quality and more profitable business. That was a bit hard to sell to some people.

'It worked very well. It went down well with our trade union. During the 1970s there was a lot of trade-union trouble. We escaped that mainly because our main trade union was USDAW [the Union of Shop, Distributive and Allied Workers]. It was fashionable in some places to think of USDAW as a soft union, but that wasn't true. It was a far-sighted union that could see we were all in this together.'[7]

The typical Tesco worker was working class and female, except for on the meat counters where, before the changes in the 1980s, there was a lot of cutting and carrying of huge sides of meat. Bookkeeping, checkouts and guarding the cash were always jobs for women. The other vital job, guarding the Back Door and examining what came in, was always a job for men. Ethnically, Tesco stores reflected the make-up of their communities, and still do.

As part of the company's drive to make supermarket jobs more appealing, Tesco advertised for more graduates. It wasn't the only retailer to do so. The Co-op was also developing young talent and it was there that one of its new graduate trainees, Terry Leahy, says he learned lessons that would change some of his views and values fundamentally.

Retail wasn't an obvious choice for Leahy – surprising perhaps for a man who would one day become Tesco's chief executive. He had spent three years 'with one eye' on his management degree course at the University of Manchester Institute of Science and Technology (UMIST) and the other on the many diversions that Manchester's student community offered, and he had no thoughts of leaving the North of England.

'I joined the Co-op in Manchester by accident. I didn't do very well in interviews. I wasn't polished. I must have come across as a bit immature. I got into the Co-op, which wasn't a prestige employer but it was local, and that got me into retailing. It all came by accident.'[8]

The Co-operative Group was made up of about 220 societies and represented between 25 and 30 per cent of retailing in Britain. Terry was taken on to the graduate management trainee scheme. 'Management appealed because it seemed easy and there was an element of leadership, so I obviously wanted to be a leader in some sense. It was about ideas. I liked ideas. It was somewhere you could have a point of view.

'Somebody had said it was a good company to go to and I didn't know any better. They had big buildings in Manchester, so it seemed to be a substantial company. At the interview they seemed professional and orderly. It was the major force in retailing.'[9]

The Co-op was also part of the Labour movement, which at the time felt familiar to Leahy because socialism was the politics he grew up with, at home and in his community. 'You had to be a union member and so I joined a union. You also had to be a member of the Co-op bank. There were some very good values. There was good intent and compassion, but it was an early lesson that good intent and compassion doesn't deliver the goods unless it is backed up by hard-nosed efficiency and effectiveness, and sometimes the two can be conflicting.

'What I saw in that movement were good values, but in amongst that organization there were people who were let loose who didn't share those values. They basically ran the organizations as they saw fit for their own gain, very often under the umbrella of that Co-operative movement, and so they didn't actually deliver down to the members, down to the consumers, the value, the range, the service, the respect that in truth the movement had hoped for. There were big exceptions and these are sweeping statements, but that was my experience.'[10]

Retailing was not for the faint-hearted, whether at the Co-operative or at Tesco. Leahy joined the provisions division of the Wholesale Society, the buying side of the Co-operative movement. The Co-operative was more modern than Tesco in those days, in that it organized its buyers along category lines. Leahy met the panoply of characters involved in bringing produce from farm or factory to customers: British tastes were changing, even in proudly traditional parts of northern England, partly because British people had seen more of the world but also because more of the world was moving to Britain.

'My job was to sell delicatessen, which is not the most promising product to sell around the mining communities of Lancashire and Yorkshire, but I ploughed on, advising the former miners that a good sheep's cheese was washed down with Sancerre Sauvignon.'[11]

He designed and ran a delicatessen training course, as well as sourcing and supplying products upon which he earned commission. 'It was a little profit centre. I pushed it very hard to grow those profits. My little graph went upwards. I was probably a bit untypical. My expectations of the line were steeper than others – that was a bit of naivety, but a bit of energy too. We made displays and took photographs.

'We had classifications of what a cooked sausage was. We showed them how to display olives. It was a purer delicatessen then than today, in many ways. People [from the Continent] had come over after the war and stayed. I learned quite a lot about fine grocery at that time, though it has never been a big feature of society. As people grew wealthier there wasn't really a parallel interest in the knowledge of food. It's a particularly British thing. There's an interest in cooking today – or more often an interest in watching cookery programmes – but there's not really been an in-depth interest in food.'[12]

His theory is that Britain's early industrialization meant most people lost their closeness to the land generations ahead of their Continental cousins, with the exception of the wealthy.

'The food quality [generally available] was not how people remember it. The food quality was not great and the choice was not great. The retailing was poor, frankly. It wasn't much to celebrate.'[13]

To a bright young graduate with a work ethic and a shiny degree, that must have been blazingly obvious. Plus retailing was lousy money. 'There were middle managers who could not live on the wages they earned. My wage was £50 a week and I had more money when I was a student with summer work and a grant. These were young people who had got married and had a house and a baby and were very, very poor. It was normal then.'[14]

Terry Leahy's generation of graduates joined the workforce in an era of soaring inflation. Unions were still strong and pay kept pace (hence the rising wage bills that Leslie Porter noted in successive Annual Reports). There would have been, however, a tangible sense of insecurity. The dole queue lengthened. Margaret Thatcher took her place as Conservative prime minister against a backdrop of 'Britain isn't working' posters.

Businesses like Tesco were as influenced by the mood as individuals were. Yet, post-Checkout, the regenerated Tesco was recruiting harder than ever. This was a fact not lost on Leahy's mentor at the Co-operative, who returned from a trip 'down south' with tales of Tesco's potential.

Leahy was looking to move south anyway for personal reasons. He applied for two jobs in 1979. The first was to be a brand manager at Alcan Foil, which he wanted, and the second was with Tesco. A fellow UMIST graduate got the Alcan job: 'Then I went to Tesco and I didn't get that job either, but luckily the person who had got the job was so good they give him a bigger job, so I was able to get that one after all.'[15]

Tesco had by then made the mental leap connecting salary levels with quality of staff: Leahy started on £6,200, 'an unimaginable increase' on the £3,800 he had been earning at the Co-operative. In part this reflected regional wage differences, more marked then than now, but in part it was danger money.

Tesco still had a poor reputation. Leahy's parents were not from the section of society that was horrified if its children joined a supermarket (as Ian MacLaurin's had been); he did, though, have friends who wondered what on earth he was doing, throwing away his career on a young company they viewed as an 'upstart' business with a poor reputation. 'I do remember saying to a Wall's salesman that I was going to join Tesco, and he said, "Well they'll eat you alive." I remember thinking, "Well, I must not be eaten alive".'[16]

MacLaurin and Malpas were demanding change, but the message had not had time to filter very far downwards by 1979. 'Tesco was much less sophisticated than the Co-op in management terms, so whilst commercially it seemed to be being successful, it was a wild, anarchic place compared to the quiet, slightly bureaucratic but professional structures and values of the Co-op, and so I was shocked,' admits Leahy.[17]

He recalls that Tesco was smaller than the Co-operative Group but it was struggling to manage its growth and lacked the necessary systems, logistics and organization to cope. 'I remember joining a business that was not successful and I remember people feeling under pressure a lot.'

He was wrong-footed when he arrived for work at the tiny central office in Cheshunt to join the marketing department. 'I found really there wasn't a marketing area. Tesco didn't do marketing. What I'd joined was somebody from the computer department, which bored me rigid.

'Essentially they had one computer in Tesco and it ran print-outs of the delivery of products into the stores. This computer chap had thought of the idea that if you looked at these print-outs then you could pick ranges and you could use the space differently in the stores. It was all very sound, and the principles of modern category management, but I think he was the only one at Tesco who had thought this. I came into this office that had no windows. There were just these massive computer print-outs.

'I thought, "I've made a terrible mistake here", and I spent the first year absolutely certain that I was going to leave this business. It was only through inertia that I didn't get around to leaving. So that was it. The start at Tesco.'[18]

He didn't like London any more than he liked the dark computer room at Cheshunt. To him it was 'frightening, fast-moving, hostile and expensive', and he missed the friendly warmth of the North. He lived first in Clapham – in those days rough and poor, and free from the million-pound price tags of today – and then moved to Enfield. The relatively safe new suburb felt better, but still the office was 'like going into prison for a life sentence.' Leahy's hours were no fewer than they were for men such as Eddie Clark, Harry Quinlan and John Gildersleeve, who were running the stores. Leahy would arrive in the crepuscular room at about 7 a.m. and not leave for twelve hours.

Eddie Clark recalls what it was like in the stores. 'I was trying to learn and get on in Tesco and I was working too long hours. I took the company's figures for years and telephoned them to Ian MacLaurin. It took time to work the figures out after half past five. Readings would be taken at six o'clock. There were thirty stores, so you added them up and then phoned them through. You might put your pen down at nine o'clock.

'If you were opening a store, you'd be there practically the whole weekend before opening. We always had a celebrity to open stores in those days. By the time you had entertained them in the evening, you'd be home between seven and nine o'clock.

'You don't go cleaning the windows, doing the gardening or teaching your children much. The children would have been asleep. You'd leave at four or five in the morning. My son says he wishes he'd known me when I was younger and that doesn't make me feel good, but that was the price you paid for a little Cockney boy trying to make good. The price was hard. I wasn't the only one. Nine out of ten of us were like that.'[19]

Leahy recalls that even the office was a hard place to be. 'There was always much more of an edge at Tesco compared to the Co-op. It was much more aggressive, very male, and people were rude to each other. You could get shouted at, and this all came as a bit of a shock. There seemed to be no structure. There were territorial wars for influence and lots of politics.

'I expected as a young person that you would go into a structure that existed and your job would be defined, and it wasn't like that at all. My poor boss was terrified half the time, from people criticizing him and taking his resources away and not allowing him to do his job. It quickly became apparent that nobody took the [marketing] area at all seriously anyway.

'The big tough areas were buying and retail operations; and then there were other people who came in to do computing or distribution or home and wear, and those people came and went. The big senior people were rather unpleasant, I found. They had been hired at big wages, wore sharp suits and were kind of rude to people who they thought were beneath them. I thought it was an unpleasant place – rather ill-mannered.'[20]

He was learning what it felt like to be under-valued and how different it was if colleagues were supportive. 'I did meet good people, nice people as well, and I remember those people who were friendly to you and welcomed you and listened to what you had to say.

'Retailing is a tough business, by which I mean it is a physically hard business. Most retailers would be used to working very hard. Tesco was a new business, an upstart business in a way. People were working-class people who came up through the business, male and often ex-army. If you think of those backgrounds, geographically and socially, they would be quite command-and-control, quite rough and abrasive, so those would be your first impressions. Like all things in life, beneath that there would be very different people, but your first impressions wouldn't be that favourable.'[21]

He recalls a company still rife with fiefdoms and ruled by the buying barons on the one side and the retail operation barons on the other. 'There were all these weaknesses [but] whilst the company wasn't trading that well, you had a sense that the leadership was going to do something about it and so you had faith in the business. That was very important. In my own small way I had started to contribute to that in terms of the broad marketing planning of how you would benchmark a better organization.'[22]

But trying to introduce change put a lot of backs up. Leahy says he was constantly amazed that he wasn't fired because he irritated so many people. 'I suppose my training was suited to analysis. What was in me started to come out. I was more bold and energetic and combative and creative. I wanted to use these things and so I pushed on. That was a bit of a shock for people, because there was this new funny northern bloke who kept making presentations and asking for things.'[23]

The funny northern bloke was noticed, though, and the ideas issuing from the computer print-out room began to transform Tesco's approach to talking to customers: modern marketing was about to arrive.

Chapter 14

Marketing for Beginners:
How Tesco Learned to Listen

'The surprise was that conventional wisdom is not often right. If you look at government or business, however well meaning or well intended, they assume they know what people need and they mainly don't.'

Sir Terry Leahy[1]

Marketing arrived at Tesco after Operation Checkout, though it took a few years to grow up. Advertising also had a fair way to go if it was going to move on from the shouty, if occasionally witty, dayglo posters.

At that time marketing and advertising were the preserve of Daisy Hyams, usually referred to as 'the legendary Daisy Hyams' as if she had an extra forename. Working for her was Lou Valencia. He had run the advertising team for a good few years before Checkout, as one of his early recruits, Robin Gray, recalls. 'He was unique. He came from Victor Value, the old food company that Tesco swallowed up. He had been doing Victor Value's printing and they made him head of advertising. I don't think he ever understood it. He ran a chain of antiques shops. He brought antiques in and fiddled around with them while I got on and did the advertising.'[2]

Robin Gray was a graduate of St Martin's School of Art in all its 1960s hipness. He decided to call up Lou one day, intrigued by this company whose boss was forever in the newspapers with some PR stunt or other. Gray would go on to run Tesco's advertising until 2007, overseeing the Dudley Moore chicken-hunting adverts and the Prunella Scales 'Dotty' campaign at the end of the eighties and through the nineties, both of which helped to expand Tesco's reputation beyond the narrowness of pile it high, sell it cheap.

Gray's description of Tesco's marketing and advertising in the 1970s in the run-up to Operation Checkout paints a colourful picture and helps explain Leahy's first impressions of the department when he arrived in 1979.

'The legendary Daisy Hyams was my boss,' Gray explains. 'I wasn't very good at keeping good time in the mornings. We had this long wooden corridor with the advertising department right at the end, so I had to walk past a number of directors' offices. I used to get on my hands and knees and crawl under their windows to get to my office. Daisy was a very tough lady. I would have been fired on the spot – because in those days you could be – if she had spotted me coming in late. I'd be on the phone and I'd hear Daisy running down the wooden corridor. She'd pull the receiver off me and slam it down and tell me she was trying to get in touch for the last ten minutes. I've seen many guys fired on the spot. She was unbelievable: very rude and very tough. She was not easy to work for. She mellowed a bit later on. She was a tough negotiator, though. She was part of the history of Tesco. I don't think any other woman after she left made the Board for a number of years.'[3]

After Checkout, Gray remembers an unsuccessful advertising campaign called 'I don't believe it'. The messaging lacked much in the way of relevance to how Tesco wanted to be seen – not that Tesco itself had really worked that out by that point.

Ian MacLaurin and David Malpas, working through Tesco's different departments as if they had a checklist, suspected that the issue was lack of coordination. Was anybody looking at how progress and change in the shops linked up with Tesco's main message? They asked John Gildersleeve to assess a range of functions, many of them in Daisy's empire.

'David [Malpas] was unhappy at the structure of the buying

function which had just bumbled along for years,' explains Gildersleeve. 'It had been the preserve of Jack Cohen originally, then of the legendary Daisy Hyams. She was very much just a buyer and a very good one, but it was a rudimentary, simple business. People dealt with individual suppliers and there was an element of distrust throughout the process. Daisy had the wall of her office made into glass rather than brick so she could spy on what the buyers were doing. I bricked it back up when I inherited it.

'The marketing department at that time had a young, fresh-faced Scouser called Leahy in it. It was more about analysing product and sales performance at that point.'[4]

Terry Leahy, downstairs grappling with computer print-outs in his dark, depressing room, nearly lost heart. He recalls, 'The problem with me was I'd have all these ideas but they weren't my department. I used to annoy all these other departments. Massively. I was by this time enjoying the work. I was able to get out more in the stores and meet more people like suppliers, so it had become a much more colourful job.

'Marketing did not really exist. Those responsibilities were handled by the buying floor or retailer operators, or even by the estates [property planning] department. There was an advertising and promoting department. Marketing was still a department without a job.

'Advertising sits naturally within marketing, but it wasn't structured in that way. It was uncoordinated. I was pulling those things into a single place for the first years, but doing it in my twenties and upsetting a lot of people along the way.'[5]

Gray remembers the resistance to the young Leahy. 'He was a young graduate coming into Tesco in a baggy suit, joining the marketing department. I could tell straight away he was clever and had good ideas. He had lunch at my desk on a regular basis and we used to get into discussions about the business. He used to ask me where Tesco could be in twenty years' time. Looking back now, even then I think he had a vision, but I couldn't know at that stage that he would be our chief executive. He was a nice chap who kept himself to himself and he was quite shy. We used to say the buyers had no idea: the tins would just turn up and the stores had to sell them.

'Eddie Clark and Dennis Tuffin and the likes of those people were the top regional managing directors and they used to wield a lot of power. Terry was unsure about that, but stuck at it [though] he wanted to leave.'[6]

Gray, ten years younger than Ian MacLaurin and ten years older than Terry Leahy, bridged the gap generationally, though his background put him closer to the younger recruits arriving at Tesco and illustrates how people in Britain, or at least in its cities, were changing. These were the younger customers that Tesco was attracting, too.

Robin and his twin brother, Peter, were born in Wembley, London, in 1947, the sons of a building surveyor and flower-arranger, both of whom loved to paint in any spare time they had. The Grays moved their five children out of their pre-fab and into a four-bedroom house with an acre of land at Hornchurch, Essex, when Robin was halfway through primary school. That suggests there was more money in the family than there actually was. Robin remembers hiding from the milkman when he called for his money and recycling coffee when the vicar called. His mother supplemented the family's small income by making wax flowers and fruit for the well-known florist Constance Spry, where her brother was a senior manager.

The children inherited their parents' artistic talent. Robin recalls that art was the only area in which he shone. 'I came head of my class for handwriting in the third year and my twin brother won in the fourth year. Secondary school was Highlands for boys, which was not a grammar school; we weren't that bright. We never hit the A-stream. We couldn't be bothered; we'd rather play cricket or football. We spent most of lunchtimes going to the girls' school. Neither of us liked school. All I wanted to do was paint and draw. I didn't get any GCSEs. I went to St Martin's School of Art in Charing Cross Road and got a diploma, [then] I spent four years doing graphic design with all the pop stars. It was brilliant. It was the best time to be there.

'We used to go to the Marquee club and see the Stones before they were even famous. [We] were all typical sixties students, great people. It was parties and purple hearts in those days. They were little pep pills that meant you could dance for three hours longer than you would have done before you collapsed on the floor. It was all jumpers and baggy trousers. You could not wish as a teenager in the sixties, when everything was changing, to be in a better place than St Martin's. All doors were open to the art college: smoking, drinking, lovely girls, free and easy. All partying and no work. I had sideburns and long hair, a Mexican moustache and winkle-pickers. Everybody did in those days. We had collarless jackets like the Beatles. I had an old beaten up MG Midget with the hood down.

'They were great days. There wasn't a lot of money but we didn't need money. We went to coffee bars. I still meet up with twelve of my friends from the youth club days when we met up and played the juke box in a coffee bar. We used to go to the youth club in the morning and church, and then after lunch we'd be straight down La Sauciere [our local coffee bar] for the afternoon. We didn't have pubs and you cannot get drunk on coffee.

'Parts of London were still pretty tough and derelict, but it sprang to life. Even supermarkets changed. It had been "Can I help you, Madam?" and then self-service took off.

'When I finished I walked into the first agency with my portfolio: you can't do it today. I was still quite young, and they said start next week. I worked on Playtex bras and Double Diamond beer, designed their packaging and poster campaigns. I went on to Lipton supermarkets because I found in an advertising agency nobody was teaching you what to do. I decided I'd like to give instructions rather than take them from a client. It was in the City Road in London and I worked for them for about seven or eight years. I wrote a letter to the advertising director of the Tesco stores saying I'd been in supermarket advertising and I admired Tesco. Somebody had just left so I got the job on Monday.'[7]

Tim Mason – later to be Robin Gray's boss and Tesco's deputy group chief executive and head of its American business, Fresh & Easy – was a Unilever management trainee in 1981 ('a jolly good thing to be') but had been stuck in the Wall's Meat Company in charge of sausages. Tesco launched an own-brand range and half his business disappeared 'overnight'. Mason explains that his reaction was full of youthful confidence.

'I thought, this is a rum do: maybe I had better go and work for them. I was flicking through a dog-eared copy of *Marketing* magazine and I saw this advertisement for a product manager at Tesco. I didn't even know they did marketing. I thought what they needed was a bright young marketing graduate like me.'[8]

Tim Mason came from an affluent, arty, southern background and as such complemented the abundance of grit, both northern and southern, supplied by other Tesco leaders. He was born in 1957 in the London Clinic, Harley Street, to parents who rented a flat in London's exclusive Bryanston Square. His story is a snapshot of a time in England when the arty intelligentsia had gained an almost celebrity sheen. His mother, Ailsa Garland, was a journalist and his father, John, worked for Shell. They had met after the war: John had had a relatively benign war in a part of Africa away from heavy fighting and Ailsa had worked at an anti-aircraft gun training base in London.

Describing his family circumstances Mason comments, 'They were getting on for the last generation of people who rented houses in Britain, and in terms of wealth-planning [they] made a mistake by not buying until their late to mid-forties and so they missed out on twenty to thirty years of property appreciation in London. They could have bought a little house in St John's Wood overlooking the canal in Little Venice for a few thousand pounds in the mid-sixties, which they could have sold for £100,000 in the mid-seventies.

'We moved to Launceston Place in South Kensington, which was extremely posh. They rented that: one of the first phrases I remember is "self-repairing lease". As the dry rot started up the street we moved to Brownwood Gardens off the Earls Court Road.

'Both my parents had gone to grammar schools, my mother in Essex and my father in Coulsdon in Surrey. I was an only child born to them late and they probably felt that what they could and should do out of the material success was to privately educate their only child. My mother was a journalist: she worked in a bank after the war and then went into journalism and was on the *Daily Mirror* when Hugh Cudlipp was the editor. She had to be around for the paper coming off the press so my parents, when a lot of contemporaries would have moved to the suburbs, steadfastly stayed in central London and that probably drove the sort of school they picked.

'She was the woman's editor of the *Mirror* when Marjorie Proops was there. I grew up with Marje as a family friend, and Felicity Green, who went to the *Daily Express* and until recently was still writing. My mother went to *Vogue* and is [its] only short-serving editor – 1963 to 1965. It was an amazing era, with Shrimpton and Snowdon, Twiggy and Bailey, but she was not there for very long. Looking back, they must have thought they made a bad hire. She was under a lot of professional pressure. She would lose her voice throughout the course of the week and get it back for Monday. Then she went to Fleetwood, part of IPC, and was a director there, so she did okay. My dad worked for Shell, in marketing, in the days when they could fill that entire building on the Embankment and it had an Olympic-sized swimming pool; but because they so enjoyed her career he only worked in London. In those days – and this is a bit of a parallel to Tesco today – if you weren't prepared to work inter-nationally it was quite difficult to get on. He turned down a number of overseas appointments. His last big thing for Shell was to do a corporate re-design, which took the Shell logo on to the red back-ground. It occurs to me now that when I did the Tesco re-design in the late to mid-nineties we put the blue into Tesco and put it into the white background.

'I had joined Tesco by the time they died, when I was in my twenties. If they had been more into commerce they would probably have said, "What the hell are you doing that for?" because Unilever, where I was a trainee, was 22-carat gold and the sort of place you

144

should build your career, and Tesco was a bit dodgy, a bit "cheap-jack". But they were okay with it and I did well quite quickly and they enjoyed that, and then sadly they both died. It was "Do your best" and I guess I have done my best.'[9]

Although Mason was one of the few Tesco people of his generation to have gone to university, he says he was never academic. 'I failed Common Entrance. I was at Westminster Under School and, frankly, would never have got in to the senior school. I retook Common Entrance at a "crammer" and I got into Stowe. Drayson, the headmaster, said, "We will accept Timothy at owner's risk." I did do better the older I got; I got terrible O-levels, better A-levels and a better degree. I liked the subjects you could talk about, which will come as a surprise to nobody. I took a degree in philosophy and English, with the emphasis being on the literature.

'We used to go every weekend to Lavenham, where my parents moved lock, stock and barrel once I went to boarding school. My friends in Suffolk were people from the village who in those days would never have been to London. Occasionally they would beat the living daylights out of me for being too posh. The best time of the year was when they brought the harvest in and the bales were still out in the fields, and you could build these forts with bales and pull the stubble out and clump mud around and make these fantastic mortar hand-grenades. There were these pillboxes, concrete structures to protect the railway line, and we used those as forts. We were told to come back when it was dark and didn't.

'Lavenham had A. R. Heeks in the village square and a shop in Sudbury called Pricerite, which was the first supermarket I can remember. It was a 1960s precinct and would later become a Tesco.

'University was okay. I did it because it was what one did. I enjoyed the people. I went to Warwick. Warwick started out being a building site: when I was there it wasn't red brick, it was a white-lavatory-tile university. It chose me. I played a bit of rugby for the university, had some nice friends and girlfriends and lived in a house in Leamington Spa. I didn't much enjoy being an undergraduate; it was a means to an end. My academic CV was not brilliant but I managed to put together an unusual outside-interest CV. I spent three months working for a PR agency in central London in my last summer vacation. The advice I was given was join Procter & Gamble, Unilever or Mars and go into advertising from there. I became exposed to the trade papers as part of working in PR and they became the subject of every interview I went to. It made me look probably better than I was.'[10]

Mason went to work for Unilever and was given a role at Wall's, a subdivision. 'They were just moving from Willesden Junction to Banbury. I married Laura in 1981, aged twenty-four. We bought 1, Gatteridge Street in Banbury. My wife's uncle was a London solicitor and chairman of Everest Double Glazing and he gave us the deposit of about £1,000. I moved to Tesco the year after that.

'Tesco accounted for about 30 per cent of the Wall's meat company's sales. Tesco was every second word at Wall's. The IGD [Institute of Grocery Distribution] started a diploma in marketing. We three graduate trainees at Wall's were sent on it. I miraculously came first and won a United Biscuits prize. I did my dissertation on Tesco, which I quoted from in a Board meeting in New Tesco House last week. Somebody had tracked back and looked at the fortunes of the business and how they correlated with the square footage that had been opened. It isn't the most insightful thing to know about retailers, that they grow if their space grows.

'A secret revolution was taking place at Tesco. I don't know if they knew what they had got when they employed Terry Leahy. Terry started working for [them] in a room full of computer print-outs. He was making a bit of progress and was allowed to hire a few people, and I was one of those first people that he hired. It was a quiet revolution. I met Terry in 1981 in the ground floor of the building we are sitting in now [New Tesco House]. He had sent out his first lieutenant to beat me senseless in an interview and he then came out to deliver the *coup de grâce*. I thought, "My God, I have never met people like this in my life", but for some reason I came to work for them.

'Tesco was a business of tremendous scale, but all of it was potential. It was big and made about £50 million when I joined, but it was always a bit touch and go. If it could improve its marketing it could be a very successful business. I've never been a big fan of the technicalities of marketing; if you were you wouldn't be a retailer. When you are spending 30 per cent of the revenues of a product on marketing then it really matters, but in a business like this you are only spending 1 per cent. It is more about getting the business facing in the right way, responding to consumers in the right way. Retail is so much about the substance of what you actually experience. If you are selling a soft drink you are selling an idea. You can make a commodity so much more valuable by the idea associated with it. That isn't the case with a retail business. It is three-dimensional – it is all around you. You kick it, you touch it, it speaks to you and you take it home with you. It is a much more experiential thing and therefore it is much more about organizing the business to be customer-facing and do things that matter for customers rather than how you talk about it.'[11]

Mason would go on to lead some of Tesco's most significant developments, and there is another interesting aspect to his relationship with Tesco: his second marriage, to Lord MacLaurin's daughter Fiona, creates a family line back to Jack Cohen's era.

'Ian comes to stay in the States [Mason's base as head of Tesco's chain of Fresh & Easy stores] regularly. I take him round the shops. He is fantastic with the staff to this day. He chats to them and tells them he was chairman. They love it. He's awfully posh. His father-in-law was Edgar Collar, one daughter [Fiona] did nearly twenty years [with Tesco], another daughter [Gillian] worked here, so Millie [Mason's youngest daughter] has more than 100 years of service of family members leading up to her. I don't know if she will ever work here, but people with high energy levels, good values and enthusiasm can make a tremendous contribution and have a tremendous career here. I would be delighted for any of my children to work in this business.'[12]

Mason joined with a small cohort of other new recruits. By then, Terry Leahy's status had risen: he had a room with windows.

'We were in a corner of the ground floor of New Tesco House. We were supposedly the bright young things of the marketing department. There were fifteen people, I guess. They reported through Terry to Keith Clark, who left in the end and went to Asda.

'Tesco was a strange business. Most of the senior people had left school young and had emerged at the top of the company by masses of hard work, personality, drive – the most testosterone-fuelled people you could ever hope to meet. They were bright enough to realize that Terry could make a difference to their lives and Terry was bright enough to take them with him and not alienate them.'[13]

The 'bright young things' had the tacit backing of Ian MacLaurin and David Malpas. 'Marketing was new. The original plan was to do range control: what products a store would stock and where it would put them.

'Stores had bought locally. If the Peek Freans salesman had been good down the road and the Nabisco salesman had been good in another [shop], there'd be a big display of one in one store and another in the other. When Ian and David went from being poachers to gamekeepers they said we're not having this any more. You had to know what you were selling in order to manage the margin.'[14]

Category management began to take shape. For the first time, rather than just being swayed by the product salesmen, Tesco would join up all the information it had about what customers actually bought: the sales and profitability of different products would determine the way the stores were stocked and how they could be merchandized.

The business also took a leap into the unknown and began recruiting people with real expertise in produce, known initially as produce technicians. George Marston was one of those people. Marston was born in 1944 in Nairobi, Kenya. His London-born father had moved to Kenya at the age of sixteen, in 1923, to join a friend who was working on a ranch. George's parents married in 1938, two years after they met when his mother was visiting friends in Kenya and his father was returning from a trip home. 'It was hugely courageous of my father to go on his own at sixteen. He thrived on it. He loved the people and had a great respect for them.

From my perspective, he did a really good job on the ranch, producing beef cattle on 64,000 acres.' In 1975 the Marstons moved back to England, to Evesham.

George was brought up about 150 miles north-east of Nairobi on the family farm, which started out as a basic dwelling without electricity or running water. 'It was a very primitive, simple life. It was a privileged existence. I was so lucky to be there. We had the Mau Mau [an anti-colonial uprising] until 1956 which wasn't pleasant, but otherwise people were very happy. It was a wonderful childhood.' He didn't go to school until he was eight, and he resisted his mother's attempts to teach him to read or write. He did, however, learn to speak the local language, Swahili, and he developed firsthand knowledge of produce. George was sent to prep school and then boarding school (in Nairobi), where he preferred sport to academic study. In 1964 he moved to England to pursue a farming career of his own, initially on a dairy farm in Cheshire but then on fruit and vegetable farms in Worcestershire.

He spent ten years on English farms and five years marketing fruit and vegetables to the supermarkets, so had developed an understanding of crops, the produce industry and also the people who worked in it. It was the summer of 1983 and he recalls that Tesco 'was in a precarious state'. 'I applied for [one of] the first produce technologist roles at Tesco. Dealing with the multiples then there was no loyalty: they were ruthless. I was piggy in the middle [at the produce marketing firm] between retailer on one side and producer on the other.'[15]

Tesco was set on big change, driven by the need to improve quality on its shelves in order to survive against other supermarkets whose quality was better then. 'The ownership of quality used to stop at the farm gate,' says Marston. 'It had to become the ownership of everybody in the chain from the field to the point of sale. To change the mentality was one of the big challenges we all faced in the eighties. The science of controlling quality was new. We had to ensure that the quality the customer perceived and bought gave them satisfaction.'[16]

'Merchandizing in 1983 was horrible. Product was pushed on to the shelves through lack of knowledge and expertise. Conditions in the store were "unfriendly". There was 20 per cent humidity, high temperatures, dehydration and rapid deterioration. It created customer dissatisfaction.'[17]

There had also been some progress in terms of Tesco's message. By the early 1980s the people at the top had decided that all the investment going into improving the quality of what Tesco sold should be championed in the advertising.

The technical revolution, however, would not have overnight results: Marston says it took at least two years for each improvement to take effect. So a campaign devised by McCann Erickson foundered because the reforms of the early 1980s had not made enough difference in the stores. Robin Gray explains: 'Robert Carrier, a chef, came from Canada to head our campaign about the wonderful apples and pears, and the lovely cuts of meat we had. He was a strange chap who came with minders to the shoots. He made some good adverts – we made about six commercials – but our stores weren't ready. We were advertising quality at a time when our stores weren't delivering quality. We had to pull that campaign because we were saying how good our produce looked in store, but it didn't.'[18]

What could be done to bring the stores into line with Tesco's ambitions? Rather than ask the stores again, the 'bright young things' decided to go and ask the customers.

Terry Leahy's management degree had covered technical subjects such as economics, but it had also covered psychology and the new consumer research operation that he ran, known as Trade Off, was the most sophisticated that Tesco had ever undertaken. It was developed with the Mars Corporation's assistance and focused on just one area of the country, Coventry, which was chosen because in 1983 it had a Tesco and a Sainsbury side by side.

Leahy says, 'It was a very profound piece of research because it was the first accurate assessment of the state of the two businesses and how big the gap was: it was massive. When asked to choose, most customers chose Sainsbury. It was the world's most successful, the world's most profitable supermarket business and so you had right on your doorstep the perfect benchmark. From that we basically sketched out the model of how we had to change.

'Trade Off was a research vehicle developed by the Ford Motor Corporation when they launched the Fiesta to compete with the [Volkswagen] Golf and needed a research technique that allowed them to reliably assess people's comparison of the two products, because straight testimonial is not always reliable. You have to find techniques that actually draw out what people really think about two things they are comparing. We wanted to find out what people really thought was important about shopping.

'The technique is you are given hundreds and hundreds of paired choices, such as "Is queuing more important than prices?" "Is quality more important than service?" and you ask so many times it is quite difficult for the interviewee [subconsciously] to fix the response. People tend to give responses that they think are socially acceptable, that sound and feel right.

'Mars had operational researchers who devised the first pairings and our young research people learned how to do it over time. We've always had good research people. The main thing you need is statistics and to understand probability.'[19]

Leahy's team went into the stores to recruit customers who wanted to talk about shopping and who didn't mind answering questions. The technique taught Tesco about its customers, and what it needed to do to serve them better and retain their loyalty; it has been the basis of its customer research ever since.

David Malpas, who was monitoring the findings, had noticed Leahy as he roamed around departments explaining to senior managers how their jobs should be done better (as Leahy describes it). Through fairly regular presentations, the Board learned that it had become overly concerned with conventional wisdom as expressed by external commentators.

'The surprise was that the conventional wisdom is not often right,' says Leahy. 'There are things that matter deeply to people that casual observers – writers, commentators, sometimes practitioners, retailers – don't really pick up on. It gave me a great inner belief – which has been reinforced over the years through talking to people and doing further research – about what really matters to people. You best understand it as part of somebody's life, what's important and why and what they are trying to do. It has been good to think of retailing as basically trying to make people's lives a bit easier. The main thing that really comes out of research is that you find that people are extraordinarily wise; they have enormous insight into their own circumstances and what they need. That is in contrast to [the attitude of] most of conventional society, which is patrician really in that it believes that educated people or people in positions of power know best what people need. If you look at government or business, however well meaning or well intended, they assume they know what people need and they mainly don't, so that's been a wonderful insight.

'We just had to be better on lots of little things around the shopping experience – the stores, the service, the lighting, the range, the pricing – but [customers said] a lot about the quality and so that had to improve a lot. In the second half of the 1980s we did make good progress on a lot of those things and particularly on our quality.'[20]

In late 1985, having been very suspicious, Tesco's commercial team was beginning to see that the technical team brought benefits. Marston says, 'After strong lobbying it was decided to increase the strength of the technical team across all foods and in particular in produce, as customer perception was low. I had to recruit fourteen technical managers to start to begin to manage the supply chain. That took a year.

'There were already fieldsmen, who had worked in retail and sourced product from the docks. There were five of them. They became part of the team. They were old school and they used their knowledge of fruit and vegetables, but Tesco had to move on. It evolved through '86 and '87. It was an exciting period of change.' He worked closely with a produce marketing manager, Andy Dewhurst, a partnership that helped ensure the 'science bit' was supported by good packaging, presence and promotion. One of the early schemes Marston drove through was the introduction of nutritional inform- ation on produce packaging.[21]

The Robert Carrier ad campaign was pulled and the agency replaced by another London team (Grandfield Rork Collins) who devised adverts featuring well-known actors and, rather bravely, the Glaswegian comic Billy Connolly. 'I had to go to the Monday morn- ing Board meeting to present the Christmas commercial to Ian MacLaurin,' recalls Robin Gray. 'I don't think they had been briefed by anybody. I played the two or three ads. If you've ever wanted the floor to open up and you to drop through, that was the time. There was this stony silence, which seemed to go on for an hour.

'Ian said, "Oh well, if nobody else is going to say anything I'll start it off. Robin, I think they are dreadful. What made you choose Billy Connolly of all people?" I said, "He mixes with the right people, he is friendly with the Royal Family and he does not smoke or drink any more. Look at the contents – the products look good. This is what we've got and I want to play them out [begin broadcasting them] tomorrow."

'Ralph Temple, the finance director, sitting opposite me, asked me what they cost. They were £200,000. The ads went out and in early December I was called up to Sir Ian's office: "Robin, just to let you know we are having a fantastic Christmas and people keep telling me how great the ads are. Maybe I got too close to them and didn't see it, but well done."

'It shows that you may not like an actor, but the ads may be right for the business. How do products look? Are the prices right?'[22]

Tesco needed this new image. Ian MacLaurin and Robin Gray were just ten years apart in age, but that decade made a big difference: Robin was a child of post-war Britain, which was a very different country from the one in which MacLaurin grew up. Beneath the layer of Board directors was a group of managers who had done parties and pop music and projects at buzzing colleges, instead of National Service in isolated institutional military bases, or even active duty. Would the mix of experience strengthen the company, or would it lead to in-fighting?

Chapter 15

A Fresh Look at Food: Britain's New Appetite for Quality and Convenience

'We would have sold more butter by value than all our fruit and vegetables when I started out in Tesco. Today fruit and vegetables outsell butter by nearly 100:1. It's been the most remarkable shift in eating.'

Sir Terry Leahy[1]

'In many instances we weren't being terribly original. We just had to go and look at what Marks & Spencer and Sainsbury were doing.'

John Gildersleeve[2]

The new, young marketing team had hit its stride; now it was time to shake it up. 'David Malpas had been discontented about the performance of the buying area and the role of the marketing function I had created,' explains Leahy. 'It was a cuckoo in the nest. It had grown up and it was sharp-elbowed and aggressive and it didn't sit comfortably with the rest of the structure. It was coming up with lots of ideas and analysis and criticism, but it wasn't operationally responsible for enough things. They tried to combine a lot of marketing process with buying process and they were trying to kill two birds with one stone.

'You get this in all organizations – a constant search for a better organizational structure, although there is no holy grail, so it's better not to become obsessive about organizational structures.'[3]

It fell to John Gildersleeve in 1986 to make sure the reorganization happened. He says, 'I asked Terry to relinquish his role in marketing and to take over a commercial role responsible for fresh foods. He wasn't overly enthusiastic about it. I wanted him to do commercial for two reasons: one, I thought it would be good for him in terms of his development; but, more importantly, I thought he would bring all his energy, intellect and ability to bear and I'd have somebody on the same page that I was, to try to sort out the muddle.

'I appointed another commercial director in charge of grocery and another in charge of non-food. Instead of having people in charge of a supplier, we had people in charge of a category – meat, or soft drinks, or dairy. We said we'll give you some tools that will enable you to measure the performance of your department, individual products, the space you need and the data to enable you to have a much more constructive relationship with the supplier base.'[4]

The way Leahy remembers it, the move was a bumpy one. 'I was thirty. I didn't feel good. I'd grown the marketing department and it was all I'd known. I felt a great loyalty to the people in it. I was young and very emotional about all this upheaval and losing all my people to various parts of the business and I was worried by it. It was felt that the marketing department was good and full of good young people, but actually to really make a difference you really needed to improve the buying side of things because they determined the ranges more directly.

'I was responsible for all of the purchasing for all of the fresh food. I had to build a structure of directors who would look after fruit and vegetables or meat and dairy or bakery or frozen food, and they would have buyers and technologists. It was a big part of the business for somebody at the tender age of thirty with no real experience of purchasing or of primary industries.'[5]

A snapshot of that era shows hopeful as well as horrible events. In 1986, for example, the Channel Tunnel was given the go-ahead, but the American space shuttle *Challenger* exploded and the Russian nuclear plant at Chernobyl erupted. The human genome project was launched, but BSE ('mad cow disease') was identified and officially acknowledged. Culturally, *Top Gun* and *The Color of Money* were on in the cinemas, *Dynasty* and *EastEnders* on television. These were just some of the influences on people's aspirations and expectations.

British businesses had to keep pace with the transformation. Tesco reformed its food-buying to reflect new consumer trends. Six categories [the five listed by Leahy above plus grocery] were established, with a fair amount of upheaval as new skills were sought and very experienced leaders transferred to new functions, such as Colin Goodfellow, who moved out of food management to run stores.

Leahy describes his own approach to personnel changes as characteristic of somebody young and inexperienced. 'I wouldn't have had a lot of wisdom in terms of how to get the best out of people. I brought in all these young people from outside the business, which was an odd thing to do when you look back. They were all people like me: ambitious graduates. It was not smart because we were all too much the same, but the sheer energy and opportunity that was there carried us through.

'[Food-purchasing] was under-resourced. I was chosen for the role [because] I was seen, by David Malpas and by Ian MacLaurin, as somebody on the up and a bit sharp-elbowed. There were people already in role. I had to dismiss one or two. It was difficult, because they were senior people, longstanding in the business and the industry. Probably if I had my time over again I'd have done it slightly differently. Some people I could have probably got more out of. It is all part of learning. I brought young people in who didn't have a lot of experience but did have a lot of energy and they picked up the experience on the way.'[6]

The new team included Tim Mason, Colin Smith and Simon Uwins (who would one day establish Fresh & Easy, Tesco's US stores, among other roles), David Wild, Andy Dewhurst (who would go on to lead Tesco Mobile) and Ed Owen. These six translated the Trade Off research findings into practical progress. A key priority was shifting Tesco's range and quality so that it caught up with consumer tastes.

'We would have sold more butter by value than all our fruit and vegetables when I started out in Tesco,' says Leahy. 'Today fruit and vegetables outsell butter by nearly 100:1. It's been the most remarkable shift in eating.

'Many more families had mum and dad at work. People had less time, but they had cars and more money. They could afford to buy things all at once. They didn't have to spread it out. They had fridges. This idea of the one-stop shop grew. So they were quite happy to find that a supermarket now sold milk as well as cheese and a ready meal as well as a bit of steak. You had an appetite for being able to buy everything under one roof.'[7]

Technological advances, from refrigeration and transport to packaging, made it possible for the stores to carry dairy and pre-prepared foods. The days of milk needing to go daily from the dairy to the doorstep were numbered. Marston says, 'There was no knowledge in the distribution chain from supplier to retailer about checking the quality. Those people in the Distribution Centre (DC) could see if food or packaging was damaged but they were not expected to understand the intrinsic qualities of a mango or spring bean or cauliflower. You got variability of supply from people supplying the same product. But intrinsic quality is the most important thing for customers. Retailers had to change their focus. That led to much more detailed specification for packaging, temperature, weight and colour. Resource was put into DCs – quality-assurance people came in. That had a big impact on the industry, which had to comply with stricter controls, so the growing of the crop had to be better. You could not harvest poor-quality produce, as it did not pay. That raised overall quality standards of horticulture and fruit production.'[8]

Leahy says, 'Milk has always been one of those products that is very price-competitive. You wouldn't make your greatest margin on milk, but you would always make an extra sale, so it became a very important product in terms of cash in the till. It was quite a bit cheaper than from the milkman, so some people stopped getting their doorstep delivery and some people had both.'[9]

The same logistical developments helped expand the range of fruit and vegetables from the leeks, onions and cauliflowers that were long-time staples of the British diet, and there was a general move beyond purely local produce.

'The idea of genuinely local purchasing had started to disappear from the very beginning of organized multiple retailing,' Leahy reflects. 'The Co-op, where I started, had national purchasing of fruit and vegetables. There had always been an international trade in citrus fruit and bananas.

'What you did see was the creation of big, central distribution centres for fruit and vegetables, which allowed the quality to be checked, and growers had to deliver their produce into those centres. What that tended to mean was they didn't take their fruit and vegetables to markets and so you saw markets decline. That was probably no bad thing, because the way that markets worked actually was that they never guaranteed any price to the farmer. People remember the nicer aspects because it is human nature, but they don't remember some of the problems. With supermarkets you knew what price you were going to receive when you shipped it in and you did get paid.'[10]

Growers were indeed guaranteed a price, says George Marston, and those who embraced the evolving quality checks and agricultural science did well. There were, however, those who could not or who would not keep up. 'Those people who weren't willing to come into that mindset were left behind,' he says. 'Because margins were tight, a lot of people left the industry. On the plus side, those growers who understood [it] invested in quality and management of crops from growing to point of sale. Collective responsibility manifested through the nineties and is common practice today.'[11]

Marston, who was to spend more than two decades in Tesco's technical operation, adds that the pressure kept up on the supply chain as expectations of fresh produce kept growing. Tesco invested in 'chilling' the chain with advanced technology, including distribution centres for different temperatures as well as vehicles. Marston says suppliers and growers had to look after their part of the chain because if one link was poor, the entire process failed. 'We had difficulties within the company and with some suppliers who did not like what was happening. We had to manage that and then start to increase the science of the supply chain.'[12]

As well as his nutritional labelling, Marston recalls a debate about date-coding produce. 'It would help stores manage their stock, but it would also create bigger wastage. It had a big impact on the way things were done and it cost a lot of money. But the directors were bold and brave: to have date-coding, to have chill chain distribution and merchandizing . . . the perception of Tesco by customers was improved.

'[But] that put more pressure on the supply chain. We suddenly said if it didn't meet the intrinsic quality in the specification, we would reject it. We set up an audit process. We compared one supplier against another so we could analyse who was delivering the best product. The buyer could switch emphasis to suppliers who would give us, and the customer, the best product. That had a huge impact.'[13]

Kevin Doherty, by then one of Tesco's most experienced store operators, who was running a group of stores in and around London, describes the impact on the shops of the new approach to buying. 'It was the first time we began to realize we had to manage range and space very carefully. Take chocolate biscuits – nobody knew what our sales were across the company, or our market share compared with Sainsbury and the national figures. [Tesco] really started analysing products.

'We had always had products with the Tesco name on, but there wasn't a lot of focus by food technologists to make sure that if it had a Tesco name on it that it would be as good as the leading brand. It had all been based on price. We did a lot of tests: we opened the food-technology centre for trading law and consumer law. Every single product was benchmarked against the leading brand. Our quality image improved. You knew if you bought our burgers they would be as good as Birds Eye's.

'If we brought out our own sausages we had to make sure that the managers always stocked them. That hadn't happened before. Customers wouldn't buy them and then the managers would see it as waste and [delist them and so these products] never got a chance to take off.

'We had bigger, brighter stores with our own products. We were managing the space better and we had a real clean-up. There were no supplier stands on the shop floor because we had had lots of customer complaints about clutter in our aisles.'[14]

Inevitably, the new way of working meant mistakes were made. Customers were not always ready for food that at the time would have been viewed as exotic, such as cherry tomatoes and peppers, and waste levels rose. Customers wanted something new when they shopped, but it took a bit of trial and error to work out what they would stomach.

'Generally, customers have always been pretty calm about a new product,' says Leahy. 'They like seeing new things because they have to go shopping on a regular basis – twenty-five or thirty or a hundred times a year, depending on how you do your shopping. It can get pretty boring. Like watching repeats on the television. So if something's new, customers like that. They may not buy it, but they have a look and if the price is right and if they have a few extra pence in their pocket then they might try it. It's a gradual thing.'[15]

Sometimes the idea would be popular but the product would have to go through several variations before Leahy's team got it right. The buying team was very immature in a corporate sense and numbered about ten people in 1979. Even in the mid-1980s there were no more than thirty. They learned a lot by watching the competition.

'In many instances we weren't being terribly original,' admits John Gildersleeve, who was the director responsible for buying and marketing. 'We just had to go and look at what Marks & Spencer and Sainsbury were doing – in quality and innovation, Marks & Spencer were ahead of anybody, but for brand integrity and customer loyalty Sainsbury were paragons of virtue. For a good long while we didn't have to have over many brain cells devoted to quality and innovation: we had two models out there we could just copy. We wanted to catch them and be as good as them and then better them.'[16]

Marks & Spencer invented the ready meal. Terry Leahy's team looked on. 'They showed that you could prepare meals you might make at home in a central factory and, by very careful management of the hygiene, safely cook it and chill it and bring it through into stores and to the consumer. That was a very, very impressive achievement. We tried to copy that and we didn't do it very well. There was a lot of skill involved right through the chain: suppliers, technologists as well as the buyers. There was a lot of trust involved on the part of the consumer. In our first year our sales were £2 million and most of that was thrown in the bin. But we stuck at it and slowly but surely we did develop a business. We had to create all of our own suppliers because the Marks & Spencer suppliers would not work with Tesco; that meant that it took more time. In the end we developed a very big business. The life of the product gradually improved from three or four days to seven or eight days and it made it more practical to move it through the warehouses and the stores and gave it three or four days in the customer's fridge.

'We did stew and dumplings, a range of British foods, all copied off Marks & Spencer, I'm sure. I do remember chilli con carne, because it was the student meal that had become popular at the time and the poor factory had forgotten to soak and cook the red kidney beans: you had the beans like hard pebbles. That was a big setback, but we survived.

'One of the main objectives was to sell good quality. This was a time when Tesco set its stall out as being able to sell quality as good as the best, which was quite something.

'In the early years ready meals were intended to appeal to the yuppie, the busy professional. It wasn't imagined in the beginning that a family would want a ready meal, but gradually, as the scale increased, you found you could offer better value on a lasagne or a big pie and it became simpler to buy a lasagne pre-made and to heat it up for a family. They were quite inexpensive in comparison to buying the raw ingredients. Whether they tasted as good or not depended on the cook.'[17]

John Gildersleeve remembers ready meals were a hard product to get right – and Tesco's surprise that families as well as yuppies grew to love them. 'The first time we launched it customers didn't want it;

second time the product wasn't good enough; and the third time customers were more ready for it. Part of the problem originally was building trust in the Tesco name on the product. It was part of our learning process, discovering a supply base that was reliable. This is a high-risk product that requires a lot of skill in production, and investment in the facility.

'We went and wrote the list [of meals we wanted to sell] out of Marks & Spencer. It wasn't rocket science. It was only in the latter years, when we became arguably the leader in some of these markets, that we had to do the real pioneering stuff. By then the teams had built up enough expertise and understanding and contacts and supply base that it could do things first. But for a whole shedload of time all that Terry and I, and Tim and others, did was copy the rest. Imitation is the sincerest form of flattery.'[18]

Customers' demand for convenience was growing, but many people inside Tesco were of the view that a ready-made sandwich was a step too far for a supermarket, even if Marks & Spencer had got it off to a fine art.

'Tesco brought them in at the back end of the eighties,' says Leahy, who remembers store managers arguing that it would never work. 'We weren't very good at it at first, but we stuck at it. David Samworth was a very well-regarded meat manufacturer. We came to him one day and asked him if he'd thought of making sandwiches. They had never made them. Today they are the world's largest sandwich-maker.

'They were aimed at busy people, I suppose. It's still a lunchtime thing. The British had taken to having lunch in as short a time as possible, so the sandwich was a natural solution.'[19]

Few women now could rustle up a tasty meal from a beef tongue or a pig's trotter, as their grandmothers managed to do. Lack of time or knowledge or inclination are the usual explanations. Some say 'a good thing too'; others make a career in television reviving lost skills.

So-called 'recipe meals' – lasagne, chilli con carne and spaghetti bolognese – became commonplace, meaning that demand for mince rose. The front end of a cow had never been so popular. The back end – cuts like skirt and flank, braising steak and shin – lost appeal. Cattle continued to grow the same way in defiance of customers' changing tastes, and this gave retailers a challenge.

At the same time as customers were becoming more adventurous in their tastes for foods from abroad, and wanting more luxurious eating, they were finding less time to cook. As more product was offered that you didn't need to know [how to cook] – you just needed to heat it up or eat it – then people preferred to do that because it was easy, says Leahy. 'Many more women were at work. Each decade there was a big change. Mums didn't have the time to make pastry and pies and trim beef. There was a bit more money around, so even though making a pie might cost a bit less, when you threw the time in they were prepared to pay the extra to have a ready-made pie.'[20]

Changing consumer need, whatever its cause, meant that super-markets stopped trying to compete with nearby butchers shops and instead left the specialist cuts to them. Previously Tesco had prided itself on its improved meat counters – as Kevin Doherty recalls, the in-store butchers would continuously check what was on offer in butchers in their neighbourhood and try to out-do it, because meat could be such a huge department in terms of profitability. Now, Leahy's new team of food buyers decided to centralize meat prepar-ation, finding that it was almost impossible to sell less popular parts of the whole carcasses that still arrived in stores to be broken down. A lot of the in-store butchers became store managers while some went to work in the central plant and others left.

These were small steps towards making a reality of the revealing customer research. By the end of the 1980s, Leahy and his team knew what they wanted for the shops. The challenge was, would they find anybody willing to work with them to achieve the vision?

Chapter 16

The Supply Side: a Taste for Chicken Kiev and Iceberg Lettuce

'In the old days we were crash bang wallop. We used to lean on suppliers, change suppliers rapidly if they wouldn't give us what we wanted. But as you get bigger and bigger and bigger you rely on suppliers, so it is far better to sit down with them and plan the year ahead.'

John Gildersleeve[1]

'There was a transformation in fresh foods available at affordable prices, led by Marks & Spencer. They took that obsession for quality and applied it with their partners to fresh food and innovated some amazing foods that transformed the way Britain ate.'

Tim Mason[2]

'You had to get new suppliers and it was difficult, because they were committed to Marks & Spencer and to Sainsbury. So we had to find our own suppliers and they didn't know what they were doing either.'

Sir Terry Leahy[3]

From fish to fairy cakes, Leahy's team of young category directors worked their way through Tesco's food aisles – also undergoing a marked makeover – to see what was not selling and how to improve what was.

'The sheer desire to make things better meant we stumbled on things that worked,' explains Leahy, who is the first to say that the process was unrefined. 'The stores were small and needed to get bigger. There was a big emphasis on getting more space for fresh food. It was a crude yardstick, but it worked. We doubled the space our department was given and we developed the range to justify that.'[4]

It helped that John Gildersleeve, Leahy's boss, had the final say on space in stores and could argue the case at Tesco's director level. Half the battle was won, but the second stage was tougher, even with the marketing and buying activity in one team.

'We gathered information about the market,' explains Leahy. 'There would always be somebody much bigger than Tesco selling more. You'd look at their range and your range. Theirs always seemed so much better. We developed a range of own-brand product in the main, and we tried to get packaging design and price point right. There would always be problems at launch: its quality, and not turning up on time. Generally the result of all that was sales moved forward. It became the habit. We'd push and push. We didn't get to market leadership at that time, but we certainly closed some big, big gaps.

'In some of these categories Sainsbury was selling two or three times the amount, not just 50 per cent more, and you'd often find Marks & Spencer selling more than you were. In some senses that made the job easier. We were so small and so lacking it wasn't all that difficult to make an improvement, even if you didn't know what you were doing. We copied, mainly.'[5]

But Tesco desperately needed food manufacturers who would work with them. Leahy adds, '[We] had to get new suppliers and it was difficult, because they were committed to Marks & Spencer and to Sainsbury. So we had to find our own suppliers and they didn't know what they were doing either.'[6]

'We made a lot of progress quickly,' says John Gildersleeve. 'We found some ways of working that differentiated us from our competitors, not least in our attitude to suppliers. I was always convinced that, whereas we wanted the best deal available in the marketplace, we wanted our suppliers to continue to be prosperous. We never wanted all of the cake. All we were ever arguing about was our slice of the cake compared to theirs. We also tried to give them an emotional reason to want to work with us. Suppliers now [after his retirement] are probably more honest with me – but they still tell me they would rather do business with the team at Cheshunt than the team at Asda or Sainsbury or anywhere else.

'In the old days we were crash bang wallop. We used to lean on suppliers, change suppliers rapidly if they wouldn't give us what we wanted. But as you get bigger and bigger and bigger you rely on suppliers, so it is far better to sit down with them and plan the year ahead as far as price structures and promotions. It is in your interest as a retailer for your manufacturer to earn a profit so they can reinvest in their business and be innovative and create excitement in their brands. So it is a case of being hard but fair, and making sure that the suppliers were honest with you and you could see them making money so they could reinvest in their brands.

'The relationship before I brought commercial under one team was largely adversarial. That doesn't mean conflict disappeared. It was constant. But I encouraged people to think of it more like a family relationship: sometimes they don't do something you want them to do and you have a row, but you still sit down and have breakfast. We need each other. We just have to make sure their need of us is greater than our need of them.'[7]

Own-brand was not new. Sir Jack Cohen had often fallen back on making alternatives to branded goods, such as Golden Ring, Red Glow and Delamare; he did it again when manufacturers squeezed retailers during the Resale Price Maintenance rows in the 1950s. So, in the 1980s, when the food-buying team could not find branded versions of what they wanted to copy, or manufacturers willing to supply them, the answer was to transform own-brand.

'Tesco was ashamed of its brand,' John Gildersleeve believes. 'Nobody had the courage to put "Tesco" on the front of the can or packet. There was concern about putting "Tesco" on a bottle of wine in case it devalued it. [But] we recognized it could give us lots of benefits – delivering better value to customers by removing the marketing cost a brand suffers or enjoys, depending upon your perspective. It would enable us to break duopolies that existed in many markets and give us a negotiating position with the existing supply base, and it would give customers a reason to shop with us: if you liked Tesco baked beans, we were the only place you could buy them.

'The challenge was to find a supplier base who would do the own-label. Marks & Spencer had Northern Foods, who made everything, and they would not make for anybody else. I had one or two heated conversations with Christopher Haskins [Northern Foods boss]. He just said, "I will not make those products for you. I have a deal with Marks & Spencer that I believe is right for Northern Foods." I tried to explain to him that he was backing yesterday's business compared to tomorrow's business, but he would not listen. Northern Foods [now] is not the business it was fifteen years ago.

'Terry and I found small businesses around Britain by force of argument and by economic incentive, but without any contracts, to build a factory to make tiramisu or whatever it was. Occasionally it went wrong, but most of the time it was a brilliant success for both parties. When people talk to me about impoverished, browbeaten suppliers, I say to them that I could line both sides of Delamare Road with Rolls-Royces and Bentleys that our suppliers own as a result of doing business with us and I'm really pleased that they've done that well. Tesco have been responsible for the creation of thousands of jobs in food manufacturing as a result of own-label. We went through that evolutionary process through all the categories.'[8]

In 1984, two years into his Tesco career and in his late-twenties, Tim Mason was trading director for provisions and was facing a tough task. 'I got those key areas of fresh foods where Marks & Spencer were absolute leaders and Tesco was nowhere: chilled dairy desserts, chilled cakes, yoghurts, sandwiches, recipe dishes. They defined the Marks & Spencer shopping trip. My bosses said, "We want some of those. Go and get them", and off I went.

'I had three departments. Michele Jobling, who eventually became chief executive of Liberty, ran added-value dairy products. Mark Williamson ran added-value meat products. Charles Gardener ran commodity dairy – milk, cheese, butter. We started to employ women and it became a bit more like a normal reflection of other businesses and society.

'I was in effect a salesman for Tesco. I was convincing manufacturers to build capability and, in the end, factories to enable us to create a range of products that would enable us to compete with Sainsbury and Marks & Spencer. Tesco was pile it high, sell it cheap. None of the classy ones like Northern Foods wanted to do anything with us. They were far too posh and far too happy with their relationship with Baker Street [then the M&S headquarters]. It sounds rude to say, but if you had made a decision to back Tesco not Marks & Spencer at the time when it looked mad, then it paid off. There were much longer odds and your horse came in.

'We never had contracts. We do now, and we do in the US all the time because you can't do business there without a contract. But we never had them then. I was finding people who were in adjacent industries – people who made pies and hams would make some pasta ready meals for us. We did it on the shake of a hand.

'The good times were a little bit longer in coming than I had described in the selling. The relationships were okay. We were people of our word; we didn't renege. By and large most of these people built a very nice business or built a business they could sell to somebody else. We were persuading people to invest, and in the end we were getting some decent returns for those people. Start-ups, don't I know it, tend to cost you more than you thought and take longer to get where you want them to. But in Tesco's case they usually get there in the end.'[9]

Terry Leahy remembers specific instances of how much courage was needed to forge the new road. 'I met a lot of good people over those years: brave suppliers who committed to Tesco, put money in and built factories. There were a lot in Ireland, because at that time the Irish industry was beginning to get organized. The farming cooperatives were beginning to be run as food organizations, like

Kerry Foods and so on. They came to the UK looking for business. They were keen, and pushy as well. We developed what turned out to be vast business between us, but they had very small bases.

'The first meetings were often difficult. I remember Trefor Campbell at Moy Park in Northern Ireland. They had been in the textile industry and gone into poultry-breeding as a way of creating employment. At our first meeting I took away all of Trefor's frozen business. The message, which was a very hard message, was [that] he could never be competitive on frozen product, which was a big commodity area, so he decided to get into fresh added-value poultry and his business never looked back. Nearly twenty years later he's got a vast business in Northern Ireland based on high-quality, added-value poultry, which he sells into Tesco and other people. So between us we developed a huge business.

'There's no good way to deliver bad news, and if you're young and inexperienced you don't do it very well. I would know now much better some of the feelings and emotions in the room and I'd handle it differently. I was always honest and always [had] the right intentions, and despite the hard edges I think that the suppliers who dealt with me and with the young people [at Tesco] recognized that. These were tough, uncompromising people, but at least they were honest, straight and trying to do the right thing.

'[Trefor Campbell] was older, more mature than me and he reacted very positively. In the 1980s the last word in cuisine was chicken kiev in Marks & Spencer and we didn't have one. He came along and said, "I can make you a chicken kiev and it will be as good as the one in Marks & Spencer and it'll be cheaper." He took me along and showed how he would re-form the poultry meat and put the breadcrumb on. The range was fantastically successful. It went on from there, from project to project. It was good cooperation when it worked well. Mainly the recipe ideas came from the suppliers because they had greater food skills, the kitchen and the manufacturing understanding. In good collaboration you got the best of all worlds – packaging, price point, ranging.

'We were never really very original. I remember Yorkshire ham, a type of ham process. For the money it produced a ham that tasted as if it was much better quality than it actually was. That became an extraordinarily successful product we had made with a division of Unigate. We then sold them our bacon-packing facilities.

'There were some fairly daft products. Out of all of that trial and error emerged a core of products that were successful. Later on, in years after I left the area, it became much more professional in terms of how it approached product development and how it launched products.'[10]

Own-brand could never, though, replace Tesco's need to stock brands such as Heinz, although Marks & Spencer held out for a further three decades. Tesco shoppers in the 1980s, like British society in general, were becoming a more complex, broader mix and most of them expected to find household brands on the shelves of their supermarket.

'We always wanted to have as many brands as we could,' says Leahy. 'There was always a limited amount of space, so picking a range meant difficult choices. The first range I ever picked in the early 1980s was the biggest we'd ever had, at 4,000 products. In a similar range today we'd have maybe 25,000. There's been an explosion in the amount of products on sale, even in grocery. We've needed bigger stores to cope with that.

'Sometimes the brand manufacturers were a little bit superior in terms of how they treated the grubby upstarts of the supermarkets. In fairness, it was difficult for the brands: it was changing from many small retailers to a smaller number of large retailers, and it was difficult for them to come to terms with that. Rank Hovis McDougall, British Bakeries and Cadbury and Rowntree's had good brands and they were very important to Tesco. Generally relations were always good. There were lots of personalities, as in the fresh-food area you tended to deal more directly with the agricultural sectors.'[11]

Leahy's new role entailed visits to hundreds of farms and factories – something he had not enjoyed since his time at the Co-operative Group. He bought entire crops of apples and fields full of vegetables.

'You had a big order book to fill. People were eating more fruit and vegetables and we were increasing the space given over to it.'[12]

Sir Jack Cohen was buying produce from overseas decades before Leahy was born, so international fruit and veg was not exactly new, but sourcing it fresh rather than in tins was a different challenge.

'Produce was poor in the UK and so was choice,' explains Leahy. 'These were relatively new ideas, that you could get grapes or lettuce or tomatoes all year round. But storage was never ideal – your apples by February or March tasted awful, so we started to bring apples in from the southern hemisphere, like Chile or New Zealand, and new varieties started to come in.

'The UK didn't grow a lot: it has a maritime, temperate climate so it grows certain things well and some things not. It's not very sunny, so it doesn't produce the sugars in the fruit and get the flavours up that we are used to. Because product had to travel a long way and the fruit and vegetables tended to be picked too young, to stand the bad logistics, things tended to be sour and hard. With better logistics and supply chain you could pick things riper, so you got sweeter flavour and got more varieties coming in.

'You were looking for ambition and expertise. Somebody who could offer something new, product, variety or season – "We can supply you these a month earlier" – a good story, you were looking for.

'Generally cost was not a problem because these areas [of the world] had big comparative advantages: favourable climates, lower labour costs and sometimes they had government support. There were tariffs to get through into the UK and the CAP [Common Agricultural Policy]. I'm not sure we bought very well, I have to be honest, but we were so keen to get the supply.

'We developed some good partnerships and businesses. I don't think we sold any iceberg lettuce and then it became huge – people learned how to grow it in the UK. The UK never produced any peppers: a lot of the glasshouse know-how has been taken from the Dutch into the UK.'[13]

Produce expert George Marston describes how his technical team worked to help buyers find new sources. 'The need to have a continuity of supply forced the technical managers to go out and be innovative and find ways for the customer to have these products all year round. Exotic foods like sweet potatoes and yams and squashes were not then in the offer, and that evolved. Salads were mostly UK-produced, except for winter tomatoes, which came principally from the Canaries. In 1983 it was only Marks & Spencer that were just about starting to sell iceberg lettuce: that was the new wonder product, which was crisp, had an eating crunch and it lasted, which UK lettuce didn't. It was an American product. So we had to go and find it, get it locally grown and then, in autumn, winter and spring, from the Continent. Colin Kitchen [one of the technicians] spent a couple of years trawling Spain, Portugal and Italy trying to identify the best regions with buyers and growers – then all those varieties like Little Gem came into the offer.

'Flowers were hardly on the horizon at that time. It was decided we should put real energy into our flower and plant offer. That became a huge business through the nineties. We had to go out to find the best source of roses, carnations, azaleas and so on. Holland is the hub through their auction systems. Eventually we went from relying on the Dutch systems to having our own supply chain sourced directly from country of origin. Kenya became an important procurement base for roses, thanks to the fantastic agronomic skills of the Kenyans. Vegetables like mangetout, sugar snaps, salad onions – we knew suppliers who didn't have the controls and continuity in place, so we went out and worked with them to understand the growth. Mangetout we had to move from East Africa to Zimbabwe to India and South America. The whole time we were trying to find new crops, things that customers were talking about, and get them on the shelf. It mushroomed. Once you have the process of identifying the suppliers, you could then make sure they developed the growing capabilities. In those days 40 per cent of fruit and vegetables would have been UK-produced because of the need to grow in warmer climates. As the business has got bigger [we take more from the UK but] that has probably stayed about the same because of the amount required.'[14]

Sourcing overseas brought responsibilities, he adds. 'The Ethical Trading Initiative made contact with the main retailers to get them to agree a code of practice. We worked with that as the principle of good people care.' In Marston's native Kenya, the Lake Naivasha area was becoming a significant source of supply for many British retailers from the eighties and nineties. Marston recalls how houses, schools, medical facilities had to be built near the farms, because trucking workers up to 60 miles each day was impractical. 'You had to make sure you had a workforce happy, well looked after and able to supply the skills to grow the flowers to send to the UK.'[15]

For the first time, British shoppers were being presented with new varieties of all kinds of produce. 'Up until then Continental cheese would have been Brie from St Ivel and that would have been it,' Tim Mason observes. 'There was a transformation in fresh foods available at affordable prices led by Marks & Spencer. They took that obsession for quality and applied it with their partners to fresh food and innovated some amazing foods that transformed the way Britain ate. Sainsbury's heritage was the provisions merchant. Tesco was the dented-can merchant and we were coming from a long way behind.

'There was a whole opportunity to put some fridges in and to sell some chilled gear. Frankly, butchers and greengrocers weren't very good. We thought surely we could do better than them, and off we went.

'It wasn't difficult to walk into Marks & Spencer and look at these lovely products, but it was bloody difficult for us to get them: a decade or fifteen years of work and hundreds of millions of pounds by manufacturers and Tesco in plant and equipment and supply chain. Billions, in fact. The great thing about Tesco was its tenacity and steadfastness in "We are going to have a world-class fresh-foods business." You didn't have to go far to see the benchmarks, because they were in the UK.'[16]

Tesco's managing director, David Malpas, had taken a risk by crunching the product-management team into the buying function.

Having expanded Tesco's ranges, the group of young men now set about ensuring the kind of display and space they wanted store managers to provide for the new products. That went down like a cup of cold sick on more than one occasion.

Tim Mason remembers a 'defining moment' run-in with Tesco veteran Eddie Clark, then a regional manager of stores, in the manager's office at the store just outside Cheshunt. Like most rows, with hindsight the trigger seems trivial and even ludicrous. Mason's role included developing a range of bakery and morning goods (buns, pastries and such like). Clark took Mason to task over the quality of his iced buns – another imitation of Marks & Spencer. The icing slipped off Tesco's version, whereas it stuck to the original, and Mason was finding it hard to match the quality. Gunstones made the original and would not then supply Tesco. Mason decided to back his buns, poor though they were, to Clark's (reasonable) fury.

If buns were that day's battle, the wider campaign was to shift Tesco into new territory, as Mason recalls. 'Everybody at the top of the company had been in retail operations and they wanted to run the business, whereas the previous era was property developers and wholesalers. We built the systems and processes that enabled the business to be centrally controlled. The store managers didn't like it. We had unholy rows with people who were much older and much more senior. People hoped we would get the sack.'[17]

As 'old Tesco' encountered 'new Tesco', the people in the stores and the products in the stores were undergoing a transformation. Tesco's bosses, Ian MacLaurin and David Malpas, were looking closely at the stores themselves. The last bastion of Sir Jack Cohen's original Tesco, the boardroom, was to be altered for ever after one more tussle.

Chapter 17

Changing Times: the MacLaurin Era

'In the early 1990s, when others were pulling back a bit, we went on and that was a crucial time for us.'

Lord MacLaurin[1]

People old enough or political enough to recall Dame Shirley Porter often assume that she ran Tesco before she arrived at Westminster City Council and became its controversial Conservative leader. However, although Sir Jack Cohen's sons-in-law rose while he was still ruling the business, it was different for his daughters, who played only supporting roles at Tesco.

After their marriage in 1949, Shirley had been used to accompanying her husband, Leslie Porter, on buying trips all around the world, and she had maintained a keen interest in Tesco all her life. By the mid-1980s, although her father had died and Sir Leslie was about to retire, Shirley longed for a bigger part in Tesco's management to maintain the Cohen interest in its development. 'I would have hoped to have continued an association with Tesco and it would not have been so difficult to have had a woman on the Board in the shape of one family member, even though it was public. I felt I had something to offer. But it wasn't to be. The resistance to a certain extent puzzles me, but perhaps I was seen as too much like my father. I was told it was the Board, but I think that the Board was led by the chairman.

'Leslie would have liked it very much. Whenever it's a family business and [other] people take over they want to professionalize it.

176

The financial advisers would have liked to spread it out a bit. Just because you're family shouldn't mean you aren't good at it. I understand you have to broaden things, but one member of the Board wouldn't have destroyed anything. You can be outvoted.'[2]

The chairman, by 1987, was Ian MacLaurin, who took up the post when Leslie Porter retired aged sixty-five. MacLaurin recounts his version of events. 'Irene and Shirley were two very different characters. The Porters were much more rumbustious [than Hyman and Irene Kreitman]. Leslie was a trader through and through. Shirley was determined that she wanted to get on the Board, particularly after her father died, and went to no end of lengths to do it and it caused no end of aggravation between me and her, and I am really sad that that happened.

'It was a sad thing for us. You can look back on it now. She didn't have the experience to be au fait with the way that Tesco was moving.'[3]

Ian MacLaurin was looking for fresh faces – on and just below the Board – to push through the changes he and David Malpas wanted in the stores. They also wanted to shift perception of Tesco in the City. Internally, the image debate was sufficiently serious for the Board to have considered changing even Tesco's name itself. They only stuck with Sir Jack Cohen's tag because Tesco was such a well-known brand that there was a significant downside to ditching it, so instead they focused efforts on changing not the name but what it stood for.

One new appointment was made after a chance encounter in the spring of 1985, when Leslie Porter and Ian MacLaurin, Tesco's chairman and unofficial chairman-in-waiting, were on the golf course.

A young accountant at British American Tobacco (BAT) called David Reid (now Sir David Reid) was, in the normal run of things then, too junior to have been invited to a grand golf day with various leading lights of British business. He landed a pass only because his boss could not go at the last minute and Reid, having arrived early as usual in the office, was offered the chance to take part. As a keen golfer and ambitious accountant, he seized upon it.

Interestingly, at that time Tesco, although radical reforms were underway, was still vulnerable and open to takeover attempts and Reid's employer, BAT, which then owned retailers including Argos and Saks Fifth Avenue, was one of the hunters. A restructuring at BAT, which floated off Argos and sold the supermarket chain International Stores to what was then Gateway, meant Reid would have less to do with retail, which he enjoyed, so he had decided to look around. He was working in Bristol, consolidating the Gateway transaction, when the golf day came up. He recalls, 'There were all these industry statesmen there. Leslie was of course interested in how Gateway/International was going. Ian said, "How's it going?" I said, "Okay. They have offered me a job in the new organization and I can't complain, because a lot of people have lost their jobs, but I don't think it's going anywhere." He called the next day and said there was a vacancy. There were a number of interviews. In April 1985 British American Tobacco looked at Tesco and turned it down on the basis that it wasn't a big enough company. It is interesting that they rejected it. In 1985 Tesco was just starting to change.

'Joining Tesco at that time was better than being at the consolidated Gateway group and the leadership was about to start things motoring. Tesco wasn't known as a good, strong company in those days, but you could see straight away they had some very good people who knew what they were doing.'[4]

Sir David Reid was born in February 1947 in Ndola, a town in what was then Northern Rhodesia and is now Zambia. His father and mother, both Scottish and graduates of Aberdeen University, went there after the Second World War. His father took a post with the Colonial Office, starting up farms and teaching locals how to manage maize and tobacco production. He stayed until 1965, eventually becoming deputy director for agriculture for Northern Rhodesia before independence, when he returned to the United Kingdom to run the college of agriculture at Inverness.

Life in Ndola was hazardous but happy. David was the eldest of three brothers who were not encouraged to go wandering around the bush, which began at the end of the cleared area around their house. The yard was baked mud: that way, the family stood less chance of being surprised by snakes. Rabid dogs were another matter, and David was lucky to escape an early encounter with one. The Reid family grew their own potatoes and carrots, and picked fruit from their own trees, to supplement the local staple, maize porridge. Other shopping was done in the Indian-owned stores. David went to the local school along with children who were mainly from Afrikaner farming families. At seven years of age he arrived in Montrose, Scotland, to begin boarding at Lathallan School.

Initially he thought he wanted to work in an area connected to the land: that was what Reid men did. His paternal grandfather had been a tea planter in what was then known as Siam (now Thailand) and he later farmed in Scotland. David's maternal grandfather was a Gordon Highlander who bought a farm after he came out of the army and it was here that David stayed while he was at school and then at university. He helped to work the farm but, like many others in the 1970s, it was to go bust.

Boarding school meant that David knew his father ('Sir') less well than he knew his Scottish uncles and his very Presbyterian granny ('If she had ever thought Tesco would open on a Sunday, she'd have had a fit,' he observes). School passed by, he says, without it really registering that he was away from his family: 'I was never unhappy while I was there.' He became head of his house: 'I never thought I was better than anybody else but I also felt I was as good as anybody else.' He lost the Afrikaans accent, though he can still reactivate it with ease. 'As I grew up I realized Africa was where I was born rather than where I was really from. I came to see myself as British and Scottish, but I still feel a great attachment to Africa.'[5]

Failing to gain the exam results to read metallurgy at Leeds University, David opted for chartered accountancy instead. He worked and studied at a company in Aberdeen on £2 a week, completing five-year indentures. Then he joined Peat, Marwick, Mitchell in Paris in 1970, finding French easy to master. He returned to

London in 1973 to work for Philips, the Anglo-Dutch electronics business then based in Croydon, Surrey. He remembers that it had become too difficult to be a foreign firm operating in France thanks to the protectionist leanings of then president Charles de Gaulle.

When he arrived back in Britain, however, he almost wished he had gone elsewhere. Prime Minister Ted Heath was battling the miners, meaning power-starved offices were sending people home at 3 p.m. There was UK price regulation to keep a lid on inflation (a massive issue for Tesco and other retailers, who bore the costs of inflation and who were the only part of the retail chain unable to raise prices accordingly). David recalls, 'Philips had 40,000 products and armies of accountants working out which of them we could apply to raise our prices on. The maximum pay rise was £2 a week. It was terrible. I spent most of my time trying to work out how to get out again.'[6]

His French diet had ill-prepared him for English fare. 'Food in the UK was pretty primitive. The French were always much more into natural foods.'

After six years in Croydon working on internal audit, David had brushed up his advanced financial accounting and had enjoyed his part in the technological revolution that brought video recorders and CDs into millions of homes, but Philips, despite having 'a five-year lead on the video recorder', lost out to Japanese competitors and moved production to Asia.

Reid applied for a job at British American Tobacco through head-hunters, losing out first time to the same Tom McNab with whom he later joined Tesco, but picking up the BAT job second time around after McNab went elsewhere. A few years and promotions later came that golf-course day in 1985.

Reid recalls that the finance director, Ralph Temple, didn't want to hire him. 'He didn't want anyone. Tom McNab and I were from a modern generation who were drivers of change, people who wanted to get the accounts out within a week not months. Ralph Temple was an old-fashioned accountant who looked at the small things, not the big picture.' Reid remembers him not having a good working relationship with his colleagues on the Board. 'Something had to change.'[7]

Reid remembers that Tesco was 'in the Dark Ages' when it came to accounting, which was not properly integrated with the practical side of the business. 'You get no prizes for producing accurate data. The prizes are for what you do with it.' He wanted a 'proactive function rather than a back office producing numbers'.

It was almost the end of the Cohen family era, with their particular style and personality. 'Leslie Porter was jovial, friendly, charming, with big blue eyes, a big smile, and he was engaging, but you wouldn't go playing cards with Leslie: you'd lose some of your fingers as well as your money. He was very competitive. His skills were different from Ian MacLaurin's. Leslie was more like a street trader: do the deals, drive the money. Ian was a leader who put people in place who could really drive their function. He joined up the fiefdoms.

'A lot of people thought Ian was a dictator, but he wasn't: he was always keen to reach consensus, but he did force people to make their minds up.'[8]

Tesco was centralizing its operations, Reid explains, and almost doubling the volume of products being channelled through the warehouses instead of being delivered straight to stores. 'They got control of their business, which enabled them to develop own-label and build the larger stores.

'I was attracted by the consumer side of it. I'm not a scientist – managing people and motivating people is, for me, what's interesting. When I arrived at Tesco, they needed new people. The older approach was clogging the department.'[9]

There was a 'pretty unpleasant' fortnight in 1985 when established people were eased out. Contracts were honoured, but, nevertheless they were being 'asked' to go.

Reid brought in two colleagues from BAT: Rowley Ager, who became company secretary, and Bharat Patel. They began to reconcile the paperwork process – all the delivery notes and store invoices were being handled manually until then. Tesco had to become more efficient in the back office or the changes in stores and product ranges would fall short of their potential to transform customers' shopping trips.

At this time, Tesco was putting 20 per cent on its bottom line every year. 'The old customers stayed because it was still great value: new products, stores, new shopping experience; but at the same time we were attracting new customers – C1s, C2s, As and Bs – especially the younger generation, because the environment was more dynamic,' explains Reid. 'If you took a forty-five-year-old mum who had shopped all her life at Sainsbury, you could shove water uphill but you may never persuade her to shop at Tesco. The younger people saw the new stores as interesting places, and we deliberately positioned marketing to market to young people: it's better value, the shops are nicer, the staff are nicer. During that era we got a lot right in terms of hanging on to loyal customers and winning more and younger customers.'[10]

Reid's snapshot of the Board as MacLaurin prepared to take over from Leslie Porter, in name as well as in practice, explains how the era of bruising, lapel-grabbing encounters moved into a time of consensus. Reid recalls, 'I bridged the old days and the new days. In some ways you regret things and wish you could go back to the old days, but if you are asked would you, the answer is no because life has moved on. Those stores were run like fiefdoms. They had no financial controls.

'Dennis Tuffin had come up through Tesco. He knew when to put up and when to shut up. John Gildersleeve was larger than life, self-taught and highly motivated. He had run all of the major functions, including elements of property. He was very high-energy and a very good manager of people. He was very good at change programmes. He settled down to be commercial director. Michael Wemms [who replaced Dennis Tuffin] didn't always voice his opinion on every-thing, which was unusual. He brought in a lot of the more modern approach to managing people and developing people.

'People trusted each other so they were forthright, but once they reached agreement there was no politics. There were probably politics and power battles outside the meetings, though. One of the strengths of Tesco now is that it is not a political place. The only politics that matters is "What does the customer see in the shop?" because the rest doesn't matter. In the old days it was "Whose fault was that?" Now it is the fault of all of us. It is about let's find out why, not who.

'I can't ever recall there being a vote by the Board, whereas Ian can tell stories about issues coming to the vote, like Operation Checkout.'[11]

Reid illustrates the less adversarial approach with a story about a site purchase that Tesco was considering. Francis Krejsa, definitely 'old guard' but, interestingly, one of the directors from Jack Cohen's era to win respect from the new faces, spent a lot of time in those days appealing to the Department of the Environment for permission to build new-style stores. On this occasion, Francis had what he hoped would be a stress-free site.

'David Malpas used to run the property meeting. He had decided he didn't want the site. Francis made this impassioned retail plea (he wasn't a retailer) – he was very flushed up. David said, "No, no, no." Francis started again. David asked, "Have you bought this property already?" Francis said, "Yes." David said, "Right, next." There would have been no repercussions. Francis knew he had done wrong.'[12]

As a result of the MacLaurin-driven era of modernization, although the number of shops fell they were better looking, better stocked and in better locations in terms of what modern shoppers wanted. Tesco had 384 stores and 8 million customers at the start of the new decade. Turnover was £6.3 billion (ex-VAT) and pre-tax profits were £426 million, up 28 per cent on the previous year: twenty new stores had opened and two had been significantly expanded. Growth had happened at breakneck speed: 23 per cent of Tesco's total selling space in 1991 had opened since 1987. The strategy to bet the farm on 'large, modern, single-storey superstores' resulted in 68 per cent of Tesco's profits coming from the new-look shops. For an investment of £2.8 billion over three years, the Board needed to see these sorts of statistics. It planned to maintain the pace of expansion: having added 900,000 square feet of selling space in 1990/91, the ambition was to open 1.1 million square feet in 1991/92 and 1.25 million square feet the year after that.

MacLaurin explains, 'In the early 1990s, when others were pulling back a bit, we went on and that was a crucial time for us. It enabled us to get a lead on others. We knew we were successful. We knew the stores were good. We had a feeling that if you go into an economic decline, you aren't going to be in it for ever. Why stop getting sites and putting a brake on the development of the business? It did come good for us. If you look at the profitability of the company after 1991/92 we had a slowing down then it accelerated away. We had the units to do it.'[13]

Property was so central to Tesco's development that four members of the main Board met every Wednesday with the estates team to review all possible acquisitions or closures. The government, in which John Selwyn Gummer was Environment Secretary, had brought in a planning law that limited out-of-town superstores. Tesco adapted by requesting extensions on superstores that it already had, for example at Camberley, Cheshunt and Southall. This created a new challenge: how to fill them. The range of products in ambient grocery (mainly products in packets, tins, jars or bottles) alone had risen from about 4,000 to 20,000 by 1990, but then the economic climate changed the landscape, as Leahy explains. 'Recession meant the larger stores were a bit big for a food-only shop,' explains Sir Terry Leahy, by then on the Board. 'So really, to find something to put in the space and make the food department a bit smaller and easier to shop, I decided to put some non-food back in.'[14]

The store he chose was Milton Keynes Kingston Extra in 1994. 'It sold reasonably well. Food turnover went up because it was a simpler shop. So we went back into putting non-food next to food [in all our stores]. But we [also] had bigger stores so we weren't forcing the ranges down in any way. We cobbled together a bit of clothing and general merchandise and put it in the front and back of the store. It wasn't terribly impressive but it went okay.'[15]

Home 'n' Wear was rejected as a label, although it had never really gone away and the buying office in Hong Kong had not shut completely, only been a bit quiet.

'Home 'n' Wear had got a bad image, not entirely fairly, within and outside the business. We wanted to move away from that. We had no name. We just made the stores bigger with more to buy and that was fine with customers. It didn't need any explaining. Often the simpler way is better.'[16]

So non-food arrived, rescued from total decline: in fact, John Gildersleeve says it had nearly been abandoned altogether. It would be one of Leahy's central goals for Tesco when in due course he became chief executive. In the meantime, it was an opportunity to be in early as shopping patterns changed.

Every overview of Tesco asserts (with reason) how critical the race to expand the right kind of sites has been, but property was not the only sizeable investment made at this time. Often overlooked, but arguably just as important for customers and where they were choosing to shop at this time, was the investment in ranges that would then have been viewed as novel, even trendy.

In the early 1990s Tesco invested in three ranges: Healthy Eating, Green Choice and Nature's Choice. George Marston's team developed the quality-assurance scheme, Nature's Choice. 'We were trying to bring produce standards up through the whole of the supply chain from a pretty base level to a sophisticated level within ten years. It was a privileged experience. If the buyer and technical manager were in harmony, you could tell by the standard of the product.

'We had the experience of new legislation at the same time. Safety issues around produce concerned the use of agro-chemicals, certainly in prepared salads, which we were just starting to develop. Micro-organisms were a risk so we had to develop our own standards.

'That led to the greatest initiative embarked upon by the produce team, the development of Nature's Choice, a code of practice of how

Tesco interpreted what customers wanted. We embarked upon this way of working with professional people from industry, from our technologists and three or four trusted suppliers. It was a massive change – you are asking people for more rotation, better care for environment, better control of waste, a lot was legislation but not all suppliers did it, being able to trace your potatoes back to the field. The supply chain didn't like it, didn't want to invest in that kind of discipline, so it was a massive challenge and not just in the UK. There was resistance. Some [of that] was healthy, because it made us adjust the code of practice. It was a complex, detailed, demanding document. We introduced that in the mid-nineties. It provoked great energy from government, particularly the NFU, to come up with something similar, then supported by other retailers. We stood alone for a long time because we believed what we had was better than what the NFU came up with. We had a passion for it. Then Europa came up with something similar. So we had three elements. [These were eventually brought into line.]

'The initiative improved belief in quality. Suppliers all responded. They didn't all bow to it, but the energy they put into it, reassuring customers, was tremendous. It made a real difference to the integrity of the supply chain. It made suppliers aware of what Tesco wanted. It produced greater continuity of product in terms of standards. It made a difference to the true, intrinsic quality of product.'[17]

The ranges introduced at this time set new standards for quality, production and supply from source to shelf and reflected how consumers were becoming much more concerned to know that what they bought was good for them and also good for the people who made it. Compare that £3 billion investment on good food with the £2.8 billion spent on property during the same period: the inevitable conclusion is that it was pointless building large supermarkets unless the food inside them was the best that customers could buy. Otherwise, they would go elsewhere.

Joe Doody, the Irish-born store manager with a talent for taming tough areas, tells a story that illustrates this point. He had managed Tesco's stores (old and new) in Brixton from just before the time of the riots in 1981. He realized it made sense to work with the local, predominantly ethnically West Indian community and by 1989 he wanted to do more than not stock South African 'apartheid' products – he also wanted to stock the sort of things they wanted to buy. 'I wondered, how could I take advantage of being in Brixton? I wanted to sell some ethnic products. There's some shops round here and you went to see what they sold. I thought we could do some money on this. I started ordering from local firms. I got ackees [fruit] and salt fish, which was hard, like rubber, but you put it in water and it turns out like a normal piece of cod.

'One mod [retail shelf unit] became two and within the month I had ten mod fixtures. I couldn't get it in quick enough. I couldn't get enough deliveries, so I had to buy a lot once a week. It had its own problems. Within three or four months I was taking £10,000 a week from this Foods of the World [range], which we made up on the spot. All the buyers and directors came to see these products. Soon, instead of going into Foods of the World it was going into the main store.

'All these products had been refined and put into better packaging because it was cheap and nasty. There was a fortune to be made. I'd find out what local shops were charging: on some of those lines those people were making 300 per cent profit and I was happy to make 30 per cent. I was able to make the decision on the price because the company didn't list these products centrally then.

'I sold sweet potato, fresh ginger – we'd buy ten cases of fresh ginger and could get a really good deal from the wholesaler; we'd get an extra case for free, which was great for the stock results.

'Robert Thomas, the security manager, was born and bred Jamaican. He told me what to sell. We did tinned ackees. They grow like wild flowers in Jamaica but they were £1.79 for a tin. For comparison, I was charging 10p for a tin of peas. The smell when you went down the aisle was powerful: curry, salt fish, chilli. I sold mountains of red-hot chilli sauce. My biggest problem was supply: I couldn't get consistency.

'I had a baker in the store who said West Indians made a heavy fruit loaf and a ginger bun. He made me a few and we tried it out. This loaf was so heavy, it must have been 5lb in weight there was so much fruit in it. I sliced it in the canteen and the staff tried it. Then he made these ginger buns like a mega-pancake and we all tried them. I got so much heartburn. The fruit loaf was beautiful and reminded me of brack cake in Ireland, but twice as heavy. We charged £4 for this cake sixteen years ago. Customers were buying them by the dozen. [But then] some silly bugger in the office said we couldn't sell them legally. Instead of saying "We want to sell it, how do we make it legal?" he said "Stop". I remember being furious. I lost the battle.'

Doody also sold an Irish cheese, Galtee, to the Irish community until it was discontinued on the grounds that only forty cases a week were being sold across the whole company.

'Nowadays it would be different. You have a store-specific area, so if you can sell Galtee because your store is in an Irish area then you get it.'[18]

Doody's Brixton store was the start of a move into ethnic ranges – World Foods – and today Tesco sells more than 1,000 lines, including Polish, Turkish, Chinese and, yes, South African staples.

Another shopping innovation that arrived in the late eighties and early nineties was scanning technology, which had been trialled for a few years at Tesco before it was ready to roll out across stores and warehouses.

Kevin Doherty remembers that as a result of 'the massive change of the eighties and the impact of Ian MacLaurin and David Malpas' he had to re-apply for his job. He was rewarded with a bigger role, overseeing stores in a sort of crescent around London that stretched from Oxfordshire to parts of Essex and up to Northamptonshire.

'In London you spent a lot of time firefighting – trying to keep your good staff. Suddenly I was where people didn't leave and it was wonderful: I could concentrate on making some money.

'Dennis Tuffin was retail operations director on the main Board and he gave me a number of projects – [reducing the loss of] trolleys was one of them, [and introducing] scanning [at checkouts] was another. Sainsbury was well ahead of us on scanning. We had tried it but made a mess of it. It had cost a lot and wasn't managed well. We had five or six stores [where we trialled it, which] we called IBM stores, after the name of the computers. In 1986 Dennis Tuffin asked me to be project director. I didn't have a clue what I was doing. The great thing about Tesco is that they will give you a clean sheet. They sent me on a couple of courses about project management and I chose Flitwick in Bedfordshire [for our trial]. It was a store of about 25,000 square feet and there was not a lot of non-food. Twelfth October [1987] was the date I put on it [for starting the trials]. I didn't want to risk later because of the Christmas trade. I put a steering group together.'[19]

Earlier work on store-based ordering meant many products had bar codes, enabling much better stock management, which in turn helped negotiations with suppliers because the (very useful) sales data was available. The bar codes meant that scanning at the till was possible. Even so, it was uphill at first. 'There was a lot of stress getting it off the ground and a lot of people didn't really understand what it was about. It touched every part of the business. We had to have rooms built to house the main-frame computers.'[20]

Doherty was the first to admit that the technology was a few levels above his understanding, at least at first. He fell back on the technique that had worked well for Tesco before: he copied the leading competitor. 'I went round to Sainsbury on a number of Saturdays. I could see this girl filling up – I said, "Could you tell me how that works? How do they train you?" "I'll show you," this girl said. This guy, who looked like the manager, showed me all their computer systems. "This is the reports we use, this is how we manage it." It was giving me ideas of what I should be looking at.

'The cost of the learning curve on a project can be horrendous. I decided I could either learn by default or capitalize on what was already working. I looked at our own six scanning stores and although they were in pretty bad condition I got an understanding. I started speaking to suppliers who had bar codes. I phoned up

Sainsbury and asked who was in charge of retail scanning. [The receptionist] gave me a telephone number for a Mr Crick. I phoned up Ian Crick, who is still with Tesco today [he is Tesco's planning and response director]. He had been through the whole thing with Sainsbury. I wanted a balance between people from outside and Tesco people: why go through all the pain when there are people out there [who had been through it]? He wasn't sure about joining. "You haven't got a good reputation," he said. I had to persuade him we were going places. I told thirty-three stores across the UK to stretch the supplier [of bar-code equipment] and we took 20 per cent of the time it took Sainsbury to get scanning off the ground.

'[We deployed the checkout plus system to a further thirty-five stores within the next nine months.] The night guard at [our Welwyn Garden City office] used to bring me a flask of tea and some rolls about four times a week. I knew we would get through it, but sometimes it just felt there was so much work. We were doing something so huge for the business. We had to triple-check everything. If you design a system and you get it wrong it can have horrendous effects. It was the biggest pressure I have ever had, I think. Suddenly everybody knew who I was. I was presenting to the Board every six weeks. "How are you going to deliver the benefits, Kevin?" I'd do it again if I were younger. It was fantastic.

'When you work as hard as you do in Tesco you have to have a real passion for the business. I wasn't very good at managing the hours. I was cancelling holidays and all sorts of things. If there is another saint it should be my wife. She was so supportive. She understood. I'm very lucky.

'At the [launch in Flitwick] I felt a hundred years old I was so tired. I had invited all the key executives and anybody who was a director was there. There must have been 150 people standing in their suits behind the checkout. Customers were wondering what was going on. I said, "Let's give the shopping free to this first customer." This woman came up with a pair of children's briefs and some soap powder and I took her down the wines and spirits and put some champagne in her trolley, then I put some salmon in and some toys for the children and she had about £300 worth of shopping for free.

'As the first customers came through, people were concerned about how slow the cashiers were, but I tried to explain that it takes people time. People were quite frightened of the systems in those days.

'There were a lot of problems at first, trying to get some stability. We opened that store at unbelievable speed. For the first six weeks we kept all the stick labels as well, as we had a number of problems. If the system broke down we still had to be able to serve customers. It took us about six months to stabilize the system.

'Because of that we suddenly realized how much information was coming through. We wanted to know how to shape the data so we understood our customers: how could we turn that into an effective management tool? Nobody actually knew how they would use this data until they prioritized what was really important: stock management, which was what we were selling, and how much space we were giving it. Our profitability margin then was based on what was delivered rather than what was sold. We could manage our margin based on what was going through the checkouts.

'The cashiers now had to understand what the whole range of produce was unless it was packed. If it was loose it had to be looked up in a book with pictures and then weighed. It took a long time to get that right. The buyers had to keep the books up to date. We used to check baskets with the cashiers when it was quiet and give them scores out of twenty, and if it was too low we'd give them extra training. Nowadays you just push the buttons: apples, colour and so on.

'Scanning put an end to fiddling. Collusion used to be a big problem in certain parts of London. You could have a customer paying £3 for £50-worth of products if they had a friend on the checkout. It was only by luck you could catch it. We designed a system so that in the cash office we could log into any checkout and watch a till receipt go through on a screen as it was happening. It is sad you have to do that: some people don't appreciate they have a good job and they make it bad for other people who are working really hard. The shrinkage result became much better in stores. We started developing security tags for products like razorblades.'[21]

In one year alone – and a decade after the trials began at Tesco – £190 million was invested in the new technology. By 1992, 80 per cent of the shops' turnover was scanned and this produced immediate benefits in terms of productivity.

Combined with sales-based ordering – an advanced computer system in those days, which automatically worked out what stores needed based on what they were selling – the heavy load of paperwork and manual tasks was becoming lighter. Managers no longer needed to fill in store-order cards manually, or set staff to the mind-numbing task of pricing hundreds of tin cans with a sticky-label 'gun'. They could accurately assess stock without having to count it packet by packet. They had more time for their teams and more time to plan.

By the end of 1991, 247 stores were operating sales-based ordering for groceries and twenty for fresh foods. The depots were modernized and linked to the store systems. Tesco expected to save £15 million every year as a result of its investment. The knowledge was shared: 900 suppliers were linked up to the system at that time. Scanning was in 300 stores in the same year.

In the decade after Sir Jack Cohen's death, Tesco had transformed itself. In 1991, Ian MacLaurin described the step-change: 'People who haven't yet had the chance to shop in an up-to-the-minute Tesco store can only guess at our new standards of quality. It is hardly surprising that research shows there is still, for some people, a degree of uncertainty about what to expect from Tesco products and Tesco stores. This uncertainty is a result of our history and the speed with which we have transformed ourselves. It is quickly dispelled by actual experience of Tesco shopping and Tesco products.

'It is clearly in the company's interests to make all our potential customers aware of the high-quality reality of Tesco today.'[22]

Tesco would do this, he explained, with a major television campaign featuring the actor Dudley Moore, which would launch in

64535 Air Mechanic Cohen, J., joined up in March 1917; marrying Sarah 'Cissie' Fox in January 1924; and TESCO tea, the label Jack created after meeting tea wholesaler T. E. Stockwell.

Above: Street markets kept Londoners alive, offering keen prices during harsh economic times in the twenties. Croydon was one of Jack's earliest sites.

Above: Sir Jack Cohen returns to Frith Street, Croydon, five decades after he first worked the market there.

Above (left to right):
Packers at the Ashton-under-Lyne food depot in 1984; the novelty of supermarkets and savings stamps means long queues in the seventies – especially on 'double points' days; pile it high, sell it cheap is a hit at Dalston in the sixties.

Left: In 1978 Sir Jack Cohen, with Daisy Hyams, returned to his Hackney barrow beginnings at Well Street to celebrate the opening of a Tesco. Kevin Doherty re-created the market stall and Cohen bantered with customers.

Left: An artist's impression of a new sort of store, Small Heath in Birmingham in 1963, where Tesco launched Green Shield Stamps.

Tesco's Board of Directors, 1970, with recently knighted Sir Jack Cohen symbolically at the centre. *Clockwise from top left:* Laurence Leigh, Lesley Porter, Ian MacLaurin, Ralph Temple, Robin Behar, Daisy Hyams, Stanley Berwin, George Wood.

Tesco Board of directors 1970

FINANCIAL TIMES

Friday January 28 1972

No 25,667

rage
10.62

TESCO LEAD THE WAY —
by opening their fourth new hypermarket

chairman promises five more by 1977

Jack's successor as chairman, his son-in-law Hyman Kreitman, talks to the *Financial Times* in 1972 about the changing face of British retail.

Below: More than a decade after retailers brought savings stamps over from America for British shoppers, Tesco ditches them. The decision caused a boardroom row, with Ian MacLaurin and Jack Cohen on opposing sides. Tesco launches Operation Checkout, slashing prices and re-setting its course. It sparks a price war and the 'first bit of excitement in the High Street for years!' according to cartoonist Franklin in the *Sun*.

TESCO STAMP ON GREEN SHIELD

GREEN STAMPS SHOCK

'Price war' warning as

Tesco scrap

£19m deal

From Thursday June 9th. Tesco gives you something you want more than stamps.

TESCO Checkout

Price cuts that help keep the cost of living in check.

STAMP BUYING IS BEST!

NON-STAMP BUYING IS BEST!

INTERNATIONAL

TESCO

FRANKLIN

"First bit of excitement in the High Street for years!"

Sir Jack Cohen celebrates the launch of Tesco's first own-brand champagne under the De Georges label in 1973. In the same year, the company moves from Old Tesco House directly over the road into New Tesco House. The no longer state-of-the-art concrete-and-glass offices remain Tesco's home four decades later.

Ian MacLaurin replaces Sir Lesley Porter as Tesco's chairman in 1983 and talks to *Marketing Magazine* about plans for larger stores, better ranges and improved quality to meet modern customers' needs in the eighties.

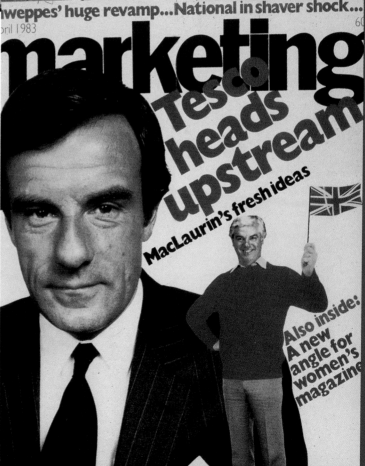

...weppes' huge revamp... National in shaver shock...

April 1983

60

marketing

Tesco

Tesco heads upstream

MacLaurin's fresh ideas

Also inside: A new angle for women's magazine

Tesco takes on architects to design the new wave of edge-of-town stores in the nineties: they come up with the 'clocktower look'. Shops follow the customers back into high streets through the decade with Metro stores – this is the first one in Covent Garden – and then the Express convenience format.

Lucy Neville-Rolfe, Tesco's executive director of corporate and legal affairs, developed Tesco's first Community Plan.

Terry Leahy goes back to the shop floor to TWIST (Tesco Week in Store), as all head office managers do each year. He is seen here in the warehouse at Rickmansworth store in 2007, ten years after he became chief executive.

Above: The first 'Regeneration' store is opened in Seacroft, Leeds, with a large proportion of the new 'Value' own-label range.

Above left: Widnes Extra, one of Tesco's most recent Regeneration partnership stores.

Left: Dudley Moore is 'Our man from Tesco', seeking out the best cheese for customers in Bergerac, France, in the nineties advertising campaign; launching 'Computers for Schools' – enabling shoppers to collect free tokens and donate them to buy equipment; the Clubcard scheme, launched in 1995.

Left: Philip Clarke was a Saturday boy at Tesco from the age of fourteen, was managing one of the biggest stores in his mid-twenties and ran Tesco's Asian business before becoming chief executive in 2011.

Above: Tesco opened a new hypermarket in Beijing, China, in 2007, with many features familiar to its customers in the UK.

Above: Tesco Lotus, in Thailand, opened its first zero-carbon store in 2010. When flooding hit the country in 2012, this photograph of customers walking across upturned trolleys became a symbol of resilience.

Right: Tesco's first foreign success came in Hungary from 1994 as it brought modern display and distribution practices to a state-run chain of shops.

Right: Tesco's virtual stores in South Korea – pictures of products on shelves with bar codes – enable customers to shop with their mobile phones and have the groceries delivered.

May 1990. 'The essential objective of the campaign is to establish Tesco in the minds of the public as "the leading quality food retailer in the United Kingdom today" in terms of quality, innovation and product range. The campaign's performance is constantly monitored by research; early signs indicate that Our Man from Tesco, even if he hasn't found his chickens yet, is well on the way to achieving his intended effect on the attitudes of the shopping public.'[23]

In the late eighties Tesco's advertising agency GRC had been swallowed up by Saatchi & Saatchi during its acquisitive splurge. Robin Gray, who was then in charge of advertising, recalls that the relationship with Saatchi & Saatchi was going nowhere. He describes how the 'Our Man from Tesco' campaign came about.

'After 1989 we decided, after having had no great campaigns of any substance and more battles than creative work, to have a huge re-pitch. Sainsbury's was the dominant brand. Business at Tesco was suffering a bit – we were not doing as well as we wanted to be. Sainsbury had a clear proposition. They had quality. They had a fantastic campaign: the recipe-collection campaign. Every time they put one of those out, the ingredients for that recipe also went up at Tesco. Tesco was still seen as pile it high and sell it cheap, despite all the advertising we had done and the money we had spent.

'We shortlisted six agencies, sent them a brief, gave them a week and then got them all in one place on the hour every hour, one in the front, one out the back. Lowe Howard-Spink came in, headed up by this incredible guy called Frank Lowe. He was very flamboyant. He came in wearing a yellow cravat, rolled-up shirt-sleeves and in jeans, but he had no material. He sat down and said, "Look, I haven't come in with boards, I've got nothing to show you, all I'm going to say is I've read your brief and I will guarantee your Tesco brand in three years' time will be right up here." We were gobsmacked. It was music to our ears. He said give us the business and we will come back with a coordinated campaign which will be so stunning and memorable that it will blow your heads apart. We saw the other three but we gave it to him.

'We locked ourselves away with Frank and the team for a few

weeks. We had an idea about somebody chasing chickens around the world. Frank said, "You've got free-range chickens you buy from a farm down in Bordeaux." He had some names: Rowan Atkinson, Michael Palin and Dudley Moore. Frank said, "[Dudley's] a friend of mine, he lives in LA and I bounced this idea off him and he'd be very keen." We flew Dudley over on a special plane and took him round about twelve stores one weekend to give him a feel for what we were trying to do. That was the beginning of the Dudley campaign in 1989.

'It was a time when Tesco was struggling. All the other adverts we did were one-off ads. We decided to write to all the commercial directors at Tesco and ask them to come back with a list of the quality products and find out if there was a particular story: do we have any unique wines exclusive to Tesco, from a vineyard run by a family? I had a list of about thirty products, such as peaches that hung on the trees two days longer than anybody else's peaches.

'The launch advert was a 90-second blockbuster at Bergerac in France. The set was an old farmhouse and we were flown down there and stayed in a nice hotel. We were in this field with the legendary Dudley [and] with Paul Weinberger, who is now chairman of Red Brick Road [agency] but he was the copywriter on the first script. Dudley couldn't get one word right. He was making it up as he went along, getting hold of my script and saying he'd do it his way. This was costing half a million pounds and we'd paid about £2 million to sign him up and he wanted to do his own campaign not mine. We said, "Let's do ours first and then yours later on." We were doing a range of cheeses down there. Dudley was brilliant for the two or three days: very honest and a very nice person to work with.

'The Board loved it. We made another thirty commercials in three years with Dudley. We shot probably two-thirds of the commercials in LA because it was cheaper than the UK. He lived near Venice Beach. We also shot a lovely commercial outside Perth at Loch Tay for whisky. Then people started to write in to ask if Dudley was ever going to find the damn chickens – we had positioned it that Dudley was looking for the chickens but stumbled across other lovely products on the way.

'There was a shift in the UK. We had been seen as downmarket. We wanted to be seen as classless and good quality and contemporary and Dudley did that for us. We asked him to do some really strange things. If we asked him to put a duck on his head he would; he was always very obliging. He did all his own stunts. He was unbelievable. He was a Dagenham boy made good and he fronted our campaign very well. It was sad towards the end [in 1992] that he had trouble with some of our scripts, but we realized so many years later it was the beginning of the illness that took his life.

'That campaign met all of our objectives, but life does not stand still and the campaign finished in 1992. We had recession hitting hard, all the German discounters coming in, Asda were on the scene and Sainsbury were banging out quality and that proved very difficult for us.

'We started to wonder where we went from there. Dudley had to find the chickens eventually and we did that at Christmas time when everybody was feeling good.'[24]

As Dudley found his chickens and Robin Gray's team pondered their next move, Terry Leahy was asked to work out what was wrong with Tesco and find out why customers were still choosing other shops, and Sainsbury in particular. With so much already in place, the solution would become known as 'Bricks in the Wall'.

Chapter 18

Bricks in the Wall: the Research Revolution

'Success and failure is very finely balanced in our industry. In a room of a hundred people if two leave that means failure and if two join that means success. If two slip out the back and don't say they're going it's pretty hard to notice. We had to find out who had gone and why.'

Sir Terry Leahy[1]

'We said: we will create the piece of junk mail people actually want to receive.'

Tim Mason[2]

The beginning of the 1990s was brutal in Britain: the country was in recession. It was tough being young and looking for a job, or being in any line of work that relied on public-sector money. Also, interest rates were high and rising, so that meant even less money in people's pockets. Things were not so chipper elsewhere in the world either, but in Tesco terms the universe was still confined to the UK and its immediate neighbours.

Whatever the causes of the descent into recession following the 'Lawson Boom' of the mid–late 1980s (named for the Conservative Chancellor of the Exchequer, Nigel Lawson), hundreds of thousands of families found themselves saddled with negative equity in the early–mid-1990s. Old industries vanished, devastating whole communities, and the UK had yet to establish itself as a global powerhouse for financial services (let alone to discover that this status should come with a health warning). The City was still licking its wounds after the square-shouldered, champagne-fuelled yuppies encountered the fall-out from the 'Big Bang' market liberalization of October 1987. The term 'Macjob' was coined – work with relatively poor pay and prospects. Double-digit interest rates meant that even those whose homes were still worth something could barely afford the mortgage payments.

Inevitably, retailers suffered along with everybody else – although some suffered less than others. If your customer base was relatively affluent, chances were that they had savings and were helped, not harmed, by the high bank base rate. If your customer base was less well heeled, as Tesco's was, then chances were you had a higher proportion of borrowers. And they were being hammered.

Tim Mason had been transferred out of Terry Leahy's product-management team to be a regional managing director of the stores from an office close to the Dartford Tunnel. His fellow directors reckoned he was proficient in 'director-speak' thanks to his head-office experience, as well as public-school and university education; he therefore became a conduit for their 'constructive comments'. He recalls, 'The end of the eighties and the beginning of the nineties were pretty ugly. It was not a great time to be in charge of stores. Our like-for-likes [comparable sales figures] were horrible. Ian MacLaurin would ring you up every week and ask you how trade was, and you would tell him and he would shout at you. Well not quite, but it wasn't great. Retailers don't like working in conditions when the growth is slow: it is no fun and it puts your costs under tremendous pressure. I had written a couple of notes on behalf of the regional managing directors saying we were off the pace on service, price and quality.'[3]

He thought at the time that he was not helping his own career prospects, but had a sense that MacLaurin wanted somebody on the ground to tell the Board the tricky stuff.

Outwardly, MacLaurin remained resolutely upbeat, but the

numbers told the story: profits were slowing and the gap with Sainsbury was opening up again. David Reid recalls the impact on the business. 'You had to keep your costs down. We cut our costs back as customers were buying less. We made our deli counters a bit smaller, for example, to survive the recession. We probably lost a couple of points of like-for-like sales growth and that made life tough. We had let our price levels get too high, our service levels weren't great and we'd cut our range too far.'[4]

It was not entirely hopeless. Tesco was in fair shape: superstores were established as the format that fitted customers' lifestyles, ranges had been expanded to meet changing British tastes and the culture inside Tesco was less military, more modern. The business was held in general to be well run, if unexciting. But still it trailed Sainsbury and Marks & Spencer, and still it would not have been first career choice for many aspiring retailers.

One new recruit in the October of 1990 remembers just how low down the pecking order Tesco still was. Jason Tarry, then a twenty-three-year-old accountancy graduate, was not long back from a year travelling the world after his time as a student at Stoke Polytechnic. He applied for four companies; only Tesco asked him for interview.

Tarry grew up in a Kentish village close to Maidstone, attending first a local comprehensive and then a grammar school. His parents shopped locally, not in supermarkets, and his grandmother would not have gone near the town's Tesco, preferring Sainsbury. Somehow, he had owned (and loved) a pale blue jumper from Tesco's Delamare clothing range: that was the only positive experience he had of the business. But he needed a job. 'My impression was they were a bit cheap and cheerful. When I first joined people would take the mickey: "Oh you work for Tesco – it couldn't get any worse." It never bothered me.'

Tarry would work his way up over the years, eventually running clothing and other general merchandise lines [in 2012, he became chief executive of clothing]. Back in 1990, he was just pleased to have a graduate-trainee position in the finance department with £12,000 a year.

One of his early jobs was for a very new part of Tesco's customer offer: petrol. Tarry says the post was not attractive internally, but it enabled him to get out of finance and into buying. 'We had decided if we were making a destination store we were going to provide petrol to give customers another reason to come there. We did deals with Texaco, Esso and BP and they would supply us as they would supply a franchised station.'

Tesco decided to compete on price, because there was no other way to add value to petrol, which was regarded by consumers as a necessary evil. Big oil companies habitually reacted immediately at the pumps to rises in the oil price. Tarry says, 'Oil would go up, so petrol would go up. We wouldn't play that. We wanted to create a brand around price. Clearly the oil companies didn't like this. We ended up with differential pricing against them and undercutting a lot of their local petrol stations. We found our deliveries were being mysteriously cancelled. No one will ever say it was deliberate, but suddenly our supply wasn't as reliable as it used to be.'

So Tesco decided to work with the independent refineries whose storage depots were right alongside the brands' facilities close to various British ports. 'We had to secure supply. We found that the oil companies had been charging us as much as they could on the basis that we didn't have any option. They would compete for the contract but it provided them with a healthy margin. We ended up dealing with companies like VSO, who tended to be oil traders with links overseas in Scandinavian companies, in particular, such as Statoil.

'They were churning out lots of product and had to find a home for it. We formed good relations with these people. We linked it to the refined price, which moves daily. We could undercut the oil companies – though in the UK they should have been able to under-cut us because it was refined locally. We rented storage and bought tankers of refined fuel. I was on about £28,000, parking my Ford Escort outside a terminal in Purfleet and trembling to see this tanker full of product that I'd bought and worrying about what could go wrong. The responsibility in buying was on a different scale from being in finance. I wasn't sure I could cope with it. Shell and Esso refused to supply us but others saw we were the future. Texaco, Elf, even BP at the end worked with us. Our strategy was working in terms of growing a business. Seventy-five per cent of the price of petrol is duty taken by government – the margins you make are so thin, but if we hadn't done what we did, I guarantee you'd be paying twice as much for your petrol. You might say with climate change that's not a bad thing, but the history of Tesco is being for everybody, making things affordable for everybody and it was a privilege to be part of that. When everybody else was moving up, we were holding it for as long as we could and people recognized that.'[5]

Ian MacLaurin describes it as a critical time. 'Some of the observers of Tesco thought we were running out of steam and profits started to slow, but there was an economic downturn at the time. This was a crucial time for Tesco going forward because everybody else – Sainsbury, Asda, all the big boys – was pulling their development programme and we didn't. We went on getting sites for the future so we knew exactly what we were doing. We were able to pick up sites when other people were pulling out and that is the Tesco of today. Many of those are Tesco Extras and are doing very well. We weren't losing our way.'[6]

It was in this climate that Terry Leahy was appointed marketing director. It wasn't a promotion he was looking for. He was anxious about the responsibility – and exhausted juggling young children with the day job. He took up the role in 1992 when economic recession was severe and two German limited-range discounters, Aldi and Lidl, were making themselves felt in the UK.

'Tesco was in squeeze,' he remembers. 'If you wanted quality you went to Sainsbury, if you wanted price you went to these new discounters. The combination of not trading very well and the gloomy prognosis put the business under a lot of pressure. There was a big palace revolution.'[7]

'I had always wanted to be on the Board. It was a great privilege, I was thirty-six, but I was horrified at having the responsibility for solving all these problems. It was as if the entire expectations of the company were on my shoulders. I'm sure it wasn't intended like that, but that was how it felt. I was back in this very abstract area of marketing to find out what the hell was wrong with the company. It is always hard to do that when you are under enormous pressure, when everything is going wrong.

'Prior to that recession you'd had complete faith in Ian and David. It was a father-and-son thing I think. I remember it happening with my father – the moment he looks to you for the answer is a very shocking moment and you feel the responsibility for the first time. You feel that terrible weight. Even *they* are looking to you for the answer. They probably weren't even aware that they were doing it. That's what I sensed. That was why I was so daunted.'[8]

The Leahy promotion caused internal ripples again. It entailed splitting his boss, John Gildersleeve's, role. 'John was very good at giving people a lot of room and I took to that. At that time the relationship was very good. He was the boss and that wasn't challenged in any way. He was a considerate boss. He gave you lots of leeway and was supportive if you needed support, so he was great to work for.'[9] But the new dynamic upset the balance. 'It was personally difficult and it took us a long time to work through,' Terry says.

David Malpas remembers the period in general as a time when the Board knew what was wrong but not quite how best to fix it. 'At the end of the eighties and the beginning of the nineties we had become a very efficient money-making machine and had begun to lose sight of the primacy of the customer and had begun to accept that customers would come to us because we were so successful. Our stores were less and less friendly. Some even used to boast crazily about "retail engineering", as though customers were something to be manipulated around the stores. The stores were becoming cramped. I was allowing our marketing department to almost auction space to the merchandise departments that could produce the most profit, and the result wasn't a happy one. We got ourselves into the doldrums. Turnover was hard to come by. Our competitors were making good progress.

'Terry Leahy and I went to Coventry and Evesham and looked at competitors and realized we needed to do something. I fired the head of our marketing department and three of our regional managing directors and reorganized matters. Of those four people I am still very good friends with three: the regional managing directors were old and set in their ways and I wanted to get some new blood into the system.'[10]

Unsurprisingly, the internal turmoil was noticed. Jason Tarry recalls that in January 1993, Tesco laid off 800 people. Terry Leahy remembers a sort of corporate exhaustion. 'It is a very loyal business and people were trying to make it better. Everybody had written off the company. People cared so much in the business that they were very worried and their anxiety came out in a negative way.'[11]

His light-bulb moment was more of an eco-bulb-style brightening. The glow began with his personal reverence for research. He organized the team and briefed a range of research agencies. 'We brought this new idea in of speaking to hundreds of thousands of our customers . . . letting them tell us what was wrong and what we should do. It sounds obvious now, but it wasn't at all, because a retailer prided himself on knowing what was important in shopping and knowing better than the customer what the customer needed. In some senses it was extraordinary to place the entire future of the company in the hands of shoppers and let them dictate what the company would do.

'It was high risk because we had one shot at this. Certainly I did. If they got it wrong or didn't bother to tell you, or the whole idea was daft, then that was it – you were finished.'[12]

The research was pre-Clubcard, so it was hard to match the statements that came out of surveys to actual behaviour. The answers did not come quickly, says Leahy. 'I joined the Board in October 1992 and we were researching and fumbling along, and everybody was saying in the nicest way you'd better come up with a plan quick because we've got weeks not months and I hadn't got a clue what plan to come up with.

'The research was so difficult. We hadn't got the techniques we have today. It was like working in a fog. You only had the vague impressions of what was truthfully happening. We snatched at the problems.

'Success and failure is very finely balanced in our industry. In a room of a hundred people if two leave that means failure and if two join that means success. If two slip out the back and don't say they're going it's pretty hard to notice. We had to find out who had gone and why.

'I asked for Tim Mason to come back from stores. He joined me at the latter stages of the research. [We discovered that] there was no one big thing wrong. There were lots of little things that added up to a big problem. We didn't need to completely reinvent the business, but there was a lot to do. We sketched out a recovery plan which we presented to the Board in May 1993.'[13]

Tim Mason claims the phrase 'Bricks in the Wall'. None of Tesco's failings was insurmountable on its own but, piled up, they added up to a dead-end for the business. Leahy sketched out the presentation while he was waiting for a flight in an airport lounge.

The plan was unconventional, as he describes. 'I set out a recommendation that we try to get better on a number of things at the same time, which is not the right thing to do in terms of classic management strategy. I didn't know if it was possible.

'The business thought that it was in some ways finished. The new discounters, the chains, the economics of the industry meant that it could never be the same. We said, "It can be the same." We came up with the argument that we'd attack at both ends. We'd become cheaper *and* better. All the conventional wisdom in management is that you cannot attack on both fronts. The way we did it was by focusing everything on the customer: the customer wanted us to become cheaper *and* more interesting.'[14]

The research – 'chaotic' in Leahy's memory – showed that in trying to ape Sainsbury, Tesco had lost its price edge and customers had gone elsewhere. It thought it was listening to customers, but the customers in question had belonged to Sainsbury. He says, 'The analysis and recommendations became the strategy for the company. What started out as really just a short-term attempt to stem a major decline ended up gaining a momentum that sustained the business for more than ten years. Central to the thesis was that we should stop trying to be like other retailers and be comfortable with the heritage of Tesco and play to our strengths.'[15]

That did not mean, however, trying to reinvent the wheel. Leahy's team learned lessons from others: if 'fit for purpose' basics could work for the German discounters, could they not also work for Tesco's customers? Leahy even had experience. 'One of my previous jobs was launching generics ten years earlier, so I brought back the idea and it worked very well.'[16]

Value lines were introduced in August 1993 with bold packaging. John Gildersleeve, then commercial director, having passed marketing and store-planning to Leahy, recalls choosing the now iconic blue-and-white striped design. He says, 'There was the influx of Continental discounters with a limited assortment at rock-bottom prices. Our first response was to find existing manufacturers with tertiary brands, meaningless to customers, but cheap. It was a gesture.

'There were three designs for the range of low-cost products. One was a knock-off of the traditional Tesco blue-and-white striped carrier bag. I said, "We'll go with that. We don't want to pretend it is anything more than it is: it is a cheap product but it will be fit for purpose. Let's not hide it, let's not dress it up." About a year later Sainsbury launched its economy range but it didn't look like it. With our Value range what you saw was what you got.

'Tesco own-brand had a rigorous process: if you wanted to launch Tesco digestive biscuits it had to benchmark McVitie's and if it was not as good you could not put it on the shelf. That gave us some challenges.

'With Value, you could be the arbiter. It had to be fit for purpose. It did not go through testing panels for benchmarking against brands. The team worked miracles. It was a time of a lot of change. I've always tried to encourage people to have ideas and take risks. I'd rather you have ten ideas and get seven right than no ideas and get none wrong.'[17]

It was all fairly close to the wire, as Terry Leahy remembers. 'Pretty much when I'd given up the ghost, I went on holiday to France in 1993 and thought, "I can't see a way through this. Whatever is going to happen is going to happen, but I think I'm going to be given the bullet." I got back and the Value lines had pushed the trade up.'[18]

Not everybody was happy and Leahy recalls meetings in the City with horrified shareholders who thought he had gone mad. 'They said, "You've spent ten years trying to shake off your downmarket image and now you've gone and launched Value lines that confirm everything anyone ever knew about Tesco as being a bit cheap." But it was a classic case of listen to the customers – and they started to respond.

'The Value range was fifty or sixty products that people buy every day, like milk and toilet tissue. We'd stumbled on a very modern form of marketing – to say exactly what it was. The customers had enough self-confidence not to be ashamed of buying Value because it didn't pretend to be something that it wasn't. It could easily be half the price of the brand and 60 per cent of the price of the own-brand. It made a big difference to people's shopping bills. The quality was a little less, but we were very honest about it so people knew what they were getting.'[19]

By opting for a bold, even brash, design, Tesco made it easy to spot those products. In more affluent phases of the economic cycle, customers would not have wanted cheap products visible in their baskets. At that time, however, people decided they were not going to worry.

The customer also, it turned out, hated queuing. They said so in research, but store managers on the ground knew it first-hand. Leahy recalls a routine visit to London's Colney Hatch store, then one of the busiest in the group. Retail estate being so expensive and hard to build, space was tight for shoppers and the number of tills was limited. Queuing for twenty minutes was standard. The manager observed that customers were walking into the store, looking down the checkouts and turning on their heels to leave. Even if they stayed, they became 'stressed, blinkered' and got round as fast as they could, buying barely anything, to factor in the half-hour queue to get out of the shop. The manager at Colney Hatch was of the opinion that removing queues would transform the way people shopped. Retail lore, however, was against this: staffing tills so queues disappeared was unaffordable, or so they thought.

Leahy had recently promoted a young store manager, Philip Clarke, to be customer services director. Clarke was keen and steeped in Tesco, as his story illustrates.

Philip Clarke was born in Liverpool in 1960, the first child of Norman and Elizabeth Clarke. Norman was a traditional store manager: he understood the appeal of a great display, piling it high and selling it cheap. In the 1950s, an era before widespread car-ownership, there were mobile shops that travelled to where people lived. Norman Clarke managed one around Kirkby for Home & Colonial, which was then a large, national chain of supermarkets. The shop was a high-sided van with shelving and two counters, over which groceries, produce, fresh bread and household essentials were served. Norman met Elizabeth when she walked in to buy some groceries: he knew immediately she was the one.

At some point during the early 1960s, when Jack Cohen was expanding out of the South, Norman found a job as a store manager with Tesco. So began a long family connection with the company.

'My first memory of Tesco was when one Sunday [Dad] was stocktaking and he perched me on the till,' says Philip. 'I was about six or seven and it was a push-button till with a cranking handle. You pushed the buttons, cranked the handle and it rang up – and I rang up an enormous "void" for him. He had to explain to his branch inspector why it happened.

'The store [Edge Hill] was 8,000 square feet with six old tills, everything priced by hand, lots and lots of can and packet groceries and a big counter selling cooked meat and cheeses; raw meat was sold pre-packed on the counter. It was self-service. There were lots of posters and Green Shield Stamps. On the Sunday it was closed. Shops shut at five o'clock on Saturday. There was a faint whiff of bleach. The men wore red and the ladies were all in light blue overalls.'[20]

A manager's job had responsibilities and a certain status, Philip acknowledges, but it wasn't highly paid in the 1960s. 'It was possibly in the early 1970s that the rates of pay started to increase, because a way in which managers could supplement their meagre income [before then] was by doing deals for their shop and getting things on the side: some for the company, some for themselves. It was approved and allowed. Buying was very local.'[21]

Until then, many store managers lived above the shops they ran. 'We moved from place to place,' remembers Philip. 'In the early 1970s we were able to buy a semi-detached house, four bedrooms, with its own garden and a little garage and a Ford Cortina on the drive [in Childwall].'[22]

Like a lot of teenagers, Clarke's first taste of the workplace was a Saturday job in a shop. In 1974 he joined his father at weekends, increasing his shifts when he was sixteen and fitting them around his four A-levels (all of them heavy essay subjects) at the Blue Coat Grammar School. He stayed in Liverpool to go to university, taking a degree in economics and economic history because his economics teacher had been particularly inspiring and it was the subject he preferred.

With experience (and age) came more responsibility: running the 'twilight shift' (6 p.m.–10 p.m.) on Fridays meant ensuring that a team of about twenty-five people had the shelves and shop floor fully ready for Saturday trading. 'There were some students, a lot of married women working in the evenings for more money and a couple of full-time people, men who did the physical hard work moving product to the aisles so we could do the filling.'[23]

In the days before Sunday trading, stores were prepared on Saturdays for the Monday-morning opening. 'In the morning a group of Saturday staff and I would be responsible for making sure we filled the store up. As the goods were taken from the shelves we were making sure it was refilled by six o'clock at night. In the after-noons it would be quieter, so you would be cleaning and filling and baling the cardboard and throwing away the rubbish and tidying the warehouse, because the idea was that the shop would be ready on Saturday night for Monday morning. There was a real sense of camaraderie. I learned then how critically important it is to motivate people and to lead from the front. I always wanted to be filling faster than everybody if that were possible.'[24]

The shop was on two floors and was linked to a small shopping centre. When Philip worked for his father there, the warehouse was in the basement and the food was on the top floor. 'Non-food, or Home 'n' Wear as it was called, was on the ground floor, open to the shopping centre, and the food floor was open to the car park. In practice customers would shop the food and non-food separately.'[25]

The jobs provided Philip with extra cash and extra time with his father, even if it was only in the car there and back. Before longer trading hours and larger stores brought the arrival of managers and deputies who worked more clearly defined shifts, store managers were at work every open hour, and then some.

'Sunday would be the only day we would really see [Dad]. Monday to Friday he would get home at eight at night. He was a wiry, fit man, and you had to be. I wouldn't underestimate the number of miles they walk today, but then you had to be out and about pushing people to get the job done. There would have been fifty or sixty people. Everything was manual: ordering, receiving; even the tills were hand-cranked.'[26]

Store managers had a great degree of control in terms of what was sold. 'We did sell fruits and vegetables, but it was a very small proportion of sales. The meat was all cut in the store from carcasses. We used to bring in pigs, sides of beef and lamb. I had a bit of a time of doing that, filling in. But the McLintocks were the family of butchers who worked in the store. Five of them: father, mother, two sons and daughter. You only went into the meat-prep room if you were invited or if you were my father. Then there was a delicatessen counter. All the chilled dairy products were manufacturers' brands. There wasn't much own-label. There wasn't a lot of frozen food; it was cans and packets. There was a wines and spirits department but you had to be served and pay at the till. Tobacco was sold from behind a secure counter. Everything came in and was case-cut. It was all price-marked. You had to be good with a [case-cutting] knife and good with a [pricing] gun.

'My dad was always trying to sell something new and different. Green Giant canned vegetables came to the UK and we were building massive displays to sell more.'[27]

As Tesco modernized after Operation Checkout in 1977, managers had less control but as much to do. Norman Clarke fell ill and, after six weeks off work on doctor's orders, was given an ultimatum before personnel stepped in and retirement was arranged. Philip says, 'The business was becoming increasingly disciplined and systematic in its approach and my dad was the pile it high, sell it cheap guy. The expectations Tesco had of management were changing and there was a new young breed of managers coming through. Dad was of the old school. I think we are far more considerate and caring than we were back then. There was a time when what was achieved was more important than how it was achieved.'[28]

It was a difficult period, but it did not put Philip off retail. A year after his father retired, he joined Tesco as a graduate trainee based initially at Walkden store in Manchester. Then he went to Chester as deputy manager before returning to the store he had shifted at for his father, running it for more than a year.

'That was a very difficult job because here was so much history and baggage and comparisons between Dad and myself. To show how [Tesco] were, I went into the manager's office on the Monday and he said, "What are you doing here?" I said, "More to the point, what are you doing here? I'm the store manager now." He said, "No you're not." I said, "I think you'll find I am. I'm sorry about that." He had to go and see my regional director. It was the way things were done at that time. We have developed very thick skins. It was incredibly disciplined, very hierarchical. I suppose what I have tried to do since then is to try to soften that as much as possible. But then it is a very big operation. If you haven't got processes and systems and rules, then it is difficult to keep control.'[29]

Clarke set his sights on promotion, looking to the South for opportunity. He tried for a few posts in London but went to Weston Favell, Northamptonshire, as deputy manager in 1984; it was then Tesco's biggest store in terms of turnover. So at twenty-four years old, Clarke, recently married, moved to Northampton with his wife, Linda. The couple had met some five years previously at the Belle Vale store where Linda was wines and spirits manager. Within a year, he was managing the 105,000-square-foot shop after the manager, David Orchard-Smith, moved to another store. 'Eddie Clark [the regional managing director for Clarke's store] persuaded the business to give this very large store to a twenty-five-year-old. Eddie Clark's office was in the store. His secretary called me and said, "Have you applied for the job?" I said no. She said, "Do you not think it would be a good idea?" She typed my application letter for me. Eddie Clark interviewed me. Then I had to go and see a man called David Crawford who had been brought in to run the stores for Ian MacLaurin. [After that] I was called in to see Eddie Clark, who said, "Congratulations. What car do you want?" They thought I was more than ready. I cut my teeth and a few people paid the price for my exuberance and determination.'[30]

He recalls his first battle was with a colleague who preferred to spend Saturday afternoons clearing the store to refilling shelves and trays with fresh produce. Although it meant customers couldn't find what they wanted, the staff were able to leave when the shop shut instead of waiting behind to get the floor ready for Monday morning. Another battle was with Terry Leahy, when he was running fresh produce, who arrived at Weston Favell with the meat buyer and who queried the freshness of meat on display. 'I was able to persuade him that the meat was up to specification, despite what his buyer was telling him, and it was,' Clarke recalls, wryly. 'I was argumentative so I didn't always have an easy life.'[31]

His two children were born in 1986 and 1989, and the promotion to manager at Weston Favell meant a bigger house (in 1987) and the family's first foreign holiday, in Spain. Clarke was young but had been trained in similar-sized stores, part of the new wave of big, out-of-town superstores that Ian MacLaurin and David Malpas were building after Operation Checkout. Clarke had experience of every department – from meat to bakery – as well as stock control and cash office. Plus a family background in the business. 'I saw the incredible skill and determination of my father and his team to make sure every morning that store looked at its best. I've never forgotten that. I can tell you today if a store is loved or not when I walk into it. Making a store clean, tidy, presentable, making sure the products face the right way, the meat is the right quality, the cauliflowers are not discoloured – that is what retailing is all about, that is how you show a store is loved. I am definitely at my happiest when I am walking around a store.'[32]

Tesco was evolving quickly, trying very hard to catch Sainsbury, but the attitude towards its people took a bit longer to sort out than did the physical shops. Clarke recalls that when he joined as a trainee ('the only one with a degree, so people looked at me a bit strangely') in 1981, it was about following the rules and not challenging too much. However, there was change of all kinds in the air. 'We were beginning to develop automatic ordering systems. Electronic point of sale was coming in 1985. Planograms were arriving so you knew where to put things on the shelf. People knew Tesco had to move along. There was more training. We were becoming more professional. It was a period of great excitement. We were opening lots of out-of-town superstores.

'My father and people like Mike Higgs and Harry Quinlan and Jim Potter [his managers and bosses] taught me that [you need] an integrated set of principles and philosophies, processes, systems and people if you are going to get the best out of [a store]. The thing I am most proud of about my time at Weston Favell was that a month after I left the manager said to me, "You had this place running like a well-oiled machine." Everything happened when it was supposed to happen. Stock levels were low. Shelves were full. There weren't many queues. The stock returns were fine. My team knew what they had to do.'[33]

After Weston Favell, Clarke joined a small team whose job was to open new stores that fitted Tesco's out-of-town strategy, several of which were linked to Marks & Spencer stores on retail parks. 'I had to open fifteen stores the length and breadth of England and Wales, so I got a bit more time off at the weekend but I had to travel more and stay away from home. For me this was all about my next opportunity and then the next and the next. Because I love what I do I never mind. I have to constantly be reminded that there are things other than work.

'My job was to take over the recruitment and the stocking and then [be there] for the opening and for eight weeks after that before handing it over to the regional team. I created a series of documents I issued to the store manager as a pack. You would go back every three weeks to check they followed it through to the opening. The whole organization wanted you to succeed. They bent over backwards to help. The man who ran the department – John Gildersleeve and the man who worked for him, Alan Besbrough – made sure the teamwork happened to get the job done. Then you got your day in the sun. The whole Board would turn up. My daughter was born by caesarean [on 3 April] so I could be there when Llanelli opened the day after, on 4 April 1989.

'There were lots of management-training programmes. We knew how many managers we had to provide because we knew how many stores we were going to open. Careers could develop very quickly and they did. It was two generations really. There were those who only ever were store managers but were good at it, and for them this was a proud moment. They went from small stores to big stores with a company car, earning as much as a bank manager, and this was great for them.'[34]

Then there was the 'second generation': Clarke reels off a list of names of men who were then deputy managers and who in 2012 are on Tesco's executive committee. He says, 'It was a great period for learning. Most of them are now in their late forties and early fifties, helping me run the company.'[35]

Clarke was next asked to go into head office at Cheshunt to be a buyer. He was interviewed by Terry Leahy, then the food commercial director, and worked for Richard Brasher. After Leahy was promoted to marketing director on the Board in 1992, he appointed Clarke to be Tesco's first customer-service director. He was part of the team who created the customer plan that included Value lines, Clubcard, One in Front queuing and a customer-service programme. When Leahy became deputy managing director, Clarke returned to running stores and he became regional managing director, overseeing 200 shops, in 1995. In 1998 he joined the Board, just a few years after Leahy gave him the challenge of working out how to banish queues and putting a figure on it.

Clarke was up-front, Leahy recalls. 'He said, "I haven't got a clue, but I'll go and have a look" and he came back and said you couldn't remove queuing completely but you could get it down to one person in front. We spoke to customers and they thought if there was just one person in front that would be fine.'[36]

The price tag on removing probably the single most frustrating aspect of shopping was £60 million. That was 10 per cent of Tesco's profit and was money the company did not have. The Board could try to hide it to avoid frightening shareholders, but instead, when the new system was introduced in February 1994, the company launched a high-profile advertising campaign dubbed 'One in Front'.

By now there was proof that challenging retailing wisdom could work. Value lines were selling well and the one-in-front queuing also seemed to be making a difference to till receipts. But there was another industry 'no-no' yet to be re-examined: loyalty schemes.

After the fight to get Tesco out of Green Shield Stamps, Clubcard was a brave move. Loyalty cards meant handing 1 per cent of profits over to customers, for starters.

But there was a well-established retailer who was already challenging that wisdom. 'The idea came from the Co-op dividend stamp, which issued profits to customers,' admits Leahy. 'It wasn't very much, but it was a tradition. Then I read somewhere that Bury

Co-op was trying to create an electronic dividend. Computer technology had just been developed so you could give a card, scan it, record the purchases and reward customers. Over the course of the year a customer might spend £5,000 with you. They are incredibly important people. Over the course of a lifetime they spend a small fortune. But you don't know who they are even to say thank you. So this idea of an electronic dividend to say thank you came about. Industry wisdom was it couldn't be done – it would cost a fifth to a quarter of your profits. But we tested it.'[37]

Tesco's research led Leahy's team to conclude that customers wanted a 'thank you' for choosing to put their cash in Tesco's tills. 'Tim Mason said, "The customers love this. They actually love it." So we did it. At the same time, an outfit led by Edwina Dunn and Clive Humby had devised an innovative approach to customer research. The two concepts married beautifully and the product was Clubcard.'[38]

Tim Mason starts the story at the company's 1994 strategy conference. 'There was a big debate because Ian MacLaurin and his lieutenants had taken over the business when they got rid of Green Shield Stamps, so what were they doing at the end of their careers creating another loyalty business? Sainsbury rather stupidly referred to it in their initial comment as electronic Green Shield Stamps, but of course the point was that it wasn't, because of the data.

'We [tried it out in] twelve test stores. It was going well. Eventually David Malpas said, "We should do this, and the reason we should do it is because we can." We launched in February 1995. It was just a gargantuan thing to do. To get from nowhere enough plastic cards to give one to everyone. Would the logistics work? Would the computers work? There was a guy called Grant Harrison, Jane Curtis and Fiona, who later became my wife, was their boss. Grant appointed two agency suppliers. One was dunnhumby who were going to handle the data and give us some insight into database marketing. The other was Evans Hunt Scott, who were the direct-marketing agency. They still both do that job for us sixteen or seventeen years later and we bought dunnhumby along the way.

'We said we will create the piece of junk mail people actually want to receive.' Clubcard vouchers, unlike most coupons and offers known collectively and colloquially as 'junk mail', could be spent like cash at face value on whatever customers wanted. Customers would also receive coupons for products that they had bought before or that fitted their shopping preferences. 'We were worried Safeway would launch before us because they were trialling something.

'When we were ready, we did the most unbelievable brief all over the country. Tesco was the first to do it: it was a novelty, it was something for nothing and it was a thank you.'[39]

Mason says that at first they did not really know how to treat the data in terms of a research asset. 'We decided we should do something. We had a relatively simple system: who was shopping, when, where and which departments they were shopping in, and that was the total run of it. If you knew where they were shopping you could mail them coupons and perhaps prevent them shopping somewhere else. People who had a Clubcard either threw in an extra shopping trip or they said, "I'm here – maybe I'll give Tesco meat or wine a try with this voucher." Both those things are manna from heaven for a retailer. It was extremely successful.

'We learned the most important thing was frequency. If somebody shopped with you they were very loyal. Frequency is almost a surrogate for loyalty. If you can be one of those things people use frequently you do get very high levels of loyalty. The really, really important thing about Clubcard, above anything else, was that it stopped you from regarding your sales figures as a dollop of amorphousness: we're selling a lot of broccoli becomes we're selling a lot of broccoli to those people. Suddenly you are off on a whole line of investigation, but it is all about the customer. It enabled Tesco to really be a customer-centric business without really trying.

'We would do Christmas-shopping nights for a store's 500 best customers and invite Clubcard customers. Simon Hay, the chief executive of dunnhumby, remembers that at Amersham, which was one of our original trial stores, we invited people to come to breakfast on the Saturday morning with the manager. Hundreds of people came: they were really well-heeled people who were fascinated to get behind the scenes. You can track the Clubcards of the people who went to that breakfast to this day and they are still incredibly loyal customers.'[40]

Critics of Clubcard worry that Tesco holds 'files' on members of the scheme and that individuals' lives can be mapped out in detail. Former chairman Sir David Reid says, 'There is an enormous amount of data. Despite the newspapers saying that Tesco wants to work out that we know what your name is, well they wouldn't give me that data even if I wanted it. Instead what they do is datamining. How many people are buying product X? Show me that by region. Now show me that by family size. How many people are having their films developed compared to how many people are buying films. Some parts of the press say what's the point of one per cent [Clubcard awards one point per pound spend and 100 points turn into a £1 Clubcard voucher]? But that's not how people saw it. They saw it as a thank you. And when they get the vouchers for £15 or whatever, they think that is nice.

'We continue to build loyalty. And Clubcard helps: if people move to a new area and there is a Tesco or a Sainsbury and they have a Clubcard then they may well choose the Tesco.

'Why ask if they are vegetarian? Well if they aren't buying meat, but aren't a vegetarian, it may be that they think supermarket meat isn't very good, so we'll send them a voucher to encourage them to try ours.

'You ask age and family so that you don't send a granny who lives by herself a voucher for money off nappies.

'It affects how we merchandise products: if people are not buying organics, is it that they can't find it? If in one kind of store people buy a lot of upscale wine, the commercial team will try that out in a store with a similar profile.'[41]

The way the information gleaned from Clubcards is stored makes it impossible for anybody to access an individual's personal as well as shopping details. The only times when identities are brought together with shopping data are those times when Clubcard mails out vouchers: the operation is done at high speed by computer and processes millions of Clubcard letters at a time.

David Malpas, who was managing director when Clubcard was introduced in 1995, describes the benefits that Tesco derived from the initiative: 'When we began to look at the success or otherwise of stores in a particular location, we were estimating what the total available turnover was for all the competitors included in that location and then trying to predict from that what the results would be for a hypothetical site. We were fairly quickly able to estimate what effect a Sainsbury half a kilometre away would have on us. It was fairly unsophisticated at the start. Now it is different because Tesco has the amazing tool of Clubcard. It can tell you that customers in a particular location are not buying meat there. So you can tell that the job isn't being done well there, or something is happening down the road. You look at who bought what, when and in what quantity. Then you look at who *should have* bought what, when and in what quantity based on your knowledge of shopping patterns. Then you begin to understand the cause of the non-purchase compared with the cause of the purchase. It is micro-marketing: if people aren't buying meat, why not?

'The thing about Clubcard, apart from the maniac Islington intelligentsia who dislike big business anyway, is that everybody likes it and everybody knows perfectly well that Tesco understands an awful lot about them. Anybody who uses a website will be offered things, but people like it and they understand it and appreciate it and – particularly – actually trust it. At the beginning we said, "We will not ever allow any information about you to go to anybody else, not ever and if you don't want us to collect it then we don't." A few people who hate big business think it is all Big Brother, but it isn't.'[42]

Leahy explains how Clubcard helped his team build up a detailed picture of shopping. 'We could collect all the information about your shopping on to the card and in that way for the first time we could match individual customers to shopping data, which was a whole new dimension in understanding shopping. That was the deal. The big unknown was whether people would bother for a penny.

'Not much information is on the card, but all purchases can be linked to you. It was important right from the start not to give that information to anybody, so we amalgamated it even to a group of people and it made them all anonymous. In that way it made the information secure and yet we could still get a lot of insight into how people shop.

'We hired a company set up by Edwina Dunn and Clive Humby. They did the data analysis. They were good at aggregating this data: painting patterns and pictures. People who like food, or who are interested in healthy things or had a baby: small groups who had in common shopping habits and behaviours.

'It had an enormous effect. You felt you had a basis for understanding customers and behaviours. Some things they said they were passionate about but did nothing about, and others they did. It was transformational for the business. Without that link to the customer it would just have been a slogan. It was the concrete means by which an entire organization could build all of its activities around customers.

'We changed the way we managed. There were some immediate effects and some of it was cumulative as you built skills. But it very much reinforced a way of working whereby you went out and gained insight from customers about what was important. Then you built a whole campaign of change, called a customer plan, to respond to that information. Each year since that time we have had a customer plan.'[43]

The significance of Clubcard was not appreciated when it was launched, at least not by competitors. 'David Sainsbury was persuaded to put his name to a press release that attacked Clubcard as electronic Green Shield Stamps, which he [must have] regretted because it became a big success and within a year we'd overtaken Sainsbury,' recalls Leahy.[44]

Although competitors did not react, inside Tesco it was a symbol of the step-change in the relationship with its customers. The 'Bricks in the Wall' approach was a key part of the perception shift that Ian MacLaurin and David Malpas had looked for. By luck or design, Tesco had modernized its approach to advertising just at the right time and was able to broadcast the shopping revolution with the help of a crotchety biddy called Dotty.

Chapter 19

The View from the Top:
a Shop for Everybody

'We cracked champagne. All of us had been involved in the cheap and cheerful Tesco of yesteryear.'

Lord MacLaurin[1]

'We laid out a plan. How we would go into non-food and go into services and would develop new formats, how we would go internationally. It was a very bold plan.'

Sir Terry Leahy[2]

'Every Little Helps', the phrase that finally replaced 'Pile It High, Sell It Cheap' for Tesco, can be traced back to a meeting in a restaurant in Islington in 1994.

'Things had been facing in the wrong direction and we needed to line them up like bricks in the wall so we could rebuild,' recalls Tim Mason, who was then Tesco's marketing-operations director. 'We needed to go back to our own brand, then we cheated slightly and we said there is also an issue about service. In fairness we made that up. Or Terry did. There was very little research evidence that said you are losing out because your service is no good. [But] Terry's instincts were that there was an opportunity for better service, to be more responsive to customers. In the end it led to Every Little Helps. It was a great motivator to the staff. They could really make a difference and they did.

'We had had a letter from a journalist who had arrived at the store in Chineham [Hampshire] and he said he had wanted ten *Sunday Times* newspapers with the supplement with his article in it. The newspapers in the shop had not had the supplement. He said that by the time he got home, there were ten supplements waiting on his doorstep.

'I went to Daphne's restaurant in Islington with Paul Weinberger, the creative director of Lowe's. I said, "Paul you have got to be able to bring to life the wonderful things the staff are doing. Paul came back with Dotty.

'That sort of campaign has many mothers, but I would credit it to Paul. Dotty was the mother of all shoppers who would put Tesco to the test and Tesco in the form of a member of staff would always rise to the challenge. The staff were the heroes and heroines.

'One of the first and best ads we ever made was the "cheerful sole" ad. Dotty bought a trout and showed it to her daughter and said it looked down in the mouth and her daughter said, "What do you expect? Why don't you take it back and see if they'll give you a cheerful sole?" Dotty did just that.'[3]

Mason recalls that flagging up great service meant that customers were quick to highlight an example where they felt it fell short. The example he recalls is that not everybody on the fish counters had quite mastered the art of smiling in the face of adversity. One customer asked for their fish to be filleted and it happened to be a new counter trainee who got the job. The exasperated boy, so determined to fillet the fish that he disregarded the customer's pleas to forget it and exchange it for another one, finished up by hurling the whole mess at a wall along with an expletive. The customer was sent chocolate, flowers and a contribution for a decent dinner. The press office issued an apology.

The Dotty campaign went from strength to strength. Mason adds: 'Frank Lowe's "MO" for making ads was to make them funny, make them famous and make them like polished gems. Think back to those Hamlet adverts, which were from the same stable. Prunella Scales [as Dotty] and Jane Horrocks [as her daughter] were two of the best actresses of their generations. These adverts would be beautifully done and that would flow over to the brand. Crikey, he made good ads.'4

Robin Gray, then the advertising director, says, 'In 1994 we conducted a major review at the end of the year; we looked at all our strengths and weaknesses. We needed something to take on Sainsbury and the others, and we wanted a campaign that was flexible and could talk about price, service and quality all in one. That was not easy when Sainsbury was focused on quality, Asda was focused on price and Tesco was squashed in the middle. It was a difficult brief.

'[The Dotty campaign] really put Tesco to the test. Prunella Scales and Jane Horrocks [were] fantastic casting: they had never worked with each other [but] it was one of the greatest campaigns. We spoke to commercial departments to get all these stories; a lot of research went into those. Most were shot at our Bracknell store [Berkshire], nothing glitzy like Los Angeles or Italy. They were shot at six o'clock on a Sunday morning because it was the only store within 30 miles of London that was closed [Sunday trading had recently taken off]. I could take the store over and do whatever I liked. It was about twelve or fifteen years old, it was all red and cream, but the new livery was blue and cream so we had to transform it overnight – all the décor. We had it all specially made and kept it at the back of the store and the same team would come in and do it.

'The furthest we went was Amsterdam, in the red light district. We shot a couple in the Lake District and the Isle of Mull, but it rained for three days non stop. They [Scales and Horrocks] were so professional. They never complained. We would have a Winnebago each for them. Prunella was absolutely superb. There was nothing she would not do for us and always got her lines right and so did Jane. It was always a small number of takes. My job there was making sure we got value for money because the costs were so huge and Pru and Jane's contracts ran into millions.

'Tesco was like a steam train coming up with new initiatives all the time. When we started, Prunella was ten years younger [than when we finished]. Jane had three kids [during the course of all the ads] so we'd had to shoot her being pregnant a few times.

'Dudley was good because it changed perceptions, but Dotty won all the awards.'[5]

After ten years and seventy-four Dotty commercials, Gray said the decision was that it was time to do something new. He recalls the transition. 'In 2004, when Dotty eventually had to finish, which wasn't easy, we trialled a new, simple, ten-second type of ad in a studio against a white background. It was quite simple. I don't think it has the same legs as Dotty, but having said that it has been running ever since.'[6]

Gray is among those inside Tesco who believe that the Dotty campaign helped shift perception – and product – to such an extent that it contributed to pushing the business past the line it had been aiming for since at least 1980: Sainsbury's leading market share. The moment came in 1995.

'There were celebrations,' says Lord MacLaurin. 'It was a very special moment for us. We cracked champagne. All of us had been involved in the cheap and cheerful Tesco of yesteryear.'[7]

Sir David Reid believes that the change in fortunes was in part down to Sainsbury's own operation. 'It probably helped that Sainsbury towards the end of that period were not running their business that well. It was the end of the John Sainsbury era: he was an industry giant. The staff were a bit arrogant and thought they were more important than the customers; our research picked up that a lot of people were saying they had had enough of that place. Clubcard was right for us because it didn't launch saying this is a great deal – we were giving customers one per cent off – but it said "thank you" to our customers. That touched a raw nerve. The Every Little Helps campaign acknowledged that shopping was a tedious experience but if somebody can help you on lots of little things to make your life easier ... it kind of touched a chord against Sainsbury's, which was "Sainsbury is so fantastic you can't think of shopping anywhere else". For customers it became: "Why don't you give me more detailed reasons than that?" Every Little Helps hit it off with customers who were worried about service, prices and availability.

'If you are going to be a winner you have to decide, are you going to be a Waitrose, which sells nice things to nice people, or are you going to serve a mass market and be a market leader? Then you have to have a wide appeal. In that sense Tesco is inclusive. Plenty of A/Bs go into Tesco and love it. Plenty of C2/Ds also shop there. There is something for everybody. There is classlessness. It's not seeking to say "I'm superior because I shop at wherever it is."'[8]

The acquisition of an independent Scottish retailer, William Low, in 1994 also boosted Tesco's sales. Tesco grew from seventeen stores in Scotland to sixty-seven, most of which it kept and developed. The Low acquisition was friendly – though Sainsbury also bid – and the integration was carried out over a leisurely eighteen months.

As the corks popped it was almost as if Ian MacLaurin and managing director David Malpas felt their work was done. Malpas recalls that, soon after his 'night of the long knives', he decided that his time, too, was past.

'I wanted a complete generation change, much to the amazement of my colleagues on the Board and some of our institutional shareholders. I knew it was the right thing to do. There were those who wanted me to stay as chairman. But I said no, and look what has happened.

'I lit upon Terry [Leahy] because he had demonstrated in everything he had done so far that he was an incisive and brilliant thinker, that he was more knowledgeable about the trade and the business than almost anyone else. He had the happy knack of knowing himself very well and his shortcomings very well and correcting them damn quick.

'In his younger days he was a bit brutal and not a good manager of people, but he corrected that very quickly and has become the person we know now. His approach and manner and attitude, if not appearance, were all about chief executive of a large organization and in particular of Tesco.'[9]

MacLaurin recalls debating the succession with David Malpas. 'We decided we'd miss a generation. John [Gildersleeve] would have been brilliant and it was difficult for me to tell John. He's a very adult person, John, a very special guy. He asked for some time to think. He said he didn't agree with the decision but he said he would give Terry his very best support.

'We all took it over when we were in our early forties. John was fifty-something; Terry was forty. We saw Terry as a mirror image of me and David Malpas and the crew. He had a very good chairman in John Gardiner, a pithy character, very bright. [Gardiner] knew the City inside out and had clear opinions about everything.

'We were looking for an all-rounder. Every chief executive has his own way of doing things. We decided to go at sixty. We saw Jack go on to his late seventies and that was very detrimental to the business. We could have gone on to sixty-five easily and the City would have been very happy about it. But we really felt that we ought to go on to do other things. It was right for the company and right for us personally. You have to have these young people coming through. You need to go and do something else in time.

'Terry was very unlike me. He's a Scouser for a start. He is a very bright guy. He thinks hard about what's going on. He has been very good with the other senior Tesco people who have come through. When John Gildersleeve left, Richard Brasher stepped in. We breed. We very rarely bring people in from outside at Board level. We have a particular Tesco culture. It's like playing for a successful football or cricket team: once you are playing with the brand leader, the best, you don't want to leave provided you are looked after well.'[10]

The 'young' team who had strained so hard to break free of Jack Cohen's rule had become the old guard themselves: having taken Tesco to the top, they prepared to hand it over in what was to be a two-year transition.

Leahy had been instrumental in taking Tesco to the top of British retail in 1995: he observes that his style and drive were largely a direct result of his background. In common with many of the Tesco people described in this book, the Leahy family story illustrates how a sizeable section of British society lived, were educated, worked and shopped.

Without a fluke on a dog track at St Helens on the Wirral, Terry Leahy's life would have likely as not begun in America. His Irish father was the ninth of ten children brought up in a railway-worker's house in Sligo Town. His elder siblings crossed the Atlantic; he and his youngest brother, Gerry, got as far as Merseyside. 'He was also going to go to the United States, but he won some money on St Helens dog track, so he thought he would hang around and he drifted into Liverpool,' explains Terry. 'He was about sixteen years old.'[11]

He became a construction worker before the Second World War, when he joined the merchant navy, serving on the North Atlantic convoys dodging German U-boats to bring provisions to Britain. He was torpedoed more than once and eventually a shrapnel wound, followed by tuberculosis, meant he had to be invalided out.

Like lots of Irish immigrants, he married within his community: Terry's mother had left a farm in Armagh to train as a nurse in pre-National Health England and, aged sixteen, had worked her way from Exeter to Liverpool. The couple met after the war in Toxteth, married in 1951 and set up home. Terry, the third of four boys, was born in Liverpool in 1956 in the Oxford Road Maternity Hospital. Home was a prefabricated house. 'It was actually a very good house, though it was cold,' recalls Leahy. 'It was made of aluminium and not insulated. The built-in cupboards were aluminium, the table was metal, but it had a fridge, which was an amazing thing then, and an indoor toilet.'[12]

The Leahy boys shared bunk beds in one of the two bedrooms. There was linoleum on the floor, painted chipboard lining the aluminium walls, a radio tuned to BBC comedy and from 1962 there was a television set around which the family gathered. His mother's pride and joy was a dressing table.

In 1966, long after the 20-foot by 30-foot prefab's supposed ten-year lifespan, the Leahy family moved as caretakers to a farm that had been bought and earmarked for housing development by the council. Then in 1970, needing space for Leahy senior's greyhounds, they moved to a council estate, which was to be Mrs Leahy's home from that time to this.

Terry, like his father before him, won a place at a grammar school. He recalls his father's frustration at not having made more of his intelligence and says that left a clear impression.

The Leahy boys did the usual things that English boys did then: 'football and scrapes', though he says he wasn't much good at football and was not keen on school, so regularly ran back to his mother. He came to reading late on, lacking books at home, but started to pick up prizes from about ten years of age. If Liverpool was past its economic best, culturally it was exploding. 'Literally there were people down the street who ended up with Top Ten records.' And of course there was Everton. 'I went to my first football match when I was seven, so they were heroes.'[13]

If Liverpool in the sixties was exciting culturally, in the seventies it became politically interesting. 'I took great pride in being part of the great city. When Cunard left in the 1970s it was a terrible blow to the city. It was one story after another of firms and factories leaving, the big decline of the docks – 10 miles of docks that employed tens of thousands – and they were closing with containerization. The sense of loss was greatest there. My father blamed the management: for him, the ruling class was the cause of the problem. As I'd never met anyone who was ruling I had no reason to doubt him. In later life it's interesting to look back at how views get baked into a community. Harold Wilson was a Liverpool MP. There was a lot of pride in that.

'We considered ourselves a poor family – working class, except my dad didn't work, so the poor end of working class.'[14]

A bit of money came in through gambling on greyhound races at unlicensed tracks, which carried their own risks – 'I remember one chap coming around with a grievance and a revolver,' says Leahy – and a bit more money came in through an invalid pension. From 1963, when Leahy's youngest brother was four, their mother worked part-time. 'Mum worried a lot about where money would come from and we never had much. We never had a car, but we always found a way to pay the rent. We were never hungry. We didn't have lots of clothes, or holidays, or things, but it was a very loving family and we certainly never felt deprived.'[15]

The local shops were characteristic of their era. 'Mum did the shopping. There was a row of about six shops built in a prefabricated way. These were tiny shops. They covered what you needed: a butcher, a greengrocer, a dry-grocery store, a haberdasher and a sweet shop. You literally knew the stores as Ronnie the butcher's or Harry the sweetshop, so you knew the store by the name of the proprietor and they were there all the time. Inside, the prefab shops were very small; the only light came from the front and the stock was there, some of it in security cages. The stores took their character from the proprietor. Harry the sweetstore was sunny. The greengrocers were a bit older and more miserable.

'Business was all assisted service. That went on until 1966 when the prefabs were knocked down. We didn't have a local store when we lived on the farm – we had to travel to go to a store. There weren't actually many shops around. People talk about an absence of shops now but there never were local shops, something people conveniently forget. This area of Liverpool, the Childwall Valley, was planned to have 70,000 people in it, which was why they knocked down the prefabs. I suppose the store we used must have been 3 or 4 miles away. It was called Crazy Cuts. Prices were remarkably cheaper – I was only ten years old but even I could see that. Then after that there was a shopping centre built in about 1970 for this big area. It contained a Tesco and a Safeway and you saw shopping more like you'd see it today.

'We made frequent shopping trips. When you had money it affected when you shopped. We ate well: I remember cabbage, potatoes and bacon. We had a big tradition of a big hot meal each day, whereas some families were already not doing that. We had meat every day: bacon, pork, or lamb chops and a roast on a Sunday. Some days it was home-made soup of some kind. There wasn't much poultry, which became popular much later.

'I didn't have my first pasta until I left home at eighteen. Or yoghurt. I had those at university. We probably never had rice. It was always fish on Friday, quite often smoked haddock. It was easier to get some taste into. My mother was working full time from 1966 and my father did most of the cooking. It was bacon, egg and chips every night then. We had tinned fruit and Neapolitan ice cream for Sunday tea.

'Nobody ever really drank anything with a meal – even water. If you had some money you bought a drink from the shop – Tizer or White's lemonade. They weren't round the house. Sweets were the same: you bought sugar confectionery because it went further and lasted longer. You nearly never had chocolate. Our American family sent us over chocolate bars and that was a huge thing, so it must have been pretty rare.

'Crazy Cuts seemed huge, but it wouldn't have been. There was a high ceiling, lots of light and cut cases to make it look cheap. It was busy, exciting and a bit daunting.

'In town you went to the department store to get good cooked ham from the fine food halls, which seemed well lit and had better-dressed people serving. At Coopers you had the added smells of cooking. We used to have tea in Owen Owen's canteen, so there was a treat. I enjoyed looking at things. Lewis's was the biggest department store in Liverpool, and Blacklers. I liked them because they were so big and they all had a different character. Blacklers seemed to have lots and lots of linens and haberdashery and the Christmas trip was the big one because there were lights and there was a grotto and everyone got a present.

'My mum never bought herself any clothes, so clothes-shopping would be for the kids. We went to T. J. Hughes in London Road and occasionally Marks & Spencer and Owen Owen.'[16]

It was school that proved to be Terry's passage to something different. 'The school was absolutely fine, but I missed my mum and it seemed to me like an intelligent choice to run home. There were fifty in a class. At seven you went to the junior school. They were all new schools built by the parish. One person came from a private house, which was unusual. They were from working families – [their fathers worked] at Ford at Halewood and the docks. The school prided itself on getting a lot of scholarship places. I passed a scholarship to St Edward's, which was the Catholic Institute that had been founded in 1850 to teach the Irish and which was the best school in the city. Four boys went there from Our Lady's. It was a private school but the council bought places, which they awarded to brighter kids from some of the schools in the city.

'It was a bit of a shock. I don't know how Mum afforded the uniform. There were middle-class kids there and scholarship boys from the council estates. My friends tended to be the ones from the council estates. I didn't much like it in the early years. I didn't like the discipline. I responded by using humour and a little bit of rebelliousness, and generally would end up being somewhere near the bottom of the class and get into trouble. It was a big rugby school, one of the best in the country, and I got into the team, which gave you a bit of standing. When I was able to choose my own subjects for A-level I did very well, which was an unexpected transformation. I enjoyed the freedom and the respect as I got older.'[17]

He took geography, history, economics and general studies. 'I owe an enormous amount to those schools because to get from a prefab to here can't be done without those sorts of schools.' He can recall and name the teachers who inspired him, even if discipline at the Christian Brothers-run school was tough. 'Discipline was severe. I remember getting strapped a lot. There was no great resentment of it as I can remember. You were naughty, you got caught out and that was it. Occasionally they would expel a few, which was sad because it didn't reflect what went on. I was lippy, looking for a joke, and I was probably a pain in the neck.

'One teacher, Tony McCann, was big and intelligent and a natural leader. He always talked beyond the subject and the classroom, so he was lifting your horizons. He made you believe that you could join society and do as well as anybody else, and that was the critical thing for kids from this background. Some families didn't want their children to do exams because they couldn't see the point, so why have the pressure? The parents wouldn't know what was possible because they had no knowledge. The teachers bridged the difference.

'It was normal at that school to do exams and go to university. There was no experience in the family of professional or business people. I didn't have the slightest idea what business was like. My brothers had engineering apprentices at Tate & Lyle. I got A grades for all the A-levels, which amazed everybody, including me. I went to UMIST in Manchester and took a management degree there. It was broad and interesting and meant carrying on the behavioural sciences. There was a bit of economics, psychology, sociology, law, economic history and a bit of maths. Economics and psychology gave you a better insight into human behaviour than a more specific subject like marketing.

'It was a good university and a good course – probably better than the students on it. Manchester was a very lively place with lots of distractions. Every one of us did the course with one eye on other distractions. I had the full grant so I was quite a wealthy student: £750 a year and work in the holidays meant you had plenty of money. I met great friends there who I'm still in touch with. There were probably very few people from council estates: it was largely middle class and I was a bit conscious of that, I suppose. The self-confident South is less aware of, or interested in, the North.'[18]

For Leahy, parental input into his career choice was minimal. Unlike Lord MacLaurin before him, there would be no shock when he announced he was joining the Co-op, or subsequently when he joined Tesco. 'They almost wouldn't presume to give advice, so you made your own decisions. I don't think Mum ever knew what degree I did, though they were proud that I'd gone to university.'[19]

The Co-op suited his values at the time. 'I was brought up a socialist. At the Co-op I had a sort of mentor, Brian Whitelegg, who wasn't a Labour supporter. I'd never met a small-business man. He told me a lot about his life – earning money, paying tax, meeting regulations, employing staff, being responsible for things. I saw another side of life. He was a good, decent person and I learned a lot about ordinary, decent people trying to make a living. I had a big belief in the Welfare State and government and this was an interesting contrast.

'I was a product of my background. I was educated, which had all been given to me for free. I was a Labour voter. I was a social liberal. In my background these were absolute truths. There just wasn't another way of doing things, so I was quite certain in my views. I'd even gone through the management degree – economics, marketing, business – and none of that had unsettled these views. So it was Brian Whitelegg, as a small-business person, and the reality of the Co-operative movement that started to give unsettling thoughts about the difference between the good intent and what is produced from that good intent.

'It was a very turbulent time – you felt the inflation but I never really sensed the problems, in part because we'd never had any money. I was better off than I'd ever been. I never felt the decline in the 1970s. I was from the Labour movement so I didn't feel the impact of unionism. I was reasonably confident, which must have come from the Welfare State: that you'd get on, that it would be okay.

'I was feeling my way in business. I had no idea about capital markets or ownership or anything like that. I always saw myself within an organization because I never imagined there would be anything else. You earned a salary and worked for a firm.'[20]

Leahy's move from the Co-operative to Tesco has been described in earlier chapters, as have his first impressions of Tesco. He found it a tough place, but he believes his background enabled him to withstand the first shocks and the battles with people above him in the hierarchy. 'I was young and quite tough, so I suppose I could give as good as I got. I would fight back. I didn't have the art of sidestepping, but I also didn't have a backward gear so I had to go forwards. That worked out okay, but there should have been another way. By the time I was in my late twenties I was working prodigiously hard and that never stopped really until I couldn't work that hard any longer. That was the kind of drive that came from deep in the background.'[21]

He had to overcome an aversion to making presentations as he took his ideas higher and higher up Tesco, pushed on by a boss who could do the politics but wanted to harness Leahy's proposals. 'I was good at the arguments, the policy and what should be done. He was good at getting an audience and getting it out there. I forced myself to do more and more presentations because I was so nervous. In some senses I was tough. I'd come from a background where you weren't expected to do well in life and so you felt you had to run faster and harder than other people to stay above water. Tesco was a very abrasive environment where people were not always helpful and would actually cause you a problem if you weren't careful, and that combination of things tended to make you quite competitive. There's a small dividing line between being demanding and being a bit too tough. And you're young and you haven't learned the full ways of getting the best out of people. On the other side I've never particularly favoured people or been hard on people in isolation.

'I wanted to do well. Not for financial gain. Not for any other reason than to not fail in life. I think that when you grow up in the environment I grew up in you could see around you that nobody was guaranteed success so you could well imagine yourself failing in life, not having enough money, not being able to make ends meet. That was the norm. So the main impetus was to do a good job and not fail. It's been with me all my life. I don't think you can take that out. I'm still the same. There are more layers of sophistication so it's not seen on the outside, but you can't really alter your early experiences: they affect you, so you have to come to terms with it and make sure it doesn't cause a problem for other people.'[22]

Leahy found a supporter in David Malpas. 'He was an inquisitorial and demanding leader with a very good sense of humour, very dry, but he was no pushover.'[23]

He says he did not realize at the time how tolerant and helpful people were being. His own management style was, he recalls, instinctive. 'I tried to be very careful in the selection of people, although I didn't really know how to. I would work closely with them in quite a challenging way. I don't think people would always have enjoyed it, but I didn't know any better so I did the best I could.

I did change my management style around the person. I didn't realize I was doing it, but every person has different strengths and weaknesses so instead of making them change around me I would change around them.

'I always have been very challenging. In the early days a lot of that was driven by fear – fear of failure. As time went on it would be more measured. By asking questions it would help people to get to the answers themselves. You've got to really encourage and sometimes force people to get to the truth of things and then if they do that they can usually work out what to do next. It's not much fun if you're on the receiving end, but that's always been my style.'[24]

Leahy's experiences of running the commercial aspects of fresh food, as has been described in earlier chapters, led directly to his promotion to the Board in October 1992. He did not feel that there was anything inevitable about promotion at that time. 'When I walked into the room, I thought I was being fired because I always thought that people would think I was doing a worse job than I was. Tesco has never been very good at telling people they are doing a good job and I am about as bad as everybody else at that.

'David Malpas and Ian MacLaurin said there's going to be some changes and we're going to ask you to join the Board as the marketing director. I think they were disappointed that instead of being delighted the colour drained from my face and I came up with a whole series of worrying questions. It was difficult for John [Gildersleeve] and me. I was now his colleague. He had made a legitimate claim to run the business and this was maybe a signal that that wasn't going to happen. It was personally difficult and took us a long time to work through. I had different relationships with a lot of people. Not everybody would have wanted me to be successful in that role and yet I had no power base. I needed the support of all the people in retail operations, buying, finance and so on because there was no marketing department to speak of. They did come round and support me. Any success I had was given to me by their support. People like Michael Wemms, David Reid, John [Gildersleeve] and others.

'The first Board meeting was quite terrifying. It was a struggling business and I didn't know if I could do this job. These were my bosses who I now had to work with as colleagues. The age gap seemed difficult. Occasionally there was fighting like rats in a sack and that was unsettling. In the end it calmed down. The customers provided the direction and I was the cipher for that. We started to be more successful and things fell in behind that. Ian was like a team captain. He was disciplined but he would worry about every member and make sure they made a contribution.

'There was friction and there were debates, which if I had lost would have put the business in a different place. Largely all of the contributions were well intended. You have to have debate. It is interesting that it is a battle of wills sometimes and there are some things you cannot afford to lose. Ian [MacLaurin] and particularly David [Malpas] always gave me that bit of extra support that I needed at the important moments and that made a difference.

'I've been very straight to a fault. I am basically shy. I couldn't network or hang around corridors of influence. I could only tell it like it was. I got a reputation for being honest. That became a much more valuable commodity than anything else. People might not agree, but they knew you were being honest. I'm not particularly talented at speaking or writing but I can speak in pictures. I could get a message across. I see a problem and I see a solution and I describe them. Pictures are much more engaging. I was able to lay out in a simple way what we should do and I've always been an optimist. They weren't strengths I knew I had, but looking back they made a difference. In management theory you find a picture of where you are, then you have a vision of where you want to be. The simpler the better if you have to engage tens then hundreds of thousands of people.

'You have to know what you're good at and not good at and learn to use that. When you are shy you tend to be more acute at listening. That's good for picking up on things. If you are very confident that sometimes means you don't listen or see things.

'In a stubborn way I've stuck to what I've thought was the truth.

Over time people trust you. The words and actions are aligned. That matters terribly in terms of leadership. They might not like you but they don't have to: the important thing is that they trust you. David Malpas said I was stubborn.'[25]

'Terry's appointment as chief executive wasn't controversial or a surprise,' remembers Sir David Reid. 'The succession of Ian MacLaurin was also smooth. Other retailers have had real difficulties and a good part of that was lack of succession planning: Sainsbury and Marks & Spencer are good examples of that. Their leaderships made some choices which proved to be not good and a few hundred thousand people found themselves rudderless.'[26]

Leahy says, 'I had two years to get ready, which proved to be very important. I suppose I was doing the job a year before anyway. We did two things. One was to look at a new strategy for the company, because although we were being really successful following that work with prices, service and Clubcard – and amazingly we overtook Sainsbury's in 1995 – it couldn't go on for ever. There was a world industry beginning to grow up and we were hearing about Walmart and Carrefour. These were companies that were big and ambitious, going into other countries. They had non-food as well as food, whereas we were just a food supermarket.

'I took the Board abroad to Asia and Europe in 1995 and 1996 and we identified the countries that we would go into. That developed our strategy. The ten countries we chose were the ones we went in and then we added a few more later on.

'Also, at the same time, Tim [Mason] suggested that, with Ian [MacLaurin] and David [Malpas] being so much a feature of the business, we, as young people, needed to say what we stood for. We got all of our managers together in a town meeting. It was an idea that we'd stolen – there is no new idea under the sun. We travelled around the country in a roadshow. We laid out a plan. How we would go into non-food and go into services and would develop new formats, how we would go internationally. It was a very, very bold plan. Only a young person could be so naive. But the important additional thing we did was we'd been speaking to our staff for a couple of years, bringing them in in small groups. It sounds clever now, but we were stumbling.'[27]

The Board decided it had to win hearts and minds and asked the staff some fundamental questions to help move forward, as Leahy describes. 'In an afternoon we'd say two things. "You've worked in the business a long time – you describe to us what you think Tesco stands for." They would write down things to do with the customer – look after customers, research for customers, good prices for customers, you try hard for the customers. Then we asked them to "Tell us what you'd like Tesco to stand for." They wrote down all the things around treating people as you would like to be treated. Respect people and trust people and celebrate success. They were writing down our values. They weren't inventing them. They were coming from their experience in the business but they were articulating them. We tidied it up, gave it back and they rewrote them.

'Those were the meetings at which we introduced our "Values". We wanted to be a business that was going to have values and manage true to those values. It was quite difficult to speak about business in that way. This was a very male, very traditional, very working-class business [in terms of management] and you were speaking about emotional things, about desires, aspirations, how people feel about their experience.

'It was actually the single most important thing that I ever did. It made big changes, because some people had to leave the business because they could not work that way. Like lots of businesses, its management style had come out of the army. It was male, hierarchical and fairly brutal. It was challenging and aggressive for me going in as a young person. This different idea of respect and manners and tolerance and consensus was too much for some people. It was profoundly important because we employ tens, now hundreds, of thousands of people all over the world and their experience is determined by whether they are respected or not. You can't make people behave the right way; they have to want to behave the right way. What I couldn't realize is that it unlocked a massive desire to be like that. It's a big part of people's lives. To have an environment that's secure and supportive and pleasant is so liberating.

'We don't always get it right. I certainly don't. But generally it's better and generally each year it gets better. We work very hard at it with Viewpoint [an anonymous survey of Tesco's employees and also its suppliers] and surveys, and how we manage and train people to enable people to live or manage by these values. The strength of Tesco is in its attitude towards people in the business and what happens is when they are treated in a decent way they believe in the business and they look after customers. That's essentially why the business is successful. Shareholders never understand that, competitors don't understand it and journalists don't. You nearly can't explain it – you just have to experience it to know it. They always look for marketing ideas or commercial ideas to explain Tesco's success but it isn't about those things at all, it's about basic values and trust and respect.

'People became more consensual, more careful about how they spoke, more concerned to challenge ideas rather than to challenge the person. The only time we've ever brought in management consultants was then and they taught us management techniques. We trained 12,000 people about how to hold meetings: get expectations; confirm understanding; plan and review. We introduced the Tesco Steering Wheel, which is a "balanced scorecard" in management speak. It's a visual thing. It allowed us to put down what was important in the business and balance all the trade-offs between customers and staff and finance and so on. It was tremendously powerful: everybody could see their role in it in stores, depots and offices.'[28]

The Steering Wheel was another borrowed idea: Leahy had read about the balanced scorecard, which featured in a few *Harvard Business Review* editions in the early 1990s and was eventually published in book form by Robert Kaplan and David Norton as *The Balanced Scorecard: Translating Strategy into Action*.[29] Leahy combined the thinking with another borrowed idea – the Big Hairy

Audacious Goal, a concept set out by James Collins and Jerry Porras in *Built to Last: Successful Habits of Visionary Companies*.[30] 'The result was Tesco's Steering Wheel, a series of objectives which at that time were divided into four segments: customer, people, finance, operations. You can have one for the company – and then for your part of the country or your store, so it can be very grand, about market share or billions of pounds, or that everybody got trained, or we reduced losses on fresh food. It comes back to the same thing. It's powerful because it is simple and visual and everybody can be engaged by it.'[31]

By coincidence, years later at a London business conference, Leahy was asked to introduce Robert Kaplan. 'I thought: that name rings a bell and I realized, blimey, it's the bloke that wrote this book. He'd never met me but I was able to give him a belting introduction because I could say, "This bloke has transformed Tesco." He was a bit stunned.'[32]

The best part of two decades on, Tesco continues to use Kaplan's balanced scorecard, adapted to fit, as the basis on which the business is managed, from the chairman to the checkouts. During that period, Leahy would set about building a company that was twice the size of the one he took over.

Chapter 20

New Tesco: Adapting to a Turbulent, Troubling World

'A food desert is anywhere that doesn't have a good shop. That was a social policy concern. Tesco came up with a perfect solution. It's a surprise that the perfect solution prompted so much criticism.'

Sir Terry Leahy[1]

'We had a war with Levi's. They were selling at £50 then and we sold them for £25. That got them very annoyed. Ultimately we lost in court. [However] people understood that Tesco was for the consumer.'

Dame Lucy Neville-Rolfe[2]

When Terry Leahy stepped into the chief executive's role in 1997, Tesco was enjoying the fruits of reinvention – along with a lot of other organizations. New Labour was one of them, led by modernizers who canvassed opinion through focus groups, understood the media and swept the board in the May 1997 General Election. Staid Britannia became 'Cool', with artists, pop stars and footballers winning international recognition.

Not that Tesco's poster-girl was trendy: Prunella Scales's Dotty was the 'mother of all mothers', with her firm demands for better food, better service and better prices, but her battiness was very British and the old dear inspired affection. Even the very many people who had never been inside a Tesco superstore probably knew that Tesco had come up in the world.

There were now 568 Tesco stores in the United Kingdom and a further 190 on the Continent. Sales had risen by 15 per cent in one year to nearly £14 billion and profits were a healthy £750 million before tax.

For the millions of customers choosing to shop at Tesco, the innovations came thick and fast. Perhaps the biggest was a new home-delivery service, Tesco Direct.

Gary Sargeant was a Home Counties boy born in 1965; his family ran a business in grocery and one of his first jobs was at Sainsbury, working in the warehouse. He recalls a culture that encouraged the Back Door dodges which, as highlighted by Tesco people in this book already, was at one time widespread. The young Sargeant got caught out with some older colleagues: his copy-book blotted, he saw a chance to move to Tesco for a fresh start. Lessons learned, Sargeant became a trusted employee and rose quickly to manage one of Tesco's large stores, in Elmers End, London. He had come to the attention of Philip Clarke, then operations director. Sargeant picks up the story of the birth of Tesco Direct.

'Every other year you are invited to a Company Conference – in those days about a thousand people went. [There was] a presentation on stage of the company's first internet site that could be used for shopping. It was a demo: how you could place an order over the internet and how goods were delivered from store. The screen went blank. I remember thinking this home-shopping stuff will never work. Derek Dyson was my store director and he said, "I need to chat to you." Phil Clarke I'd seen some months before on Shakers and Movers, which was a scheme to see if you could do anything other than store management, and I'd had an interview with him. They wanted me to be part of this small team.

'In April 1997 I took over what was then Tesco Direct from Ken Towle, who was looking after it and had gone back into [store] managing. Ken started the very, very early stages of home shopping. We set about deciding our strategy. We developed the model he started [Towle went on to manage Tesco's business in China and to join the executive committee in 2011 as director with responsibility for Tesco's online businesses]. We took orders through fax, phone and very few from the internet – 1 or 2 per cent. Orders were sent by fax to the store, they picked the products into standard trolleys and then would go into the warehouse and scan through a till there, then pack and put into trays and load on to vehicles for delivery. It was a very clumsy process. The first store to go live was Osterley, then Hammersmith and a number of stores around London, and we picked a store in Leeds to see if the customer behaviour was different outside London. We persisted with that for a year.

'We got the model to work. Then Terry [Leahy] had received two of the worst customer complaints he said he had ever received about our service. So we had to look at that. I went to the Board to ask to extend the trial into a pilot to go into another ten stores – a total of twenty stores. Terry asked me in July 1998 whether we could actually make any money, and of course we couldn't. The delivery charge of £5 didn't cover the cost. That was a changing point. We switched our focus on to how we could make money.

'I had responsibility for the IT part of the operation and we were bringing in technology, which we were testing at Romford Gallows Corner. That helped a bit.' They abandoned plans for the additional ten stores and worked on what they had, streamlining the process to try to achieve profit. 'We decided we could only take orders over the internet and not phone or fax, which cost a lot. Previously pickers had only done one order at a time. We looked at how to pick multiple orders. We re-designed the whole process: the trolley they picked on to, the trays, the vans so they could be loaded in the order they would be delivered. I went to Terry for the £200,000 to do this – buy the vehicles and the kit for the store – and we launched in Sunbury in October 1998 as the very first internet-only home-shopping store. It started slowly. We were able to make a profit from each of the orders. That was the start. We worked perfecting the trolley, the flow process, the system, printing the orders [printouts got damp in the warehouse]. In early 1999 I went back to the Board to get the money to roll out the system to a further ten stores. Most were around the Home Counties and South London, because that is where the demographic said was where people with a propensity to shop lived: people who were cash rich and [had more] time.'

The operation rolled out into more than 100 stores from mid-1999, moving through the Midlands to the North.

'We had one of our fantastic Christmases – all our delivery slots were taken twelve days ahead. It was clear that Terry's original strategy, which he pulled together with Tim Mason, that if customers wanted to shop this way, we would give it to them, was right.' Stores, however, were less convinced, because internet home-shopping sales diverted sales away from their standard checkouts. Sargeant says that some manipulated the delivery slots, holding them back so that customers could not book them, which led to dissatisfaction as they had to accept slots they did not really want. The speed of development was rapid. 'We moved exceptionally quickly, which meant we got a lot of early ground. Our competitors were doing it unprofitably. We had a thin margin, but it was profit-able. Now you wonder if we had to do it so quickly, but in the early days of the internet you had to grab as much ground as you could.'[3]

There was also a new customer service centre, in Dundee; Clubcard had 9.5 million members; and financial services were under way with the Clubcard Plus payment card. Petrol was one of the 600 everyday products included in a new promotion called 'Unbeatable Value at Tesco'. Quality was high up the agenda – a new 'Chef's Club' providing culinary advice included fish expert Rick Stein. Some stores had 'cook shops' to showcase own-label products in practical but entertaining demonstrations. Kids World – a range of toys and clothing – was launched. Shoppers could buy award-winning wines, find flowers and treat themselves to food hampers. Tesco was focused on delivering an affordable, accessible version of services or products that traditionally were the preserve of Britain's better-off.

Tesco was often not the first with an idea, but it set out to deliver the best possible version. Superstores, discount shopping, the Value budget range, computerized warehouses, scanning, till receipts –

these innovations meant the business, largely unchanged in more than three decades, modernized in less than ten years.

The newness – especially the different store formats – got Tesco noticed. Several years before Leahy became chief executive, he was standing in a cash-and-carry car park with John Gildersleeve on a routine retailers' recce. He describes the moment. 'There were a lot of vans. Conventional wisdom was that small stores were in a slow decline, but actually these convenience stores, despite the emergence of the big superstores, were thriving. The logical thing then was to develop a format. We thought it would be petrol-station forecourt retailing and that format did okay. But the really successful shops were much closer to where people lived and could reach on foot. Eighty per cent of the people who use an Express go there on foot. With the rise of the one-stop shop it left an opportunity for the top-up shop that takes place in an Express.'[4]

Express opened a route to new customers, but perhaps also turned out to be the tipping point for Tesco's media image: people, especially in the London area, who had not encountered Tesco before suddenly had the shop in their neighbourhood. Perhaps it was simply that Tesco went from underdog to pack leader.

The nineties brought rapid, far-reaching changes driven by technology and accelerated by affluence; home delivery was one example of this. The appearance of a local Tesco often concentrated opinions. Leahy acknowledges the impact on shopping that Tesco's development since the late nineties has had. He believes it was positive.

'One of the great strengths of Tesco is that it has something for everyone. An Express can operate in a tough council estate, on a traditional high street, in a village or on a commuter estate. There are no people cut off, because they can walk there. I think it is sad that it has attracted so much criticism from other small shopkeepers because more people use the local parade of shops if there is an Express there.

'A food desert is anywhere that doesn't have a good shop. That was a social policy concern. Government and other people were wringing their hands. Tesco came up with a perfect solution. It's a surprise that the perfect solution prompted so much criticism.'[5]

The first Express opened with a petrol forecourt in Barnes, London, in 1994. The first Metro store – a format slightly larger than the Express model – had opened in Covent Garden the year before. At the other end of the spectrum, plans for the first Tesco to stock all of the lines then available to customers were well advanced: the first Tesco Extra opened in Pitsea, Essex, in 1998, a result of lessons learned from the company's emerging businesses in Central Europe.

In 1998, however, Leahy warned that profits would take a bit of a back seat for a few years because Tesco was about to throw huge amounts of investment at rapid development. He had some simple but ambitious goals for the business: to grow the UK core food business, to build a significant non-food offer, to open internationally and to develop retail services such as internet shopping, banking and telecoms.

'Those businesses that started since 1997 are actually bigger and more profitable than the whole of Tesco was in 1997,' observes Leahy. 'That's a big achievement. There has been creativity and risk-taking and innovation. The idea was to have most of the things that a busy household – whether a one-person flat or a full family house – would need to get through the week. It could be a torch or a duvet or some low-energy light bulbs.'[6]

This was not a new idea: Jack Cohen had brought Leslie Porter into Tesco back in 1959 to run the clothing and household departments to fulfil pretty much the same aim. Like Jack, Leahy believed that non-food would help food sales. 'Non-food attracts more people, from a wider distance. The Newcastle store used to take nearly £1 million a week. It was a highly successful food superstore. We knocked it down. It was about 42,000 square feet, and in the end it was about 115,000 square feet. Now it does about £1 million in sales of non-food and general merchandise. So the new area is taking as much as the food was.'[7]

When it became difficult to expand outwards, Tesco decided to expand upwards to get the space, which annoyed critics although again it was not a new idea. Jack's shops were often on more than one floor, opening up on a new level to put clothing, or cutlery or aquarium fish on display.

'You would not have thought it would be successful,' reflects Leahy. 'People wouldn't want to go up another floor. Actually, they seem to quite like it. They browse quietly in one area and they do their busy food shop in another.

'Non-food is just part of the natural evolution. Non-food is higher risk than food. You don't have to buy televisions or clothing but you do have to eat. You don't come to the store with those non-food products on your list. So those products have to be attractively priced, presented well and at the right time.'[8] Sargeant describes how Tesco Direct borrowed from established catalogue retailers. '*Baby* catalogue in 1997 was the first. It was linked to the Baby Club our marketing people did [which] gave advice and was linked to great products. The home shopping and catalogue went hand in hand for a while. It took £12 million. It showed us we could do a catalogue in all the product groups. The infrastructure required, the warehouse and technology, was a huge investment. A lot of the major catalogue companies had been going for a hundred years. As Tesco we were trying, as we always have done, in about ten minutes to work out how to get from £15 million to £150 million at no cost and get all the experience that had been going for over a hundred years.' Sargeant's first proposal, for a Tesco order-fulfilment centre, was costed at £80 million and got short shrift from the Board: it was a lot of money for an experiment. So he looked for a joint venture partner. 'We were drawn to Grattan, who had a state-of-the-art centre. It was all done in the dark by robots. It was German. Mail order was huge in Germany because, after the [Second World] War there had been nowhere to buy anything.'[9]

Tesco's popularity with many shoppers grew, but other traders, some non-governmental organizations and some residents' groups began to question the merit of large supermarket chains. Those arguments are by now well known: that the global supply chain damages local production, that local shopkeepers should be protected from national chains, that low prices must mean somebody is being short-changed, that supermarkets can afford to challenge planning decisions.

Leahy says his own background helped him understand some of the criticism. 'Some people, a minority, worry about global trade. It is threatening. I worked in factories in Liverpool making Meccano toys and packing sugar, and those factories are not there any more. It is very upsetting when your employment has been taken away from you. Some people feel there is something troubling about the loss of community where businesses are based in a community and everything you use, you know how it's made and where it is made. They can't get their minds around a world that's got no physical barriers or boundaries, which is understandable. But billions of people have been taken out of poverty because of global trade. It is a more challenging, more turbulent, more troubling world, but that is a price worth paying to take billions of people out of poverty.'[10]

In fact, as Tesco modernized there were genuine losers, as George Marston explains. Nature's Choice enabled Tesco to assure customers of quality and responsible growing, but suppliers and growers needed time to implement it, he says. 'It could not take place overnight. You had to give them time to give evidence that they were managing waste [and] water properly, to have evidence that pesticides [were] used selectively with thought and not prophylactically. Every crop is a one-year season. It takes a minimum of two years to effect that change. Any supplier would tell you it has cost them a lot of money in terms of resources, management time and skill. Tesco understands that, but if the supply chain hadn't invested and had had a food scare, which was possible, the cost of that would have been far greater than the cost they undertook voluntarily to comply with Nature's Choice, or Europe's Good Agricultural Practices. They needed to up the security, performance and management of the supply chain sooner or later. Nature's Choice prompted that change sooner and quicker. Tesco could do it well and quickly because we had a comparatively small group of suppliers and growers across the world. The rest of the industry is still catching up.'[11]

Tesco's own staff numbers grew by tens of thousands during the early nineties and when Leahy became chief executive there were some 160,000 employees. Possibly new recruits were tempted by leading salaries, gold-standard pensions and, since 1987, free shares in the company.

Whatever the cause, Tesco was attracting as much attention under the publicity-averse Leahy as it had under the showman-like Sir Jack Cohen. In an era of spin, it was one of a dwindling number of companies that decided to stick with a predominantly in-house team to care for its reputation. Leahy's new Board sent head-hunters to identify people who would support this approach.

Lucy Neville-Rolfe was a high-grade civil servant whose career had covered, for the most part, agriculture and environment and who had been posted at 10 Downing Street and the Cabinet Office during John Major's administration. She was still there when Tony Blair and his official spokesman, Alastair Campbell, arrived in Downing Street. Tesco needed somebody who would translate government regulation and who knew about managing reputation. Neville-Rolfe took the job.

She has a clear recollection of why she was hired. 'I had been brought in to manage the reputation and external agenda with a growing company in a society where supermarkets create change and make enemies. I was a professional public-policy person.'[12]

Neville-Rolfe herself was a bit of a departure for Tesco: she was an outsider, female and she had no retail background at all. Instead, her family story illustrates a rural lifestyle of that era – not flush with cash or possessions, but middle-class.

Born in January 1953 in the Wiltshire village of Wardour, Neville-Rolfe was the third of five children whose parents had interesting backgrounds. Her mother, Margaret, was brought up a Catholic in a fine house in Campden Hill Square, Notting Hill Gate. Neville-Rolfe's father, though international in terms of roots (India, French Canada and Poland), lived a very English life in a rural home in Norfolk. Both parents were educated privately and took degrees at Oxford University.

Education was embedded in the Neville-Rolfe household, along with politics and faith. Lucy and another sister followed their mother to Somerville College, Oxford, and three of her own sons have kept the family connection with her former college alive.

The Neville-Rolfe parents left their careers (in the Civil Service and army) and set up home in an isolated spot between the old and new castles at Wardour, seat of the Arundells, a great English Catholic family, just before Lucy was born.

'The farm started as a folly [in the park] for the modern house,' she explains. 'My father tried "farmer to freezer" ten years ahead of its time. I helped my mother look after chickens, cleaning the eggs with brushes. I brought the cows in for milking. We had pigs, a dairy herd and chickens and we used to go to Shaftesbury or Salisbury market (now a Waitrose) once a month to sell or buy stock. It got very difficult in the fifties and sixties – he gave up the farm in the early sixties but stayed in the house. He went back to university. Less efficient farmers were being driven out by lower prices as cheaper grain and meat came in from New Zealand and Australia. It is difficult if your business falters. I remember the farm sale, selling off the stock and the machinery.'[13]

Pocket money was 'how may years old you were in pence' and the children were allowed a cake when the baker brought the bread to the farm, but treats such as jelly were for birthdays. The farmhouse was filled with 'old furniture and board games'. There was no television. Shopping was done in the small supermarket at Tisbury, dark and piled with boxes and tins, or the slightly larger Tesco at Salisbury.

Theirs was not a moneyed childhood in the modern sense, but their parents' breadth of experience and their focus on education created a rich environment that could be described as privileged. Holidays were in Cornwall; there was a lake at the bottom of the garden for games of Swallows and Amazons; and the family drove to Switzerland for the first of several skiing holidays in 1965. The children were encouraged to learn foreign languages: their father spoke seven.

Their schooling was local and free. Neville-Rolfe recalls a very good teacher in the village primary school she attended. 'Wardour was a Catholic enclave so the school attracted Catholics from a 10-mile radius. The level of supervision was good in those days. There were around twenty children in one infant class and about forty in Mrs Burt's junior class. There was a lot of learning: spelling, tables and so on, and preparation for the 11-plus began with tests from about seven or eight years old.'[14]

Neville-Rolfe took the 11-plus aged nine, passed and so joined her older sisters on a free place at the otherwise fee-paying convent school, a bus ride away at Shaftesbury (Dorset). Although out of her depth with the older pupils socially, she thrived academically. Having taken GCEs at thirteen, she was sent to Vienna to stay with her mother's friends, the British ambassador and his wife. There she learned to speak German before returning to take A-levels at a Cambridge convent school. She arrived at Somerville College in 1970 to read politics, philosophy and economics. Her interest in government and economics was cemented during these years.

'Society was changing very fast. There was the issue of the trades unions – we hardly think about it now, but when I was studying their place and their history was incredibly important, for example, to the extent you were trying to control inflation. It got worse for a period, until the early eighties when Mrs Thatcher and Mr Tebbit decided they had to do something about it.'[15]

Neville-Rolfe's career in the Civil Service spanned more than two decades, beginning in the mid-seventies in the Fisheries Department looking for new fish resources. Her job took her from fishing communities to research laboratories in Hull; she recalls that there was a huge effort to get British people eating more mackerel. After a stint in the Civil Service's training college, she returned to the Ministry of Agriculture, Fisheries and Food, this time focused on cereals. The 1976 drought, with the shortage of hay and straw felt keenly by farmers, led to government intervention to support agriculture. This was her first experience of crisis management, learning skills that would be useful in later years at Tesco. The job also gave her first-hand experience of negotiating in the EEC. One of

Neville-Rolfe's last big projects in agriculture was a review of 'greener' uses of agricultural land. In 1992, as Margaret Thatcher left Downing Street and John Major entered in her place, Neville-Rolfe had been promoted to the Number 10 Policy Unit. Her projects included immigration policy and then deregulation and the Citizen's Charter. The latter gained popular infamy as the origin of the 'Cones Hotline' – an outcome that Neville-Rolfe describes as a 'PR disaster', though she believes the initiative itself raised standards in areas of public administration such as schools and transport where it introduced comparative 'league' tables.

She met her husband in the Civil Service: he was a principal private secretary and she was a private secretary. Neville-Rolfe says her ability to keep working throughout her boys' childhood depended upon having excellent nannies and two back-up plans (in the form of childminders and her parents on standby). 'Not turning up is not an option,' she says. 'In those days, you couldn't say you needed to go home for the children if you wanted any credibility or you wanted to get on.'[16] After he retired, her husband took over the management of the house.

By 1997, and with the arrival of Tony Blair's New Labour administration, she felt that the Civil Service was altering. 'Labour was suspicious of the bureaucracy. We had assumed they would use the civil servants in the way that the Tories had done, but because they had been out of power for a long time they did not believe we were truly independent. They brought in a lot of their own people, like Ed Balls, to fill those jobs. I got on well with them but I think generally you could see the way that the Civil Service would change. It is now in transition from the old, independent system towards the American system, where every eight years the top echelons move out into academia, law, business and there is a general swap round.'[17]

When a call from a head-hunter slipped past her secretary, Neville-Rolfe decided to find out about a role that sounded interesting.

'I had been dealing a lot with Sainsbury and very rarely with Tesco. John, Lord Sainsbury, was a great friend and a role model. I had some good vibes about Tesco from when I was a child and had shopped there, and I thought it was innovative and growing. Terry [Leahy] wandered into my first interview and we immediately got on. We had a conversation about risk. There was a problem about food safety and over-regulation. We talked about land use and politics. I had no business experience.'[18]

She joined in August 1997. 'I was quite surprised and faintly horrified by the mixed nature of people I was going to have to manage. In the Civil Service you always have people of a certain intellectual standard who are fairly well trained. I had a small team of fifteen or twenty people dealing with the media, with internal communications, investor relations and government affairs. Some were great characters, but the idea of them talking to government ministers given the state of their hyperbole was extraordinary. I also looked after property public relations, persuading people of the value of the property plans.

'I had had very little management training in the Civil Service. Giving strong feedback to people who were creative, and wouldn't necessarily do what you told them to, was a learning experience for me. I found warring factions. It was a challenge.

'The quality of the senior executives was extremely high – very professional, articulate, always friendly, disciplined and caring about their people. There were a lot of skills that were different to the Civil Service; it was much more different than I'd expected. You learn in the Civil Service to do lots of analysis and to write good memos. I had to learn how to talk more and write less, and to learn how to make sure I was heard in meetings. I often had the infuriating experience of making a point, nobody heard it and then twenty minutes later somebody else would make it, some Tesco man, and everybody would say what a good point. I learned that you had to be clearer and more repetitive and develop emotional intelligence as well as the intellectual and analytical skills [which are] important in the public sector.'[19]

Neville-Rolfe is one of a handful of British women to have secured a seat on the main board of a FTSE 100 company. She joined the

Board in 2006 as a member, having been company secretary since 2003. She built her team from a range of backgrounds to reflect the different specialisms within Tesco's corporate and legal affairs department. The department was arguably Tesco's most diverse in terms of functions and expertise. It includes specialists from the Civil Service, lawyers from City firms, pensions experts, insurance and accountancy specialists, PR and investor relations professionals, events managers, climate change and charity experts and former journalists. Neville-Rolfe built relationships with most journalists covering the retail sector. She had meetings with civil servants and recalls one, in February 2008, with a Number 10 Policy Unit official, Geoffrey Norris, which illustrated the type of conversations Tesco has with government. 'We discussed the competition commission, regulation, nutritional labelling – traffic lights and guideline daily allowances – and what to do on alcohol. It is incredibly frustrating, because we think it would be good for the industry to get together and try to stop the war of [alcohol] promotions. One of the ways you get people into your stores is by a beer promotion. You cannot individually, as a company, stop doing this: people will stop shopping with you. We'd prefer something on an industry-wide basis. Under competition law apparently that would be illegal. So we're trying to find a way of moving that forward.'[20] At the time of writing, the British government has ordered a minimum price for units of alcohol, following the Scottish administration's lead.

During her fifteen years at Tesco, Neville-Rolfe was involved in critical developments, in particular establishing the business in Central Europe, Asia and the United States, from Thailand in 1998 to India in 2008. Her work took her regularly to the different countries where Tesco operates, meeting international government officials, politicians, non-governmental organizations and journalists. She was instrumental in establishing Tesco's environmental pledges, an area that has come to be called Climate Change.

'We have had enormous change at Tesco, but it hasn't felt like change. It has felt like continuity because of the way we have branded it. We communicate change to our staff through our annual plan. Within that there are the customer plan, community plan, operations plan, financial plan and people plan. The key elements are reviewed each year. There are strategy sessions in September ahead of changes to the customer plan in February. There is always a bit of argy-bargy about what plans we're going to give priority to. Come February, there is a strong communication across the business so that people understand what they will be doing. People move across projects. It feels like continuity, not riotous revolution. It is the opposite in government, where not much changes but it feels like revolution. That's the way that ministers like it. They want every-thing to seem to be new and to change because that's the way they look good on telly. We're more interested in the result.'[21]

Neville-Rolfe was not the first Tesco person to understand the importance of talking to the politicians. Jack Cohen never missed an opportunity to buttonhole an MP, particularly at the height of the row over Resale Price Maintenance. Then, in the eighties, Ian MacLaurin realized the need for 'jaw jaw not war war', as he (and Sir Winston Churchill before him) put it, when Tesco was struggling to make its case for new sites. But whereas Jack had clear party-political sympathies (he was a paid-up Conservative), under Leahy Tesco would be apolitical. If Tesco sponsored an event or had a stand at one party conference, it would do so at every party conference. Neville-Rolfe recalls that it helped that Leahy was interested in public policy.

'He is a great marketer in all the best ways of marketing. He understands what is attracting people and what is going to make a difference. He has very high standards, criticizes where necessary but encourages and thanks you. He is also interested in public policy. I encouraged him to get to know the senior people – Tony Blair and Gordon Brown, not just the junior people who dealt with food. I felt Tesco was very good for society and for a party that was trying to help poorer people.

'We learned television and newspapers a bit together. Government Affairs was quite new. Tesco had realized Labour was going to win [in 1997]. I solidified the Tesco relationship with all the parties.

Labour coming back into power was concerned to create jobs for the less fortunate, the less skilled in society. Tesco was growing so it was creating jobs. We were training and developing people, so that was a fantastically strong potential bond. Our regeneration schemes linked in well with the New Deal in 1997. The recession of the first half of the nineties was still very much in people's memories.

'There were MPs who were complaining about the supermarkets: small shops felt they were going out of business because of super-markets and farmers felt they weren't getting good enough prices because of the way the supply chain worked. That eventually ended up with the competition inquiries.'[22] (The competition authorities' interest in supermarkets would lead to a series of official investi-gations; see Chapter 24.)

Supermarkets were rarely out of the news in the late 1990s and one in particular was making headlines. Asda had hit hard times until a pair of well-known retailers, Archie Norman and Alan Leighton, took it on. Jason Tarry, in 1999 working in Tesco's buying teams, picks up the story.

'In the second half of the nineties we were facing a resurgent Asda. They almost went bust, but the management team did a brilliant job. The key influence for them was the American Walmart business. Asda took a lot of influence from them. They were price-driven and a general merchandise and food store rather than a supermarket. They reconfigured, so much so that Walmart decided to buy them in 1999.

'That was a significant point in Tesco's development. We'd over-taken Sainsbury. We were starting to watch Asda as their prices were so competitive. Walmart taking over Asda, with all the threat that entailed – their scale, the devastation they had created in the States, where no one had been able to compete with them and had given up and tried to differentiate in other ways with limited success, so we were really concerned.'[23]

Tesco's reaction was to watch and learn: as ever, it tackled a successful competitor by copying, as Tarry explains. 'I remember a lot of discussion that this could be the best thing that has happened. When you are a follower it's easy. When you are a leader you've got blue sky and you have to create your strategy out of nothing.

'Asda being taken over had a galvanizing impact. I was seconded on to a small team to look at the impact. We had people looking at store development, customer service, staffing policies, pricing, ranging and sourcing and supplier management. I was looking at their supplier management.'[24]

Tarry tapped into contacts who had worked with or for Walmart, some of whom Tesco had inherited after recently buying stores in Thailand from Walmart itself. He asked how they worked with the American giant: what were the processes and cultures that lay behind the success? He was impressed by one example in particular. Walmart had a small supplier that it encouraged to take office space near its headquarters (in Bentonville, Arkansas) and increase the team working purely on Walmart to 130 people. Like many Walmart suppliers, Tarry recalls, this outfit had a lot of responsibility and worked almost as a subsidiary of Walmart. Tarry says this was the inspiration for Tesco's subsequent supplier business units.[25]

Tesco was among the businesses doing more to explain themselves to politicians and this was an era when the politicians wanted to listen. Blair's New Labour invested much time and arguably its biggest biscuit, Peter Mandelson, in wooing business. Sometimes they wanted more than to explain that New Labour was friendly. A case in point was the Millennium Dome. Almost as soon as Labour won the General Election in 1997, a decision had to be made about the controversial project that would be Britain's showpiece celebration. Mandelson backed it, but needed business to pay for it.

Neville-Rolfe recalls the negotiations. 'The most difficult relationship we had with government was over the Millennium. We all had to decide how to celebrate. The government wanted people to be interested in the Millennium Dome. It's a sign of where we [Tesco] were then that they didn't actually think of us first. They thought of Sainsbury and of Boots and were in discussion with them.

'We went to see the government. We decided we wanted to do an education project for the Millennium: a website we would create to which schoolchildren could contribute stories about themselves and their families. We spoke to Number 10 and they could see the advantage of having this linked into the Dome. They tried to get £12 million out of us. We didn't want to pay £12 million, but we did want to do the school project and we wanted it to be supported nationally. Eventually we agreed to set up our Schoolnet 2000 scheme and we showcased it in the learning part of the Dome. We had a very moving film made. That became the principal contribution from us to the Dome. We started a year before the Millennium. There was a lot of excitement. We were able to take parties of suppliers, supporters and journalists to look at the Dome while it was being constructed and it raised awareness that we were involved with education and with the internet.

'There was better buy-in from primary schools than from secondary schools; Computers for Schools is the same – there is more take-up with primary schools. Each of the fifty teachers we hired [for the Dome project] was linked to a store, they were Tesco-trained, they made project plans, they turned up to team meetings in stores and they learned management skills. Teaching at that date was not very touched by management techniques. Most of them got lost to teaching – having realized what they could do, most of them went off and did things like educational consultancy.'[26]

Tesco's regret was that the scheme did not establish itself nationally, as had been hoped.

As the new Millennium dawned, bug-free (despite widespread fear that computer dates would go haywire faced with a year ending in three noughts), Tesco's main issue remained space to grow. Planning appeals were relatively few, but by the end of the 1990s the pressure to stop large multiples expanding had hit new heights. Growth required imagination and a willingness to provide something unique in communities where Tesco's offer might be recognized as a valuable service. Neville-Rolfe remembers, 'We changed the way we did site location to keep pace with planning changes to try to encourage town-centre development – we called it going with the grain: Express, Metro and Regeneration stores. We sat down with the map of England of the most deprived areas that the government had published: they were called social-exclusion areas. We could build stores which would be the anchor for social-regeneration schemes. We added a partnership with the local employment agency, the local authority and the staff union USDAW to bring the long-term un-employed back into work. The idea was that these would all go through planning swimmingly and incredibly quickly, but of course it wasn't like that because planning is slow. However, we did get most of them through, creating thousands of jobs.

'It was satisfying to have the combination of being able to get growth for the company and also helping the more excluded in society through regenerating such areas.

'Seacroft in Leeds was our first Regeneration store. It was next to one of the worst housing estates in Europe. Southampton University did a study, paid for by Sainsbury, of the effect of the opening of this store, and the main finding of the study, totally unexpected, was that diets had improved in this deprived area and they put this down to the fact that there were cheaper fruit and vegetables. Our Value lines were readily available in this store and this had improved the diets by a significant statistical amount. We have found this again through our Express stores.'[27]

'At Beckton [another Regeneration store, in Newham, South London] sales were very poor to start with; it was a bit of a ghost shop. In time, customers came and also we were able to put our dot.com vans in and they were filling up for customers in St Katharine Docks and more affluent areas.

'Crime can be more of a problem in those areas – you have to have very good security. But it can also be easier. In a new area where people haven't really had shops they welcome it. Often these stores are well positioned on the road network, which helps distribution.'[28]

A series of controversial, food-related developments at that time caused a storm whose tail pulled retailers in behind it. As one example, Neville-Rolfe recalls the headlines that genetically modified foods created. 'Food safety should have been an opportunity not a problem. GM food was different. We stopped selling it. The focus groups were picking up the hysteria in the media, essentially whipped up by non-governmental organizations. We stopped selling it because customers didn't like it, not because we were opposed to it.'[29]

Tesco had learned from its history that being on the back foot, trailing events or competitors, stilted its potential. It was better to determine a course of action and then to throw every available resource at carrying out the strategy. Jack Cohen's high-profile rows with trademark owners in the 1950s had positioned him as the housewives' champion. Almost five decades later, Tesco again decided that it could give customers a better deal than the restricted distribution network of designer labels was allowing.

'We had a war with Levi's,' recalls Neville-Rolfe, who was interested to see whether the campaigning tactics used in politics could be applied to public relations. 'We were selling the jeans, which we bought up on world markets at half the price. They were selling at £50 then and we sold them for £25. That got them very annoyed. We were permitted to do this, but they took us to court. It ended up at the European Court of Justice. It was a high-profile row. Ultimately we lost in court. They decided that once goods had been put on sale, the trademark-owner, Levi's, could control them and we couldn't just undermine that. Trade Mark law was split into two: the European market and the world market. But in the meantime we had had a couple of years of campaigning. People understood that Tesco meant value, Tesco was for the consumer. We were trying to sell clothes (people had thought of us as a grocer before then). The campaign was very helpful. On the back of it we did special offers on Calvin Klein underwear and perfume.'[30]

Tesco also learned that it could at least build a relationship with journalists by sharing its knowledge about British consumers. There was a new appetite, in serious newspapers as well as the 'red top' press, for snippets about what people were mostly eating, wearing or aspiring to that week. Tesco, with its geographical spread across the nation and its unrivalled research ability, could help feed the demand for topical consumer information.

'People are always interested in the ways that lifestyles are changing,' says Neville-Rolfe. 'We made regional maps showing where people ate the most soup, or the colour of their socks. These sorts of stories enabled us to build relations, particularly with the tabloids. We did a deal with the *Sun*, a voucher deal, and it seems extraordinary now but they wrote favourable stories about Tesco alongside the deals. We shared the cost. The favourable stories were supposed to drive trade. That passed. I don't think the *Sun* thought it was terribly useful to them in the end in terms of the extra sales they were meant to be getting. But it helped to cement a confidence in us that we could deal with the tabloid newspapers, even the *Sun*, and in understanding from them that we liked consumers. We constantly tried to use research and stories from the stores to build this passion for the consumer, which, for me, is the really wonderful thing about Tesco.'[31]

However friendly relations with the press may have been, Tesco, like all other businesses, learned that nothing was off the record and anything was fair game. Yet media coverage was proportionate, Neville-Rolfe recalls. 'It wasn't an overwhelming wedge of press cuttings then as it is now. We didn't then have this questioning about supermarkets, and about Tesco in particular, as a tall poppy that you got from about 2004/05.'[32]

Coverage remained UK-centric. Tesco's growth abroad, though known and understood inside the company, was under-reported in the UK media. With the exception of France, the countries into which Tesco first moved were little known and even less understood. The foreign strategy, though, would be instrumental in transforming Tesco and would come to define the Leahy era.

Chapter 21

Foreign Fields: How Hungary Answered the European Question

'We had two disasters. We tried to run the Irish stores from Cheshunt. There was a great Irish rejection of Tesco. The other one was Catteau. Our team went in and the French ganged up against us.'

Lord MacLaurin[1]

'We wouldn't be number two in the world if we hadn't made that leap and taken that risk. You've got to make that stretch if you really want to stay ahead.'

Sir Terry Leahy[2]

On 23 October 1956, in a small town in the east of Hungary, a fourteen-year-old boy listened to a radio in the cellar of the technical college where he boarded. Just listening to Voice of the West was illegal under the Soviet-backed communist regime. Miklos Walastyan, whose father had been jailed because he would not toe the party line, was one of thousands of students who responded to the call to rise up against their oppressors. After an evening spent burning communist books and flags in the town square, the boys were locked into the college by the headmaster. A small group decided to escape, making it out of the building and passing each other their bicycles over the perimeter fence in the middle of the night. Four of them headed west towards the Austrian border; two of them made it together. One was Miklos. He intended to head for

South America's balmy climate and beautiful people. He wound up in a disused army camp near Swindon, England, changed his name to Mike and got a job at Anthony Jackson's Food Fare. He was not to return to his homeland for thirty-three years.

Why is this relevant to Tesco's story? Because, were it not for Walastyan's entrenched hatred of communism and his equally strong enthusiasm for Britain and for Tesco, the company's first successful foreign adventure might not have happened.

A chance encounter between then managing director David Malpas and Walastyan at the Eastville store (Bristol), which he was running, encouraged Tesco's leaders to have a look at an unlikely corner of Europe, despite the company's unhappy experience in Ireland in the early eighties and in France. Tesco was interested in going overseas, but its first forays had not been positive.

Lord MacLaurin recalls the Irish problems. 'We bought the man who started Kwik Save, Albert Gubay's, business – 3 Guys [in 1979] – because it was available. It was a good business. The Irish didn't like Tesco. We didn't do any proper research. We changed the names and it just didn't get it off the ground. We sold it for round about what we paid for it. I don't think it was anything to do with the economy. It was to do with our expertise and the way we got the trading methods wrong.

'You can say the same about Catteau [in France]. We got the management wrong. We shouldn't have left the [Catteau] family there. It was a very bad decision.'[3]

The Catteau acquisition was announced in December 1992 and completed the following June at a cost of about £150 million for ninety-two stores in northern France, the land that created the hypermarket. MacLaurin was optimistic and the theory, in his 1993 Annual Report, sounded good. 'We have been looking for a suitable European partner for some years. [Catteau] is a successful food-retailing company of the right size, with an excellent track record of profitability and growth; it offers potential for further expansion; it has a strong management team in the Catteau family and their senior executives, who will continue to run the business; and Tesco will be able to offer the local management the benefit of our buying, distribution and systems skills. Catteau will give us the opportunity to learn more about food retailing in France and about trading in the new European environment.'[4]

Sir David Reid recalls the decision. 'It wasn't a global plan: it was "Let's go into France, let's start to understand what it's like to trade overseas." We chose France because it was nearby, but they then changed the French planning laws, which meant you couldn't go there and open large stores. It became pointless. After two years of tootling along we sold out and took the money back [Catteau was sold for £250 million in 1998]. It gave huge clarity to us. We realized that if we didn't compete with the major players abroad, sooner or later they would come over here and give us a very hard time or buy us.'[5]

Tesco learned that simply transferring its domestic ways of work-ing overseas was not enough. Sorting out the shops was hard; nailing the supply chain was tricky too. Ray Allcock joined Tesco in 1984, aged forty-two, bringing logistics expertise learned in British Rail's freight department. A large part of his career was spent modernizing Tesco's distribution centres, from the technology to the working practices, and much of this was focused on establishing networks in the overseas businesses. In 1992 he was Tesco's development director and remembers going into France.

'The distribution centre was pretty grim and desperately short of space. We invested a lot of money, not least on the supply-chain side. We put in a warehouse-management system. It was an off-the-shelf system from America, rather than the one that we had developed. It was a world-beating package, but we could never make it work in France so that it gave us the benefits we wanted. Perhaps our aspirations were too high for too quick a result.

'What killed the business or prospects, however, was that just after we had completed the purchase the French introduced a new planning regulation, which put the nail in the coffin of edge-of-town hypermarket developers. Those operators that already had a good property portfolio were very nicely placed, because nobody could grow up to be a competitor to them. Those of us with aspirations found ourselves blocked. All we could do would be to buy cast-offs: the dog store in the wrong place. We withdrew and we managed to get our investment back out, though I suspect there were a lot of costs that were not put against the French business. It was a sad little business.'[6]

Fortunately new prospects were emerging. The journey to Hungary came first, via Tesco's store in Eastville on the edge of Bristol.

Mike Walastyan had been in England so long that he had forgotten how to speak his childhood language by the time the former Soviet Bloc began to open up with the fall of the Berlin Wall in 1989. He had thought about writing letters home, but was frightened about the impact it might have on his family. He had not realized that it was possible to visit before then, but once restrictions began to ease he was quick to return. Armed with newly stamped British nationality and the passport to go with it, he returned and tracked down the elder sister and brother-in-law who had looked after him when he was young because his mother had had to take a job away from home while his father was in jail. Mike's mother died while he was in Britain, never having heard from him since he fled Hungary. The emotion in his voice when he speaks of his reunion with his siblings remains strong more than two decades later.

He was making annual visits to Hungary during his holidays, during which he began to pick up his mother tongue again, when Tesco's then managing director dropped into the Eastville store. Walastyan takes up the story.

'David Malpas came for a store visit in the summer of 1993 and I had come back from holiday. He asked where I had been because I was tanned. I said Hungary. "That's interesting," he said. "We've looked at a little company there who wanted some investment, but the language is impossible so we have not done anything about it." I said I could help with the language. Within a couple of weeks I got a call from the secretary to come to the head office at Cheshunt. David Malpas said, "Perhaps you'd like to take a couple of weeks out and take a look at the company?" That was October. I hadn't known Győr as a city, or the area. I was pleasantly surprised. It was a little bit more upmarket than the eastern side of the country. The stores [called S-Markets] were a bit messy but in the main in good positions. I reported back. David Malpas said, "Take six months out and do me a feasibility study of the retail business in Hungary. We'll see how we go." I was shipped off back to Hungary assigned to Global [which ran S-Markets] as a consultant.

'They were at a stage when turnover was decreasing. To save costs they turned off refrigeration on a cold day or turned out half the lights. It was a miserable shopping environment. We started refitting the stores from 2 January 1994. I presented my report to the Board on 14 February. A decision was made that day to invest £14 million in Global. Within twelve months I was chief executive officer of the company.

'The initial improvement of the stores for me was quite simple. These stores were a lot worse than I'd ever seen before, even in the early days of self-service. I appointed four regional managers and gave them company cars, which was almost unheard of. I assigned ten or twelve stores to each. We refitted the forty-three stores by September of 1994. We were achieving a 50–60 per cent increase in turnover. To maintain that growth we needed something else: we introduced a bonus scheme. All members of staff, whether shelf-fillers or managers, stood to benefit if they reached turnover targets, and other results, like stock or productivity, were acceptable. Every light was on all the time, all refrigeration worked all the time. We opened a new store at Szombathely at the end of 1994 and another in Győr. We had planned supermarkets. The mayor in Győr said there are other, larger sites around the city where you could develop something quite large. Were we interested? We were surprised. We visited France and hypermarkets there and started to make plans. We took on a consultant from Auchan [the French hypermarket company] and some staff and brought them to Hungary. We had a site in central Budapest, which was a bit more like a hypermarket: stand-alone – flat car-parking with other shops, though not part of a shopping centre.

'There had been virtually no progress in the stores in forty years of communism. The supply chain was very weak, packaging and presentation were very weak. We suggested to suppliers what to do. We started own-label development after trying to import Tesco lines which were not successful; locally produced own-brand was.

'The industry was not geared to public demand, it was geared to be comfortable for itself. [After the fall of communism] those who were not prepared to change fell by the wayside.

'The first store we refitted was opened on a Monday – 10 January 1994. The first customer who walked in said, "Suddenly, I thought I was in Austria." I introduced promotions: buy so much and get a kilo of sugar or a loaf of bread, which delighted the customers, who had never seen that before.'[7]

The Hungarian business taught Tesco a lot about taking account of local habits – lessons already learned to an extent on home soil at stores in London such as Brixton, Hayes and Finchley, but magnified here. Hungarian shopping habits were completely different. Women 'nipped out before breakfast for fresh bread rolls', so shops opened at 6 a.m. Most women had jobs, so they stopped on the way home to buy supper. It was an issue of time rather than storage – most Hungarian families had allotments and kept a refrigerator on their land as well as in their home.

Walastyan saw the possibilities for reducing the number of trips these busy women had to make. Modern retail meant that British women no longer shopped the way their grandmothers and mothers had, and Hungary was ripe for change. Another British export was store layout: Hungarian customers were used to shopping along horizontal lines, walking 25 feet to see a whole range of fruit juice. British shoppers could stand still and scan the full range. Hungarian women were greeted by washing powders as they walked into a shop. British women encountered fresh fruit and vegetables. Walastyan says staff, as well as customers, welcomed the changes, not least the new jobs created, the overtime system and bonuses.

'I managed to achieve a similar status in Hungary that Ian MacLaurin had in the UK. Ian came on a visit. The staff were excited and the stores looked wonderful. Ian was quite clearly pleased. He said to a lady manager and the area manager, "Your store is beautiful and nicely kept – you obviously work very hard." They broke down and cried. He had this effect even though he could not speak the language. I had to translate. I was choked up. I knew they worked hard but it was nice to see he appreciated it.'[8]

Walastyan spent four years running Tesco's stores in Hungary, to his sister's delight: she regarded him as a returning hero, bringing modern shopping with him. However, opening up retail after communism brought risk as well as reward. Walastyan recalls attempts by leading brand manufacturers to corner the market with 'shady practices' that he blocked. 'Coca-Cola was prepared to pay a bonus if you kicked back Pepsi, but that was not the way to do business, though some of the buyers were doing quite well. They were not taking account of the customers and how this practice would damage loyalty.'[9]

Hungarian customers and businesses were used to fixed prices – a sort of extreme, communist-run version of the old Resale Price Maintenance laws in Britain. That meant 'there was no incentive to do it better, cleaner or cheaper'. Walastyan describes improving efficiency in logistics so that he could lower prices.

It was the Hungarian habit to keep all the fresh food in the back of the store until the goods already out on the shelves had sold through. 'Supplies went stale in the back room before they even hit the shelves. I made them put the fresh stuff out and reduce the stuff that had gone bad. Everything was Hungarian. It was virtually impossible to get fresh cucumbers out of season. All of that has changed: the growers and farmers have acquired skills from other EU states. People have moved into farming here, even though [until recently] land is rented because they cannot own it. The supply chain has improved beyond recognition.'[10]

Having identified logistics as a main issue, Tesco's distribution expert Ray Allcock was transferred to Hungary to help Walastyan. He recalls how well educated the warehousemen were in Hungary; if their practices were dangerous and inefficient, it was because the old management had set up a nonsensical system of penalties. Allcock explains: 'The warehouse was desperate. There was one man that the manager trusted. He was the supervisor, a great big, burly man with a walrus moustache who spoke not a word of English. He was in his early thirties. Nothing went in or out but that this chap personally checked it; the throughput was set by what he could check. If stock was short it came off the wages. The way [the management] had ensured wages didn't get docked was that nothing happened until it was all checked, so stores were not serviced well. There was very poor availability and it was arbitrary. The stores sometimes didn't have key products, such as cooking oil and paprika.

'A buyer would order a vast quantity to get a good price and it would get dumped in the warehouse. People were clambering over stacks and climbing up the racking. People were hanging off the top with one hand and easing a case off with the other. The chap below would catch and then give it to another chap. It was very inefficient and terrible for the store.

'In the UK we happened to have just taken over William Low [the Dundee-based supermarket group]. They had their own fleet of roll cages, which were not the same sort as Tesco's. We got them for a song. We decided to test 'rollability' in the warehouse. We had to have full roll cages. We filled one with new wheels with apple juice in Tetra Paks; [in] the other one, we put the same quantity of tomato juice. Considerable interest began to be taken in what we were doing. After a bit, the supervisor came along. A young Hungarian employee [who also acted as interpreter] was chatting away to them. The supervisor said it would be a better test if there was the same weight. I said there was the same weight. "Oh," he said, "is it?" I said, "Yes. Same number, same size." He said, "So the specific gravity of apple juice is exactly the same as it is of tomato juice?" There was a difference of 12 kilos. It made his day. All the Hungarians loved that, naturally. Thereafter we were on very friendly terms. My estimation rose of this chap as to how bright he was. He went on to make a very good career with Tesco and left his dust-coat days. He is now the number two on the supply-chain side in Hungary.

'The warehousemen were very intelligent. I was told they were very well educated because one of the strengths of the communist system was education was superb. Teachers had a very high status. Every child learned an instrument. But by 1994 teachers were hardly able to live on their salaries because inflation was rampant.'[11]

Allcock stayed in Hungary to open up the distribution centre outside Budapest, built to service the emerging hypermarkets. 'The site was an old small-arms factory, bought by a German property director who put a decent floor and doors in because he was going to make the office block into a hotel.

'Personnel said we should have similar wages in the warehouse as in the stores [which were lower]. But the effect was wages for warehousemen in Hungary were not competitive. We couldn't attract or retain high-quality people. There was tremendous turnover and an awful theft problem. I became a bit paranoid and was very grateful for the antecedents of the building because it had stout fences. I used to patrol every morning. I cleared undergrowth and raked the soil so we could see where footmarks led to the fence and goods were thrown over. But whatever we did, the ingenuity of thieves was always one step ahead of the paranoia of management. We had an awful problem when we needn't have done. We did not have that in Győr.'[12]

Allcock was one of about forty Tesco people who eventually came out to join Walastyan, who admits to having felt isolated in his 'commie block' flat. Reluctant to arouse suspicion among his still wary post-communist-era Hungarian colleagues about how much information he needed to send back to the UK, he would fire up his laptop at home at night and send figures back via a telephone modem. He says suspicion was mixed with quiet resentment towards him for having 'defected' and returned in a high position. His efforts to build relationships – a feature of work that all Tesco people who work abroad highlight – paid off eventually. 'I chose to take early retirement [in 1997]. I couldn't give a satisfactory explanation for the people here, but sixty is the age to retire here and I was not that far away. At my farewell do I gave a speech, then a senior executive could hardly deliver his because he was crying. I grew to be very fond of the people in the business and they grew to be fond of me.'[13]

By the time Walastyan retired, he had built a business whose turnover was growing by about 20 per cent every year in real terms, not including inflation. The stores had large ranges, more modern display techniques and checkouts, and good conditions for staff, including part-time working. 'That was one of the things they said would never work here, but fortunately that was not the case. People wanted it.'

It took about two or three years to turn a profit, as Sir David Reid describes. 'We get criticized [in the UK] for being too big, for making so much profit, but half of that is because we got off our backsides and decided we were going to compete internationally and now those businesses around the world produce about £1 billion. Produce is local. The stores are plugged into the global supply chain so they can have things they wouldn't have had before. We work with the growers to train them up to produce better quality: quality has improved dramatically. The stores in Hungary are amazing.'[14]

Lord MacLaurin, who retired from Tesco the same year as Mike Walastyan, says, 'When I left in 1997, Budapest was one of our most successful stores in the whole group. In Hungary, we were able to miss three or four generations of development that we'd gone through in the UK.'[15]

Sir Terry Leahy says that the French and first Irish investments taught Tesco to explore markets with clear growth possibilities. 'In the early stages there was not much research; we sort of staggered into Central Europe, really. But there were some wise decisions. We didn't go further east, which was the correct decision. Ten years ago Russia didn't feel it was making economic and political progress. With the oil boom it has made a lot more economic progress; whether the political institutions are stronger is open to question.'[16]

Reid was heading up the international development team when Tesco invested in Hungarian stores. Part of his job was to check that owners' claims tallied with what he could see with his own accountancy-trained eyes before Tesco parted with cash.

In 1995 he flew to Poland to meet Ryszard Tomaszewski and George Glinka, who owned a group of stores called Savia located near Poland's southern border. Arriving at a 'godawful' hotel at eight o'clock and finding that there was no food to be had after 6 p.m., Reid and his Polish hosts moved negotiations to the bar. 'These two had a vision,' Reid recalls. 'Over these beers, George, and Richard, in particular, said, "The reason we are doing this deal is because we think we can be the biggest chain in Poland." He promised if we gave him the leadership he would make it the biggest in Poland. That is what happened.'[17]

Tesco was not the first international retailer into Poland and the business needed an experienced hand to guide it. Kevin Doherty, then fifty-three, had run stores and regions, and had established systems, such as scanning, for Tesco. He recalls the director in charge of personnel, Michael Wemms, telling him, "'Kevin, you've been nominated, the Board have agreed you should go, but it's entirely your decision and I'm very happy to keep you – there's no black mark." Then Philip Clarke saw me in the corridor and he said, "I hear you're off to Poland."'[18]

Doherty agreed with his wife that he would commute between Poland and Hertfordshire, packed and was soon acquainting himself with thirty-three Savia stores and one Tesco shop in the former communist country. 'The idea was to understand Polish culture and the market. Out there were all the big hypermarket operators: Carrefour, German discounters, Metro, Casino (Géant), Auchan – the ten top operators in the world were all in Poland. There were 38.9 million people there. We were the latest in and we were employing about 400 people.

'We didn't have our own talent pool. The first thing I tackled was getting the Poland team on my side, asking them a lot of questions about what they thought. People in the communist regime were very rarely asked their opinion. All the other companies had their own managers so there was little progress for Polish people. I promised them that the [store] managers would be Polish and the first area manager would be Polish.

'We made a lot of mistakes. We had to go out and get the experience. Suppliers were selling us whatever they wanted to because these young buyers were going through a learning curve. You can't put twenty years' experience on young shoulders.'[19]

Doherty did what had worked for him in the UK when he was asked to set up scanning and copied Sainsbury's: he borrowed from the opposition. 'I went to the hypermarkets and looked at their ranges. Auchan was good on ambient, Géant at textiles and Carrefour at hard lines [goods such as electricals and homewear]. I took on three Polish people working for these companies. They had been trained in France; they understood hypermarkets. All of a sudden our buying margin went up. We moved all the inexperienced people we had into other roles – we didn't lose people. The people I brought in brought their buyers in. I made Ryszard Tomaszewski the first area manager. I spent a lot of time developing the people because if I was there for ten years I wouldn't have understood the market the way the locals would. We developed processes and systems and an operating model to roll out to all the other stores.

'We picked the five most important things: the people in the business; a process and a system for everything we did in the store; good succession planning for future stores; a sound marketing campaign; and a really good supply chain.'[20]

Tesco bought a further thirteen stores from a German company called Hit and integrated them in twelve weeks. Merging two head offices was difficult as people were moved into other roles or out altogether and contracts with suppliers were negotiated.

Within a decade, Tesco had more than fifty stores and was Poland's biggest retailer, picking up business awards and employing more than 22,000 people. Doherty's first driver, Bogden Felix, became a hypermarket manager. 'It was a fantastic feeling. Most of the stores we opened, about 40 per cent of the people we took on hadn't had a job for more than two years because unemployment was high.'[21]

Doherty's role meant he rubbed shoulders with VIPs at trade

events. He recalls, 'I talked to Prince Charles about how Tesco develops young people. I never would have thought that I would do that when I was growing up in Walthamstow. When I met Mary McAleese I didn't realize she was president of Ireland. She was from Roscommon and she knew the Dohertys in Cloonagh. You could run a company out there and let it go to your head, though it isn't very glamorous. You have to work very hard.'[22]

Tesco learned about discounting and non-food retailing in Hungary and Poland. This accelerated the development of Tesco's Extra format, the first of which opened in Pitsea, Essex, in 1998.

Doherty's description of Tesco's Polish hypermarkets in the mid-nineties is less startling to today's British consumers than it would have been then, although up to 90 per cent of the products in the Polish stores were nationally sourced. 'In Poland, people buy crockery by weight. You come in and on the right-hand side the aisle has a huge range of non-food, of home entertainment, bigger than you'd see here – six long runs of 60 feet each of CDs and videos and DVDs, then stationery and computers, then homewear – pots and pans, then a range of electric kettles, toasters, fifteen types of slicers for cooked meats, then refrigerators, freezers, televisions, hi-fis, baskets and bicycles. In May, because it is [Holy] Communion month in Poland and everybody gets a present, you can sell 4,000 bicycles in an average store. You have all the fresh foods, bakery and your counters right along the back wall, then facing that is a huge textile range of clothing. Then you move into grocery and down the left-hand wall is all the alcohol – beers, wines and spirits – then across the front you'd have your produce. There are anything from thirty to [sixty] checkouts.

'Then there are the shopping malls. In Kraków we had 100 shops in malls, which we owned and let out. We didn't know how to do it when we opened up. We brought the expertise on board and gradually we filled all our shops. It's a big family day out in Poland to come to the mall and shop and eat.

'There are a lot of towns which don't have the number of people to justify the hypermarket, so we opened 2,000-square-metre stores, a bit like a discount store. They are destination discount stores with a hypermarket offering.

'Finding sites is hard. Sometimes we [would] take the compromise location if we knew it was unlikely that somebody else was going to come in because there wasn't enough business to sustain more than one.

'Everybody thought we weren't going to survive in Poland and [within] three years we were ahead of everybody. We had a really good reputation in Poland. We were the only company that had subsidized staff restaurants. People wanted to work for Tesco. They knew they had a future in Tesco. I'm proud of that.'[23]

Doherty describes a cross-industry group set up to discuss ways of working. 'We thought it would be fantastic to get manufacturers to make everything [in boxes or crates] so we could make it easier for our staff to [put them straight on to the] shelves. You start putting pressure on manufacturers and retailers to make the industry more efficient. I was the co-chair. I had a lovely meal with the chief executive of Auchan in Warsaw. He had been in the business twenty-five years. We had the same passions, similar careers and similar-sized families. You can be fierce competitors and still be companions. We never talked about business: we couldn't because of trade secrets.

'In Poland, you have store-specific pricing, which is very different to here. Competitors check each other day by day. It is a really ruthless market. We had a price-checker in every store. In the early years we probably weren't very competitive, but as we became more effective in monitoring the prices of competitors we have come out on top. There's a danger you take your foot off the pedal on price. The minute you do that you are dead. You have to invest your profit in price. Prices are key. You can't stop that. That's what happened with Géant [who lost ground to Tesco]. People out there are very shrewd. They don't have a lot of money. They know if you put [a Zloty] on and they switch. As painful as it is, you have to make sure you are really competitive on price.'[24]

Polish families, he says, reminded him of the way people shopped when he was growing up and had a job in working-class parts of London. 'Normally the eldest person in the family supports the family. They don't have big refrigerators, so they shop little and often. People generally have little disposable income and as soon as they got paid they shopped. I felt for them. I remember how poor we were. It is hard to walk around a store and see this great array of televisions and things and not be able to afford them. There are some very affluent people in Warsaw – you can sell Sony televisions there, but not in the poorer cities. It is an incredible country. I was in our Brookfield store [in Hertfordshire] working in the shop in the three days before Christmas. I thought, "Look at the money these people are spending. Imagine that this could be Poland in ten years." Value lines are very successful in Poland because they give reasonable quality at affordable prices. The Polish shoppers are always looking for bargains.

'Tesco was the first retailer in Poland to open twenty-four hours, in Warsaw and Kraków. Everybody thought it was a big joke, that we were mad. But it has been a big success. You can open there twenty-four hours every day of the week. Sundays are very busy out there.'[25]

Doherty left Poland in 2004, after three parties and holding a book of 16,500 signatures and messages from the staff, which was presented to him at a party in Kraków for 550 people. 'I felt terrible leaving. When we went to the airport five of the management team were waiting there at 6.30 in the morning to say goodbye. Some of my Polish friends come out to my place in Spain. It was the second most stressful job in my life, but it was also probably the most rewarding. I thank the Board for putting that trust in me at fifty-three years old.'[26]

Kevin Doherty was awarded the OBE for his services to commercial relations between Britain and Poland.

Afterwards, he spent six months recruiting staff from Poland to come to the UK. 'They add a lot of value to our stores and distribution centres. They deserve the opportunity. They can earn five times more here. Over there, 40 per cent of their graduates cannot get jobs.'[27]

It was one of the first examples of staff travelling to different countries to gain experience: British employees going abroad and foreign nationals coming to the UK. Ryszard Tomaszewski, the original Savia man who asked for Tesco's investment, worked in the north of England before returning to Poland as chief executive. Doherty says it was one of his proudest moments. George Glinka's Tesco journey has taken him to China.

At about the same time as Doherty and Walastyan were building businesses in Poland and Hungary, a group of former Kmart shops in the Czech Republic came up for sale. Tesco's Hungarian and Polish shops were close to the Czech border so, although they were in different countries, geographically the radius was not large.

Ray Allcock was transferred from Hungary to the Czech Republic to streamline the distribution and supply networks. 'There was no central distribution at all. We had bought a set of department stores but they were nothing like John Lewis. Kmart had run them since 1989. They had changed and improved the job lot very significantly, but they still weren't awfully good and particularly not in the supply chain. Suppliers delivered straight to stores in Prague and got into trouble with the police for blocking the roads. The answer was a central distribution centre to service the department stores and the new hypermarkets.

'We hadn't been clear which format was the most successful and decided while we were there that the format would be hypermarkets. First of all, they seemed popular when our competitors opened one. Secondly, hypermarkets were the only way to grow a big market share in a reasonable amount of time. You can get from 0 to 10 per cent of a market share with six hypermarkets. They were to have 65,000 different products, compared to the UK average of 40,000. The range would include ski equipment, bicycles, gardening equipment and clothing. We have learned from that and brought the benefits back to the UK.

'We had to persuade suppliers it would be cheaper to drive 100 kilometres away to the provincial town where the distribution centre would be. People in the UK said it couldn't work.'[28]

For his part, Allcock decided UK expats wouldn't work. 'It was outside their experience and they were too expensive.' He went for people with aptitude rather than experience to operate a brand-new logistics system called Gold. They got it from a French company and felt it was superior to the American Dallas system being used by Tesco in the UK. In fact, the teething troubles were unexpectedly painful.

'We trained our unfortunate Czechs with a Frenchman using very quirky English. While you are filling up a warehouse and not shipping you can concentrate. The management team worked seven days a week, using Sundays to catch up on traumas [that had occurred] during the week.'[29]

Before the system went live, the new team felt they had got the hang of the operation. The reality of the first day came as a huge shock: so many people wanted to get into the stores and at the special offers that Allcock recalls gridlock traffic in that part of Prague. Stores had to close their doors to regulate the queues to get inside. 'We in the warehouse were hearing all these rumours of tremendous success and we waited for our first order. It never came. We phoned the store and said, "Where is your order? Just something to get us started." They said, "We've sent it off three hours ago." Our faces fell because it should have come through at once. A black hole had developed. It couldn't be resurrected. The next day the store needed replenishment badly. It was the second day we were on the phone to the store saying "What would you like? We'll send it." Little lists on backs of envelopes were made. All our work of putting every-thing in exactly the right place and the computer in the right format, all of that went out of the window. All that I'd told my management team to expect went to dust.

'It took weeks to clear the trauma. I felt I was exploiting people, but they were happy to do it and had such enthusiasm for it.'[30]

Tesco's adventures in Central Europe and the lessons they were bringing back for the British shops had given the company confidence, despite the difficulties. The 'disastrous' first visit to Ireland felt a long time ago by 1997 when Tesco made a fresh attempt. Leahy describes the takeover of Powers Supermarkets, trading as Quinnsworth in the Republic and Stewarts in Northern Ireland, when they came up for sale.

'It was the biggest corporate takeover in Irish history,' explains Leahy. 'The business was owned by Associated British Foods, which was quoted on the London Stock Exchange and owned by a Canadian family, but being bought by Tesco was seen as a much more significant change. This expression of British economic power in Ireland had political consequences and so we were not that welcome. Over five years we had to earn our permission in the broad sense to operate there. We had to demonstrate that we were good for the society, that we would understand the social consensus that operates in Ireland, work with unions, employers, suppliers, farmers, consumer organizations and work through the political and social change taking place in Ireland at the time. As Ireland has modernized, we have modernized the business there. We are a good employer and a good retailer and those things are valued in Ireland.

'The town centre in Ireland is stronger [than in the UK]. Population density is still higher. You haven't had the urban sprawl in Ireland you saw in the UK, though it is coming now. People shopped regularly; they bought less each time and shopped around more. That was partly because people had less money at the time and partly because there were less good shops, so you had to shop around various places to get what you wanted.

'The Irish government asked for a commitment to purchase a substantial amount of Irish produce. We'd made some similar [voluntary] commitments elsewhere. I don't think any Irish business has ever made those commitments. We negotiated for that to be voluntary and then we were happy to do it and happy to see it through. Perhaps it reflected this surprising concern about this large British company coming into an important part of Irish life. There is a strategy for economic development in the island of Ireland, but the politics in the late nineties were not at the stage where you could contemplate combining the two businesses. They are two sovereign nations. We don't do that anywhere else. For practical, historical, commercial and political reasons they have been kept separate.'[31]

David Potts, one of Tesco's highest-rated store operators by that point, was dispatched to Ireland. It was a conscious attempt to avoid the mistake of the first Irish adventure and to repeat the lesson of doing business in Central Europe. Ireland had to have its own executive. It would not be 'run out of Cheshunt'. Potts explains, 'Three or four of us went over. Ireland was just emerging into the Celtic Tiger era. It was getting a lot of subsidies from the European Union and unemployment was starting to fall. There remained a high degree of scepticism, suspicion and conflict between England and Ireland, and therefore all things British were not exactly welcome in Ireland. Tesco had unsuccessfully gone in there a generation ago and pulled out. I flew to Brussels and met a professor who knew about acquisition and talked to him and that helped. I asked Laura Wade-Gery [who left Tesco in 2011] to join me: she came from a consultancy. She and I laid out a plan for the Republic of Ireland where we kept the leadership team in place and we went 'softly softly' on what consumers wanted. Tony Keohane was part of the original leadership team, Quinnsworth, and he stayed with Tesco and is tremendously loyal.

'Bringing in produce would have meant centralizing distribution to Britain. There were a lot of vested interests. The government, lobbied by competitors who didn't want us, [wanted] £872 million exports from Ireland to the UK. We made that £1 billion in three years.

'I developed a lot of Tesco products that could be made in Ireland and sold in Britain and Ireland. It was a rural economy and we made good use of that land by putting technologies in to extend growing seasons and achieve better quality.

'In Northern Ireland the company [Stewarts] went bankrupt as we bought it: we had to clear an office of about 300 people and we ended up with an office of twenty people. We took courageous decisions and integrated within nine months.

'If you acquire a business you have to keep the best of what it does and if you go into another nation you have to respect the values and develop local people. We failed in Ireland first by doing none of those things. [With] Hillards and William Low [earlier acquisitions in the north of England and Scotland] we were probably pretty brutal, although they were good for growth. I feel we listened to customers and staff in Ireland in a way we had not done the first time. A bloke in Tipperary said, "I worked for you when you were here before. They used to do planograms where everything went from England and stuff came in a lorry." It was stuff like curry powder that had no relevance in Ireland then. We were very careful the second time around. We spent £700 million and we had to change everything without upsetting the government and getting chucked out.

'The UK didn't understand the Irish situation. Chaos broke out one day because the UK business had run an advert for meat – "All our meat is British – we can get it cheaper from Ireland, but we're not buying it." But a lot of newspapers printed in the UK were sold in Ireland, so the farming community went ballistic. I phoned Terry: "I've had the Taoiseach Mary Harney on the phone and this is serious. We've got farmers in the car parks." He asked me what I wanted. I said, "I want you to go and get the UK buying team to buy a load of Irish beef and promote it now", and he did it. The Irish watch your feet, not your mouth. When they saw the orders come back it went back to normal. I went to see the government and said that my UK colleagues had buggered up but they won't do it again. They took it in good faith.

'We had the RGData organization [the lobby group for in-dependent retailers in Ireland], whose mission it seemed to me was to disrupt Tesco in Ireland, briefing against us because they represent convenience retailers over there called Supervalu. Michael Campbell was the leader. He was a pain, but he kept us on our toes and made us do the right thing, so what came out of it was he made Tesco better.'[32]

Leahy explains that the timing of these moves into Central Europe and Ireland was because, by the mid-nineties, it was clear that a business that wanted to be world-class would have to travel. 'The UK represents between 2 and 3 per cent of the world's GDP and back then that was the average growth rate of the UK economy. The world economy was growing at some 5 per cent a year. In search of growth and in order to stay in the front rank you have to go out. So that's what we did.

'It is not easy, because the economics of retailing are very local so there is not much advantage in being an international operator. But we have stuck at it. We have had a lot of success, and probably more success than any other retailer in that period. It will take generations to create an international retailing business.'[33]

Chapter 22

Asian Tigers: How Tesco Travelled from Cheshunt to China

'We went on a trip and we picked the countries that we liked in terms of the culture, the politics, the economic growth prospects and so on. We had people living in people's homes, trying to get a sense for what would work.'

Sir Terry Leahy[1]

Tesco had been in Asia since Jack Cohen's day, when Leslie and Shirley Porter had made trips to Hong Kong to meet suppliers. Various general merchandise goods were sourced in the Far East – but generally through agents who acted as go-betweens for manufacturers and foreign retailers.

As Tesco watched Walmart more closely following the 1999 Asda acquisition, this began to change. Jason Tarry, part of the team exploring the American retailer's success (described in Chapter 20), observed how Walmart built direct relationships with Asian manufacturers.

'We decided to do what Walmart did. We'd identify manufacturers that had the capacity and capability to manufacture products in key parts of the world. We would form relationships directly with them. They would select ranges for buyers to approve, then do all the testing before shipping.

'You minimize the cost by going direct rather than through agents and you have got ownership and are able to protect your reputation around standards for production and for workers' welfare.

'We set up quickly and found buying teams were not ready. I was asked to head up sourcing offices and create that working relationship, embed it and develop it. I picked that up around 2001 and I loved meeting people, manufacturers across Asia, real entrepreneurs. What they were achieving was fantastic. Creating a flow of products into the UK was satisfying. We expanded the sourcing offices, opening an office in southern China and Shanghai, and in Turkey, which is a big fashion and clothing base and because it is closer you can turn around the product more quickly.'

Tarry explains that Tesco chose different locations for different products, based mostly on where the expertise was. 'It isn't as simple as choosing places where the labour is cheap. There are places in the world with skills in areas of manufacturing because of ancient and recent history. Delhi in India has a very strong reputation for tailoring because they always have made suits, and also for beading and embellishment, a tradition handed down from family to family. Beading and embellishment have been in fashion. You go directly where the expertise is and find you get the very best product at good, competitive prices. Bangalore is famous for cotton production and conversion into clothing, so that's why we went there. Southern China is famous for electronics and toys, so that's why we went there.'

Subsidies also help. 'Bangladesh is impoverished and has least developed country status with the European Union, so there is no importation or excise duty, so it's good to source from there.'

Tarry found that manufacturers had often never heard of Tesco. 'We developed presentations to inform factories about us. We talked about our strategy within their product area. We set up things to ensure it was attractive to work with us. We've got strict payment terms to make sure we pay them on time. Once the order had been fulfilled we paid within a certain number of [guaranteed] days, not waiting for it to arrive in the UK.

'If they perform to the right standard, quality and on time, we would have continuous relationships, not spot-buying. We have a couple of suppliers out of Hong Kong who have been dealing with us for over forty years and they are proud of that; they have grown with us. We're proud of what we've done with them.

'Trust and loyalty are important everywhere, but incredibly important where you have an owner-entrepreneur. Providing continuity and loyalty is important. It means you end up with a strong business relationship.

'We still buy a huge amount of product from the UK where it still makes sense to do so in terms of the quality or the cost prices; for example, all of our filled product – sofas, duvets, pillows – at the moment [are made] in the UK, [and] tights and lingerie; it's about going to the best place in the world. We go to Italy for pasta. Most of our meat is British.

'We belong to the Ethical Trading Initiative and sign up to the standards that requires. It's important that people adhere to those standards and it's important that we deal with people who are managing their business properly and ethically. This is a way of individuals being able to improve their quality of life through an export market. We're much more a force for good there.'[2]

His research resulted in Tesco transforming the Hong Kong quality-assessment office into a sourcing office, and several more were opened in India, Bangladesh and Sri Lanka.

Having made such reforms in sourcing, Tesco's knowledge of Asian countries was growing. In South Korea, a supermarket has to be more than the place people go to shop: customers want everything from violin lessons to keep-fit classes. Tesco's move into the country was made with a local partner: Samsung. The companies established a joint venture to operate hypermarkets, known as Homeplus, under the leadership of Samsung's Seung Han (SH) Lee. The hypermarkets cater for the Korean thirst for betterment as well as simple nourishment: it is the way to hold the number-one slot in that country. Sir Terry Leahy identifies this national drive to be number one as a key reason behind the invitation to Tesco to enter the country in the first place.

'Entering Asia from Europe in retailing is a big cultural challenge. Retailing is the most local of industries. You can't really export much that you have that is familiar in your home market. In the early years Korea was a relatively closed place and there were some informal barriers to entry while the local industries could become sufficiently large to be able to compete with international businesses. After the Asian financial crisis in the late nineties, Korea began to open up much more to foreign investment and to see it as a spur to its competitiveness, and it has prospered as a result.

'Tesco would have been one of the very earliest and most significant joint ventures in Korea. It was foreign to us and in a way it was foreign to Korea. It is an amazing place, with an incredible history and a very independent society having to fend off at various times China or Japan. You couldn't tell people what to do. They are a highly ambitious people. They wanted to be the best in the world. You had to prove that what you knew about retailing was the best in the world and if it wasn't they wouldn't adopt it. We had to do that by example, be patient and show we had things to teach the local management. Luckily, Tesco is blessed with some good retailers and some patient teachers. We didn't put many people over to Korea, but enough to provide a conduit through which we could help and teach as well as providing capital. We supported the Koreans, SH Lee and his team, at important times and I think they valued that. We supported them financially as well as in other respects. They have done a terrific job as leaders of the business in Korea. They have taken a lot of personal responsibility to create the best modern retail business in Korea as well as one of the best in the world. That is the advantage of local leadership. They have a sense of ownership of the business and a long-term investment in the business's success, so in a way they behave like Tesco people behave about the business in the United Kingdom. They think of it as their career and their legacy, which expat people don't always do. They are there for three or five years. To some extent your decisions can be over a shorter time-frame. It is good to have the balance where expats bring in expertise and local leadership feels ultimately responsible for creating a respected brand over decades.

'Korea is our most successful investment in Asia. Thailand and Malaysia have been very successful, but Korea is larger and more sophisticated. The business is closer to the UK business because the consumers have higher spending power. Culturally it is very sophisticated. It is a real leader of art and fashion in Asia.'[3]

One of the key moments for the South Korean business was the acquisition of the Homever chain, the second time those stores came up for sale. It was a fresh example of how critical new space is to a retailer's success.

'We had been looking at that business for a year or two. It came on the market when Carrefour [who had owned Homever] exited Korea. Walmart and Carrefour had both been in Korea before Tesco and had not been successful and had left. Tesco was more prepared to tailor our offer to the local market. In the joint venture we were more prepared to learn and be taught by the management of Samsung, led by SH Lee. Carrefour was not keen on selling to Tesco, funnily enough. We were in the original bidding process, but Carrefour sold to E.Land, who were textile retailers and good at it but had not really got experience of food and hypermarket retailing and they struggled. We were able to buy them second time around.

'It was quite important, in that it gave us a lot of stores in Seoul which had been built by Carrefour in the mid-nineties and which would be very difficult to build today, the land prices had gone up so much. These were priceless assets in a way and they gave Homeplus a more visible presence in Seoul, which has half the national GDP, and it gave Homeplus more scale and enabled it to challenge for the number-one position.

'We had had similar levels of success in Thailand and Malaysia. The scale of the Asian business was becoming more substantial and the margins were not far off what we were achieving in the UK. We quite quickly became the most successful international retailer in Asia.

'Tesco has built a unique position in Asia and there can be very few other British companies who are leaders [there].

'It has been a great privilege. I am not a lover of exotic places – I am worried by the unfamiliar. Asia has won me over with its remarkable humanity. There are hundreds of millions of people working for a better life, a better existence for themselves and their families, working incredibly hard individually, collectively, irrepressibly. People have always wanted a better life, but either the government or the state of the economy or technology hasn't allowed it, but despite the difficulties that has changed, and that has been an amazing thing to see.'[4]

To Westerners, Asian countries are often thought of in terms of just their major cities, and their sizeable secondary cities are sometimes under-recognized as considerable population centres in their own right. Selling food gives a retailer a far wider geography to explore than, say, designer handbags would.

'Because of our business, which is so local, you get out of the ersatz capital cities with their five-star hotels that could be anywhere and you get out into real places with real people and you get more of a sense of Asia, a sense of this amazing change that is being brought about, not by governments but by the sheer hard work of millions of men and women.

'The countries in Asia are very different in their history, government and climate. You don't know what will happen [and you can't] predict the outcome, although you feel you can shape it.'[5]

Those differences meant that China felt too foreign to risk investing in when Tesco first looked eastwards. Leahy explains, 'When we first looked at Asia in the mid-nineties we decided not to go into China. We felt it was too early. We needed some success in smaller places, the Asian Tigers, that gave investors confidence in us and allowed us to make the investment in China. We were late but not too late. China is a big place. It requires a big effort, a big capital effort. We will put something like £6 billion into China in five years – not all of it Tesco money, but we will be the lead investor. That is appropriate. To be a leading retailer in China, to be able to shape your future, you'll have to be a very big business.

'Of course it is not one place. China is a set of regions and so different supply chains, different brands and different tastes are successful. It is almost like entering five big countries.'[6]

Even living with families and researching on the ground for two or three years was never going to give Tesco enough local knowledge to tailor its offer for the Chinese. As with Thailand and South Korea, the route chosen was to work with a local business, Hymall, a Taiwanese-owned company that Tesco directors got to know when Tesco had stores in Taiwan. Hymall already had more than twenty hypermarkets in key Chinese provinces, plus a chain of convenience stores, a property-development company and the biggest noodle-manufacturing business in the country. Leahy explains the decision. 'China is a hard place to understand; you can look for years and not learn very much. A Taiwanese family has been there for a longer time and working with them proved to be a good idea. The Wei family [who owned Hymall] had built a good business. They were already in areas where several hundred of the most affluent people in China lived.'[7]

Sir David Reid said the strategy was to go steadily ahead of the eventual opening in 2004. 'We kept quite a low profile while we put the capability into this company. The stores are thousands of miles apart, so you have to have a regional strategy. The stores are mainly round Shanghai, Beijing, Guangdong in the south. China welcomes foreign direct investment and has opened the market up, unlike India. There are some good local operators there. They look at what you do and open up the same thing. They are very dynamic. Our stores are like street markets although they are much more sanitized. There is a hubbub over there. In China you come into non-foods first and then into fresh food. The amount of bread rolls those stores make and sell in a day is astonishing. Some of the ways fresh goods are displayed in China wouldn't be allowed here – it is too open, but in China it is more like the market. You lose some of the hustle and bustle over here.'[8]

The Chinese eat differently. No surprise, then, that the Chinese penchant for turtle meat has caused a row. Tesco's chief executive, Philip Clarke, says it is an example of having to bend to local tastes, but applying Tesco's values. He calls it 'appreciating the differences'. Clarke ran Tesco's international businesses for seven years and describes the ways in which the company adapted.

'When I was asked to run Asia and Europe, it was nine countries at the time. I was asked to help create the right Tesco in each of our markets. What Terry Leahy and John Gardiner [then chief executive and chairman respectively] were really saying was, it is all right to be different because all cultures are different and many countries have different climates and these dictate the way in which local consumers eat. The biggest difference about the stores in our Asian markets is that they are all very different from each other. Korea and China have extremes of high temperatures and very low temperatures. In Thailand and Malaysia they wear woolly hats when it hits 19 degrees Celsius because to them that is very cold.

'Our strategy was to build hypermarkets, but they look very different. The business in South Korea is called Homeplus. The business in China is branded Tesco but is known by the customers as Lurgo, or Happy Shopper because it was Hymal Lurgo [which means that] when we bought it.

'There are also incredible similarities to each other. What I really set out to do was to make sure that Tesco would be successful because it does what local customers want. The customers in northern South Korea, around Seoul, have different habits to those in the southern part. It's like the difference between the north of England and London – it is that stark. You have to be the number-one local business even though you are an international global organization.

'In the main, all the stores in China look the same as their fellow stores and the same is true of Korea. What is different are the products you sell inside those stores. In northern China, from Beijing across to Tianjin up to Shenyang is Liaoning province. The local delicacy is sea slug. You don't sell any sea slug in southern China. You go into a food hypermarket department in Dandong on the border with North Korea and there will be 50 linear feet of sea slugs. Down south, in Guangzhou, you are more likely to see a vast array of whole, fresh fish for the table. They are 2,000 miles apart, like flying from London to Greece and saying it is the same country. It is just not. The climate, culture, language are different.

'We had to recognize what was similar and only do those things once for a country or a region, such as IT, general merchandise and supply chains, but appreciate the differences and not reject them out of hand because through Western eyes it might look strange: appreciate them, benchmark what the locals do and do it better.

'We sell what customers want. We don't put in front of them things they don't want, because we've found when we do that they don't buy it. So long as it can be done ethically and humanely we'll sell what customers want. We won't sell things if they cannot be treated in a humane way. We don't sell many [turtles in China] – it is a delicacy – but there is a group of customers who will not come to your store if you don't sell them.

'The first market we went to was Thailand. The business there was opened and operated by a local conglomerate; we became a partner of theirs. It was the time of the Asian financial crisis. We took a business that already had established relationships with suppliers and governments, local and national, and already had a presence. We were able to take the strength of our operating model, of our technology, our know-how, our category management skills and our marketing skills to make it the market leader, which it is fifteen years later.'[9]

Tesco learned, says Clarke, that purely expatriate management could be problematic. 'In Malaysia we wanted a joint venture with another local conglomerate. We met with more resistance because we didn't quite take the time to appreciate where the government stood, what the non-government organizations thought. You have to play by the rules of the country. I remember in my first year the government telling us we shouldn't trade twenty-four hours because it might affect the mom-and-pop retailers. We discussed this with the CEO, who then went and traded twenty-four hours anyway and, surprise, surprise, the government said, "You won't be opening any more stores here for a while", and we didn't. We had to reverse that decision. You have to play by the rules. Malaysia, a fifty-fifty joint venture with multinational conglomerate Sime Darby, ten years later is the market leader, with a home-grown team and an expat chief executive.

'We had to learn that just because we are the biggest and best in the UK doesn't earn us any right to do anything anywhere else in the world. You have to put a lot of effort into understanding the way the land lies. In China we bought into a 50 per cent joint venture with a Taiwanese family who had twenty-five stores and today we trade out of 110, and there will be decades of growth. Because we bought into an established venture there were already a lot of people who understood. We brought our globally learned skills to apply locally. This has made us a strong force.'[10]

Tesco's success in Asian markets has been varied, and in fact after nine years it exited Japan in June 2012. The 117 shops made losses in 2010/11 and Tesco found a buyer for them. Clarke, Leahy and Reid all point to India as the country that demonstrates Tesco's ability to think laterally in order to keep growing, adapting its business model to suit local markets.

The first hurdle to operating any business in India is the country's restrictive laws protecting Indian companies against foreign competition. This means operating on the lines of joint ventures. Tesco agreed a partnership with Tata, the global giant whose international companies include Europe's second largest steel producer and Jaguar Land Rover and is run by the Tata family. Its Indian operations include the retail company Trent, which has companies selling furniture, books, music, fashion and the hypermarket chain Star Bazaar.

Clarke says, 'We entered India in 2008/09 not quite as a joint venture, because we are not allowed to invest directly in multi-brand retail, so we operate the hypermarkets for Tata and Sons. They have a lot of local knowledge. They had five stores. Now they have fifteen. They've got a chief executive officer, who runs it from their organization. We have got the chief operating officer. We've got the commercial and marketing and supply-chain organizations supplying the hypermarkets.

'When we took the decision to enter India in 2008 I explained to the Board we should consider it as an extended piece of research working with an outstanding partner, Noel Tata's Trent [the retail arm of the Indian multinational Tata], and we should think of India as somewhere for terrific growth in the next decade. It's an interesting piece of research. We enjoy the partnership a lot. There is a chance we could build in Bangalore and Mumbai, the two big markets we have chosen to be in, where we could get to be market leader with Star Bazaar. We can help them to get there. We can carry on for years in India without foreign direct investment being allowed in multi-brand retail.'[11]

Leahy, Tesco's chief executive when the decision was made to go into India, predicts that India will open up as China has done. 'India has too big a population to rely on being an exporting economy, like South Korea or Japan were in their development. Tesco has done very well in a limited cooperation with Star Bazaar. We've helped design and operate the stores. We've shown ourselves to be good retailers in India. There are consumers there who respond to an improved retail offer. Indian investment for us is still a few years behind China. It needs a few years of investment into infrastructure.

'China is more open, because in part the Chinese don't see retailing as strategic an industry as some others. That can change. But for the moment it is relatively open, whereas India is not. The concerns are in terms of other retailers, or mom-and-pop shops, or agriculture, or just opposition to foreigners in some quarters. But the benefits will far outweigh that in terms of providing an infrastructure by which agriculture can get to the market and produce more and better products. Food prices will come down relative to spending power; quality and choice will go up. The birth rate is higher in India and that will affect growth rates in the years ahead.'[12]

Opposition in India is, however, firm. 'It is a mixture of deliberate opposition, accidental opposition and lack of expertise that you have to navigate your way through. You have to have a lot of patience and humility and try to understand what the local society is trying to achieve. What its wants are. You have to try to demonstrate in your behaviour that you are a solution and can help meet aspirations, and that you are not a threat or a problem for them. It is difficult everywhere. I wouldn't pick out a place. It is difficult to do business everywhere, including the UK.

'People who are not involved in business and yet whose lives and societal aspirations depend on the success of business have to be persuaded that business, and business investment, is in their interests. Retailing is high-profile, it is physical and visible; it attracts a lot more attention than business that is harder to see.'[13]

Local partnerships, then, have been fundamental to Tesco's international growth, as Clarke explains. 'Michael Fleming is the strategy director and for fifteen years he has been responsible for finding the partners. It takes a long time. It took us nearly four years to find the partner in China and a similar time for the business in Malaysia and India. It's a lot of getting to know people. It is about relationships. Can you forge a partnership or can't you? I spent a lot of time building a relationship, understanding, making a choice. You have to share values and vision. That is what has enabled us to grow successfully.

'I had more dinners and more toasts in my international role in the last five years than I probably had in the first thirty-five. The other dimension is that once you are into the business you have to be able to create the right team. You have to bring in the Tesco know-how. It comes from Tesco people. You are rebuilding a team and a new dynamic. That's quite exciting. That's what I love to do.

'Building businesses you don't have success overnight. It is a lot of two steps forward and one back and occasionally one forward two back.

'We were determined to build sustainable businesses. We learned in the UK that you invest in customers and you look after your staff, and you get rewarded, and that's what we've set out to do. At the heart of it is the loyalty effect: you create momentum, you create sales, you generate profit, you put some back to shareholders, some back to customers, some to the staff, and it builds more loyalty, a virtuous circle.

'The big difference is that the business in the UK has been going for eighty years, it is market leader, it has the most superior operating ratios of any business of its kind in this market. The one in China is eight years old and is not making money yet. The objectives are the same. We want to pay upper-quartile rates of pay – we don't want to pay the minimum wage in China. We're close to it today, but our staff know our objective is to change that and as we generate sales and profits so will their incomes and benefits rise. We've always offered subsidized food in restaurants. The government in China requires you to, but we have always done it anyway. We go beyond that. We provide full uniform. Others don't. We have a set of values, we have ethics and we train. We do those in a similar way around the world.

'We've learned that if you look after staff they look after customers, so our objective wherever we are is to pay a living wage, not the minimum wage. As the business gets more mature and industry develops, we have a road map to get there. We start by living the Tesco Values, which are treat people how we like to be treated, and no one tries harder for customers. They resonate wherever we are: time and again our staff in Asia tell us that's one of the points of difference between us and other retailers and companies. Not only do we say it, we try to do it. We measure how staff feel about customers. We do it in the UK, we do it in all our operating businesses. It is part of our quarterly and half-yearly and annual review process, and we target for improvements which largely relate to what it feels like working for Tesco, how much support you get from your boss and so on. It doesn't matter whether you are in the US or Cheshunt or China, we work hard to improve it. We know if you hire the right people you improve your labour retention.'[14]

Leahy says doing business in such different countries is demanding. 'It can be pretty exhausting, as it is for Asian business people working in the West. The jet lag, the unfamiliarity, the difficulty in communication. But as a result things get created. We've been able to help build modern infrastructure for consumption in Asia, and

Asians have equipped our households with lots of goods we couldn't previously have afforded.

'The development of Tesco internationally will be seen as a profound turning point for the company, to have opened up a whole new chapter in its history which can sustain it for several decades if it is successful. But it has required the business to take an awful lot of risks, learn an awful lot of things and to expend an awful amount of energy. All of those things are good Tesco qualities that have grown up over very many years.

'We won't be overhauling Walmart any time soon. But the world is a very big place. No retailer has even one per cent of the market. So there is plenty of room for Tesco and Walmart and some others to do well. Size alone won't do it. It's much more about having the culture to be able to successfully pursue and survive international expansion.'[15]

Walmart's home market is, of course, the United States. What was it that made Leahy and his fellow Tesco directors think that they could make a go of America, where so many British retailers have failed, without the local partner that was central to success elsewhere?

Chapter 23

The American Dream: the Wild West

'We began to look for a new format, one that we felt would use the skills we had learned around the world and tap into something that hadn't already been done in America.'

Sir Terry Leahy[1]

'The Aquarius Project began in early 2005 when a significant number of us travelled to the USA and visited different stores and formats.'

Tim Mason[2]

American dreams tend to disappoint British retailers. A raft of household names – Boots, Marks & Spencer, Sainsbury – even the Body Shop – had a try at re-creating domestic success stateside. The question was: why would it be any different for Tesco? The business had thought about it before on more than one occasion. What changed?

Leahy and Tim Mason, Tesco's deputy chief executive and the head of its business in America, describe what lay behind the Aquarius Project. Leahy explains the decision to cross the Atlantic after decades of rejecting the idea. 'The United States had always been a natural place for us to go to learn about retailing. In the 1950s, when Britain was suffering shortages and food rationing was still in place, the modern supermarket had been invented in the United States with self-service retailing, which was the greatest breakthrough in productivity since the Second World War. Lots of

British companies felt the United States was a good place to invest.'³

During the MacLaurin era, Tesco had cast its eye over American retailers, including a Chicago-based chain and some non-food stores further south. The risk and the price had been thought to be high, particularly at a time when so much energy was being pumped into transforming Tesco in Britain in the late seventies and throughout the eighties. The early nineties were difficult for retailers in the UK and then Tesco's foreign investment had focused on emerging markets closer to home. The time had just never been right.

Leahy explains: 'By the time we came around to think about the United States again, in 2005, we'd had the opportunity to invest in other parts of the world and we'd learned to look at places through local eyes and that prepared us to take the right approach to the United States as a foreign place. We were still interested in the United States: it has 30 per cent of the world's GDP, is a democracy and is a place where, if you developed a successful format, there were no restrictions on growth. It was a good balance to our high-risk invest-ments in our developing markets in Central Europe and Asia. They were the reasons why, strategically, we wanted to do it. We knew America would be a big challenge, so it was good to begin at a time of strength when you could see through any difficulties. That proved to be an important decision in terms of timing. It is difficult if you are short of growth or trying to get away from another problem. That is not the time to go to the United States.

'We were then faced with a decision, as with all countries, in terms of how to enter. We could have acquired a big American retailer – we were strong enough financially, but time had moved on and America was no longer the leader in supermarket retailing. It wasn't the place where the ideas were coming from. It was an ageing, very good industry, but no longer the leader. It got to that point when it was an industry you would rather compete against than own. So we began to look for a new format, one that we felt would use the skills we had learned around the world and tap into something that hadn't already been done in America. There is no shortage of retail space in America; they don't need another shop just the same as what they have already got, and yet, if we found something that was new, America was a market that could attract customers and you could grow.

'The one area that looked under-invested was convenience retailing, which was a market growing rapidly all over the world except in the United States because of land availability, cheap energy and cheap motoring costs. People could really do a big, one-stop shop. Even in the United States those things were beginning to alter: transport costs were going up and people were becoming concerned about the effect on their neighbourhood of these big-box developments. So we wondered whether an investment in convenience retailing might spark growth that we had seen in other parts of the world. It was a relatively uncompetitive space and, although it was a niche, in America a niche can be a very big market. So we did our research and we sent teams over from about 2005 or 2006 to really test whether a new format in the convenience area could be successful and what its ingredients might need to be.'[4]

Tesco also had a small amount of experience of West Coast food retail following a joint venture with American supermarket Safeway (no relation to the former UK supermarket chain with the same name). Gary Sargeant was sent to apply his new home-shopping knowledge. 'In August/September 2000 the Board decided we had something we could sell to other retailers around the world. Most retailers understood why they needed to do grocery home shopping because customers wanted it, but nobody was doing it profitably, so everybody was interested in trying to learn from Tesco. They are always interested in listening how to steal your dinner but less interested in a joint venture.

'The Board decided the place we wanted to focus on first was the United States. In late 2000 I spent a lot of time cold-calling people through the States. I spent much of 2001 flitting all over. At the same time we launched home shopping in Ireland and South Korea, so I was travelling. In February 2001 I went to talk to Safeway. They had a market share of more than 50 per cent in northern California and [their business was] threatened by Webvan, a home-shopping organization out of a warehouse with huge venture capital money behind them from Louis Border, of Borders Books, and a guy from Andersen Consulting.' Safeway had invested in Grocery Works, but Gary Sargeant said one look at the warehouse showed him it wouldn't work and hadn't been thought through. 'If you were under 4 foot 8, you couldn't reach the top tray [of the] picking trays. Some of the people couldn't reach and had to stand on cases of water.'

This was in the middle of the internet bubble and Safeway could not get out of its internet venture because it would impact on its share price negatively. Tesco's model offered a solution. Sargeant worked on that from August 2001 to early 2003, as did Mike McNamara, then chief technical officer for Tesco's dot.com business. McNamara was appointed to Tesco's Board in 2011 as the company's information technology director.

'We started the service in Portland, Oregon, because Steve Frisby [Safeway's boss] lived there. We did four stores there as a trial. Four or five months later we went into stores around the Bay area. Within a year we moved into southern California – Vons stores – Safeway's brand in LA. We were in Las Vegas, then extended into Seattle. The operation now is going to the East Coast, to Washington. Without head office costs it was making money, but the expats were a big part of the cost. We handed it over to Safeway. We demonstrated that our model in the UK was exportable, and also that we could work with other retailers.'[5]

Sargeant returned to the UK and store management, running a group of stores in Central and West London. In 2012, he is still in charge of a group of large Tesco stores.

Leahy asked Tim Mason, the man he had recruited more than two decades earlier and with whom he had worked for most of that time, to go and have a look at the situation in America. Mason recalls his first 'recce'.

'The Aquarius Project began in early 2005 when a significant number of us travelled to the USA and visited different stores and formats. Before that Terry had said to me, "I've discovered this business in the United States of America called Whole Foods. I think we should buy it. Quietly, just go and have a look for me and see what you think", and I went off to the United States and I did one of those trips where I went to Washington, Texas, Florida and places like that. It's the only time I've ever been to Kentucky. I just went round for a week, round Whole Foods after Whole Foods. I bought myself a pair of cowboy boots. I just thought it was fantastic. I agreed with him completely, though I don't know whether what we had in mind would have been completely successful, knowing now what I know about the United States. I went to Austin [Texas] and visited the business-development director of Whole Foods, who clearly felt that we had parked not one but a whole division of tanks on their parking lot outside their offices. I said, "We are admirers of yours and we are much more expert than you are on things to do with the internet. Maybe we could do some work together and we could give you some help on the internet." The slight flaw in this cunning plan was that they had just lost an absolute fortune on an internet experiment; it was all very unfortunate. We did then do proper due diligence and looked at the business: their share price went through the roof. This was not long after John Gardiner had become Tesco's chairman and these were early moves in Terry's time as chief executive. We just had to back off.

'After that, we tramped the terrazzo, flying all over the place, looking at Walmarts, Publix and just generally having a look around what was going on in America. This was a precursor to Terry producing a two-page paper that said we should go into the American market, the stores should be about 10,000 square feet and the business should be called Fresh & Easy. Basically, he wrote down in a page and a half what I've spent the rest of my life doing.'[6]

Some ask why Tesco decided to go it alone in America rather than partnering an existing retailer as it has done in Central Europe, Turkey and most of its Asian markets. Leahy describes the rationale. 'You went into partnership in countries where these were new democracies and economies and they would be more opaque than the United States for an investor, so local guidance was helpful. Also you could go in with an acquisition by buying something small and rapidly expanding with modern retail infrastructure. The United States was more open, and the assets were older and there wasn't the natural growth, so you really did need a different type of entry. The thing about organic growth, even in the United States, is that it is very survivable. You would have had to acquire a significant business, which would have meant Tesco would have had to bet the company to enter the United States. I felt this was a safer route, where the downside risk would be embarrassment and a billion dollars written off, whereas the upside was tens of billions of dollars of value and transformational for the business.'[7]

Going to America would be such a significant decision for Tesco that the research had to be better than anything that Tesco had ever done before. 'We chose from our own people,' says Leahy. 'We sent a team led by Colin Smith. They came back and said we've done our research, looked at the market, spoken to customers, lived in customers' homes and we think there is an opportunity there for fresher and more wholesome food at prices anyone can afford delivered into the local neighbourhood. These were areas of relative under-investment in fresh, modern, wholesome food. There were retailers of good-quality food, like Whole Foods, but it was for the wealthy. There were retailers of very low-price goods, but they tended to be in big-box locations away from the neighbourhoods, so our objective was to develop a format that could offer the quality of Whole Foods at the price of Walmart but delivered into the local neighbourhood. It was a very tall order, but we knew if we could do that it would be a different, compelling offer and people would see it as new and be attracted to it. We had to build it from scratch, the whole system from end to end, to be incredibly efficient, to offer low prices on good-quality product, our own sourcing and manufacturing as well as distribution. Stores had to be organized efficiently and in an easy-care way to keep labour costs to a minimum. Much of the preparation usually done in supermarkets was to be done centrally on a greater scale, with more efficiency, and quality could be controlled as well.'[8]

'The concept of "neighbourhood" really meant urban or

suburban area. As is the case with a lot of big places, most people live in urban and suburban locations: 75 per cent of the United States's population could access this type of store. We chose to go in one place because we needed to build the infrastructure: the supply chain, the factory to make the foods and the warehouse to deliver the goods, and we needed a network of stores around these big facilities. We chose the south-west of the United States, which in 2005 was the fastest-growing area with real population growth and new communities being built.'[9]

Mason describes the depth of the research. 'Colin Smith had built his career in buying with Tesco. The difference between that team and every other team that we had applied to our international expansion was that there were no ifs or buts or maybes – you had to send your best people. We sent one of our best commercial people, John Burry; one of our best technical people, Ian Fletcher, because we thought it would have a manufacturing component; the guy who ran marketing in the UK and had done for many years, Simon Uwins; the human resources director from Northern Ireland, Hugh Cousins; and Steve Ryder, who was a long-term store planner and store designer who was at that stage working internationally but who had worked with Terry and me for twenty-five years. It was a very heavyweight team. They went to see what they should do and they came up with a sort of added-value, limited-range format. They built the thing in a warehouse. They sought to apply what we had learned globally – partly in Europe – about discounter retailing and to apply it to the American market, so it was discount retailing plus the best-quality chilled recipe meals, great meat, great fruit and vegetables. They did a lot of consumer discussion groups. They lived in people's houses, went through their cupboards with them, asked them how and where they did their shopping and tried to immerse themselves in the market. Eventually they came up with this store format and by this stage the team was a bit wider. There are sweet stories along the way of how John Bury and Ian Fletcher had to get the products for the store. The store had a big own-brand component to it, but the problem with own-brand is that it skews the consumer groups. If you put Trader Joe's own-brand into this store that was called Fresh & Easy, they'd know exactly what the brand stood for. So the team went halfway across the country, hired a 40-foot refrigerated lorry and went into mainly Wegmans [a family-owned grocery retailer, mostly on America's Eastern Seaboard] and bought a lorry full of product. I think the excuse was that we were making a movie set in a grocery store and that it had to have a realistic look.

'At that point, they were not even telling people where they were, let alone what they were doing. It was very difficult. They were incredibly secretive about it. Terry obviously frightened the living bejesus out of them. They had to get American phones. You weren't allowed to use company credit cards. You had to forsake all of the air miles you got on the trips.

'One of the site researchers, Benjy Meyer, was responsible for getting the milk for the mock store, so they went to a Gelson's, which is a local supermarket chain in Los Angeles, and they bought all the milk they had in the store. They got to the cash register and a slightly perplexed cashier looked rather quizzical, [so] they said desperately, "We have a café", which didn't seem to help the cashier much, so Benjy rather helpfully piped up: ". . . and the cow's sick."

'We looked in California, but originally we also looked in Denver [Colorado].'[10]

Feedback from the research was positive, although there was a nasty moment when a member of a focus group had forgotten her methadone and then had to be taken to hospital in the full throes of cold turkey. It was put-up or shut-up time.

Mason recalls, 'In the autumn of 2005 we went out to California and went through the store, met everybody and talked through where they had got to. It went to Strategy Conference [in November 2005] and it was agreed we would vote the capital to allow Fresh & Easy to be born.

'One of the problems that they had was that British business is very twitchy about the United States of America. They don't do well. Marks & Spencer has failed there, Sainsbury has failed there.

'Terry and I were getting a bit in each other's pockets and I was getting a bit grumpy with him. He was possibly getting a bit grumpy with me. So I thought maybe this is a way of doing something exciting in an amazing place. I said to Terry, "If you want me to, I'll go." When you go to California everybody thinks you have won the Pools, but there is absolutely no support network at all. I couldn't get the children into schools. As every expat will tell you, until you get the kids sorted out you're not sorted.'[11]

Colin Smith left Tesco in early 2006 and then took a job with the supermarket chain Somerfield. 'Colin and I flew out there in January 2006 [to make the announcement that he was leaving],' recalls Mason. 'We sat down and Colin said, "He's your boss now." They were absolutely flummoxed. That team of people – maybe as many as twenty people by then – was the core team, the Founding Fathers. Although they had come up with a half-decent retail proposition, they were quite a dysfunctional mob because they had had a bit too much time on their hands and they had not been closely managed, which nobody knew. They had sort of got on and done it by themselves. I don't think it was even colour by numbers: they had done the numbers and then the colouring. There was a bit of knocking of heads together, but that was all fine. We had a meeting at the Fairmont, in Santa Monica, and I remember walking round the garden with Terry and then I went in and laid it out. They were very good. They probably just wanted a bit more leadership and structure and direction, but that was a funny trip.

'When you are working with a small team of people you are bringing all your experience, your values, your beliefs and your instincts about what it takes to make a great retail business and applying those. When I arrived, there was this business in a warehouse and it had been designed but it had no heart and no soul and no reason.'[12]

Mason wanted Fresh & Easy to feel like a start-up rather than like Tesco in America. 'One of the things that occurred to me in starting a new business, particularly in America, is in reality the new businesses that start that are successful, that change the world, are businesses that are started by entrepreneurs who have a belief and a point of view, such as Steve Jobs or Howard Schultz. I wouldn't have been able to articulate it when I first got there, but with the benefit of experience I have become more determined that we have to hang on to what we believe in. Otherwise we are just a chameleon-like corporate entity and nobody will have any affiliation to that whatsoever. So what we originally did was, we sat down and said, "These are the Tesco Values. What are the Fresh & Easy values going to be? What's the belief system of the business?" We asked, "It's your business. You're creating it. What do you want it to be?"

'It is basically Tesco with an American accent, in green, but with some differences. I think probably the biggest difference was to make the product, the food, a more central part of what we did. The food in American supermarkets is not very good. It is over-processed. It's one of the things that customers said to us when we did these groups. We asked, "So what you want is healthy eating?" They said, "Sort of, but not particularly that lean cuisine stuff. Food is too messed around with." That was the overriding feeling from an awful lot of American consumers: "Just give me food that is less messed around with." That developed as a central thought of the Fresh & Easy development.'[13]

The secrecy surrounding the early research was maintained for as long as Tesco could manage. Leahy explains why. 'There was an incredible amount of work to be done to build a new format, untried anywhere in a new country and based upon huge upfront investments in infrastructure. Normally you go into a country step by step, but this model didn't allow that. You had to put the infrastructure in first – factories, computers and distribution centres. Partly that was because it is the United States and it is a very competitive place. The minute you put your toe in the water they would either have copied you or beaten you up and you wouldn't have got past stage one, so we knew we wanted to be up and running very quickly. It is amazing that by November 2007 we were opening our first stores.'[14]

A year and a half after Mason moved out to California, Fresh & Easy was ready to open.

'We opened our first store in a slightly unprepossessing place called Hemet, in California. Most people who come from California haven't been there. It's not up there with Los Angeles and San Francisco. Hemet is well inland and is residential and elderly. We opened there first because it was ready. We could open it quietly. We had a soft opening. We opened six stores on the same day in California. Then immediately after that we opened in Vegas and then Phoenix. We opened on Hallowe'en 2007. I'd been there for about twenty-two months.'[15]

In November 2007 the sunny outlook was deceptive, or, as Leahy puts it, 'That is where we got unlucky.'

Even the best-laid plans go awry. Careful analysis of growth potential and local circumstances – so effective in earlier inter-national investments because of the lessons Tesco had learned from Catteau in France and the first Irish acquisition – turned out to be incomplete: nobody had considered what could happen if first the American and then the global economy went into what is universally acknowledged to be 'meltdown'.

Leahy continues: 'That was the beginning of the recession, which would be a problem anywhere, and more so for new space than exist-ing space because people hunker down in a recession; but it was particularly the case in the south-west United States, which was the epicentre of the housing bust that caused the global financial crisis. There may have been a contraction of 4 or 5 per cent of the economy as a whole in the United States, but these places were seeing 10 per cent contraction in the whole city, and some neighbourhoods much more than that. We were opening in neighbourhoods that had been growing and were now emptying out. Literally, the population had gone. That was a big challenge.'[16]

Mason describes ghost towns – and Tesco had to adjust their opening strategy, opening stores at a slower rate than had originally been planned. Five years after the first store opened in Hemet there are more than 160 Fresh & Easy stores employing more than 4,000 people. Back in 2007 and 2008, that felt like a long way off.

This being America, not Hungary or even South Korea, and the era of instant global communication in the English language, the

British media were able to follow every twist and turn. Although Fresh & Easy was a relatively tiny part of Tesco's business, it represented a large chunk of the commentary. Nowhere else on Tesco's map would a single store opening – and that in a small town – have merited front-page coverage in the *Financial Times* and *The Times* newspapers. Accordingly, Tesco arranged a trip to America for UK-based media and analysts from financial institutions who would report back to shareholders. It happened during the honeymoon period before the full force of the recession came to be understood.

'The stores themselves really were a reflection of everything we had hoped and planned for,' Leahy counters. 'Those customers who used it really got it. They saw it was something different, that it did offer fresh and natural food without preservatives or flavourings at a price they could afford, as well as being convenient in their local neighbourhood. They liked the edited range, how quickly they could shop round the store, and they even liked the self-service checkouts which most people thought would never work.

'It got the best ever research scores for any new brand, measured by an agency that tracks brand introductions in terms of "would you refer this to somebody else?"

'The appeal also, although it was a niche, was right across income groups, ethnicities and age groups, and that is very unusual in the United States because things tend to appeal to segments. So this encouraged us to believe that this would be a big niche, but we had to get through the recession. As well as that, we had to get through a learning process that you always have to do in any new market, and get through the mistakes you make and build on the successes you have got, all of which was having to be done into the headwind of this terrible recession. So the team really had a difficult time of it.

'All credit to Tim's leadership in keeping morale high through that difficult time, and to the entire leadership team. They were under an unusual amount of press and public scrutiny; if they had been just start-ups on their own, they could have just got on with it. Every step and misstep was reported.

'The record of British businesses hasn't been great in the United

States, particularly for retailers, because it looks deceptively like the United Kingdom, so people go over and tend to manage it as the United Kingdom and it is not. But Tesco had the opportunity to look at it as foreign, to learn what is necessary to operate in a foreign culture and customer base and make necessary adjustments. We learned those lessons from being in Korea or Hungary or anywhere else.'[17]

America certainly proved to be foreign. One aspect that Tesco's researchers might have looked at harder than they did was the California labour laws, as Mason admits. 'The two things missed in the original research and development phase were the American industrial-relations background and something that an American would take for granted: that California is an incredibly difficult place to do business. California has been voted the most difficult place to do business in America for fourteen years in a row because of state laws, which they overlay in addition to Federal requirements.

'One of the things you have in the USA is workers' compensation – this is what stops you from starving to death if you get injured. We run the same business in Las Vegas, Nevada, as we do in California and our workers' compensation bill in California is astronomical compared with Las Vegas. These are the same people, from the same root stock. They all travelled west. Some just got a bit further west than others; but if you get to California, you stub your toe and you claim for it. In Arizona if you stub your toe you limp for a couple of days and you get on with it. That's just an example of this very legislated, liberal environment.

'Legislation nearly always has unintended and unforeseen consequences, which is why the Brits as a rule are reluctant to legislate. A lot of what happens in California is unintended con-sequences of previous legislation.'[18]

The state also allows secondary picketing during labour disputes. Mason says it was a steep learning curve understanding how American politics work, and in particular how much politicians depend upon large interest groups. 'It is amazing to understand that Democrat politicians do not get elected without the support of the trades unions. If you don't have union money behind you at the primary stage, you will never win the primary.'[19]

Tesco opted to be a non-union business in America, however. 'In the UK we have a very good, progressive relationship, which has been good for the business and good for everything. What we perceived absolutely rightly is that union–company relationships in the USA are the worst form of old-fashioned adversarial union–management relationships that it is possible for a Brit to conceive of.

'We've had this issue where the UFCW [United Food and Commercial Workers Union] decided that the legislation to end the need to price-mark individual products was incorrectly drafted and therefore that price-marking via shelf-edge labels and scanning was not legal in California, and so you needed to put a sticky label on every packet. They took Fresh & Easy to court. The judge threw it out and said there was no charge to answer. If we had been found guilty we would have had to have gone out and found a manufacturer of pricing guns, but all the union businesses would have had to do it too.

'The thing that is most surprising to me about it all is, if you were to talk to people who have been around in our business for long enough, they will tell you that one of the worst jobs in the world was taking the sticky labels off products when you needed to price them up. It is the worst job, and yet a union is trying to re-create this worst job that there ever was.

'We launched with assisted checkouts [popularly described as 'self-service']. You don't have to scan yourself out at all. We offer you help and staff develop a relationship and a sixth sense and judge what sort of help people need. So the person who has a sandwich and a drink and comes in every day doesn't need help and doesn't want it; they just want to get their meal and go to work. Somebody who turns up with two kids and has a huge cart of stuff wants help packing.

'It was quite a risk. It isn't the way things are done. Staff and customers really enjoyed it, I think, because they felt it was more bespoke. You have unchained staff from the machine. They actually now have freedom to act. They can give very good or very bad service.

'For the union, it was the next line of attack. These cash registers, they said, make it easier for under-age people to drink. It's just a lie. If you scan a bottle of alcohol the tills stop and you cannot complete without a member of staff coming over and ID-ing you.'[20]

Leahy describes [in 2011] how the plan for Fresh & Easy evolved. 'There is a growing number of people for whom this is the very best store they know. The business is growing pretty well on a same-store basis and in terms of new stores, but we haven't been able to grow at the speed we originally intended. The upside infrastructure costs haven't been defrayed as quickly across the growing business, which meant the start-up losses we anticipated have been quite a bit larger.'[21]

Leahy anticipated Fresh & Easy would break even in 2012/13 and then move into profit. 'The economy hasn't really recovered yet, so the business has made all of its progress on its own.'[22]

Culturally, Fresh & Easy contended with almost as much newness as Tesco did when it set up stores in countries such as Hungary. The policy on no artificial colours, synthetic flavours or preservatives – well established in Tesco in the UK for its standard and Finest ranges – created problems for Fresh & Easy because it excluded American staples from the shelves, as Mason describes.

'Periodically you would have a conversation that we've agreed to these damn food policies, but now we can't do this and it is costing us more money to do that. Have we done the right thing? Should we cheat and change it? It caused quite a lot of anxiety and angst.

'One of these things that is extremely popular in America is this thing called red velvet cake. It is the standard cake you would get for a celebration. It is basically sponge cake but bright red. The only way you can get the sponge to be bright red is you have got to put some artificial colouring in it. You can't not have one. So we developed the Hermosa Baking Company, named after the beach which is just south of where we are headquartered, which enables us to keep within our Fresh & Easy brand promises but means that where necessary we could also offer products [that do contain additives] that people wanted as part of their shopping trip. It is absolutely not cheating. The absolute point is that if it says Fresh & Easy on the label it won't have any additives, colours or preservatives, period.

'If I go back to the early days of the launch of the Value range in the UK, there was once a marvellous group discussion when customers said, "If you see the red and the blue and the white stripes then you don't need to look at the price. You know that Tesco will have nailed the price for you. We get that same response to Fresh & Easy. People say, "One of the reasons I shop there is I don't have to check the ingredients panel because I know Fresh & Easy have done the work to take out the ingredients I don't like my family to have." That's an amazing position. That's a real brand.'[23]

From the office in El Segundo, a district of Los Angeles county in Santa Monica Bay, bordered by the city's airport to the north and Manhattan Beach to the south, the view looks benign. But on 5 December 2012 – incidentally during the final editing stages of this book – Tesco announced a strategic review of Fresh & Easy.

Chapter 24

Success: At What Price?

'Tesco came from nothing and the people who work in Tesco largely came from nothing, so we don't rely on being on a pedestal.'

Sir Terry Leahy[1]

'Crises are dreadful but they illustrate that supermarkets are at the heart of the community.'

Dame Lucy Neville-Rolfe[2]

From the £4 pair of jeans and the 9p can of Value baked beans to Finest champagne, from Sunday trading to convenience stores and home delivery, Tesco established itself across a decade as a shop for everybody. Sir Terry Leahy's team had even revived the Cohen-style consumer-champion battles by taking on Levi's over the right to sell designer clothes at high-street prices.

Tesco people were perhaps so focused on customers, staff, suppliers and shareholders that they were underprepared for the new demands that success generated. New voices made challenges that boiled down to two main questions. First, if Tesco was so successful, who was losing? Second, how could Tesco share its success with people other than its customers, staff or shareholders?

There were three government inquiries into supermarkets, in 1999, 2004 and 2006. As director of group corporate and legal affairs, Neville-Rolfe and her team assembled Tesco's response each time. She reflects, 'In a way we created a problem for ourselves because we were campaigning around why Tesco is good for consumers. We had the fight in the courts with Levi's to try to get cut-price jeans.

'There have been three inquiries by the Competition Commission, the major competition authority in Britain. They have taken an enormous amount of time, and cost and energy and commitment from the business. It is difficult to believe the sheer depth of questioning, the amount of preparation you have to do to answer their questions. They go into every nook and cranny in the business: the land you buy, the contracts you have with suppliers and the way the industry has developed in all its aspects. The competition authorities have strong powers. They are judge and jury on your industry, on your company and they are also in a sense the prosecutors.

'We have had three inquiries in seven years. Every time they have come to a conclusion that, in contrast to many of the other industries that they have looked at, consumers benefit hugely from the growth and nature of supermarkets, including the leading supermarkets in the UK.

'In the last ten years inflation has probably been about 25 per cent and supermarket inflation has been about 5 per cent. Services have improved. There are more products. Rivalry has increased. There is more switching between shops.

'The first inquiry was in 1999. That looked at whether there was a monopoly under the Fair Trade Act of 1973. They gave us pretty much a clean bill of health but they did bring in a code of practice regulating relations with the supply base, making contracts more transparent and trying to get rid of concerns that had been expressed.

'The second inquiry [in 2004] was when first Morrisons, then Asda, Tesco and Sainsbury all entered a bidding fight to take over Safeway, the failing fifth supermarket, and the inquiry looked into who should be allowed to buy it. They again concluded that the market was highly competitive and good for consumers but they felt that only Morrisons, the smallest, should be allowed to buy Safeway because otherwise there was a risk that the competition and rivalry would be reduced.

'The third one [in 2006], which was beginning to feel very burdensome and unnecessary, came about again because of the combination of small shops, suppliers, farmers and the non-governmental organizations like Friends of the Earth who don't like the rate of change or modernization that supermarkets have had. It is not unique to the UK. It is one of the reasons why working in supermarkets is so interesting: you are at the heart of this debate about the nature of society and how it changes. People work. They want to bring their families in a car to shop. That has led to a huge change in the nature of our towns and suburbs. Supermarkets have essentially responded to that, but it has raised questions. Those questions then get brought back to politicians. Politicians, finding them very difficult because you are going to disappoint somebody, have handed them to the statutory regulators the OFT [Office of Fair Trading] and the Competition Commission.

'Yet again [in 2007] we have found that there is rivalry, this has been good for consumers, prices have come down, ranges have improved and we haven't been engaging in anti-competitive behaviour. Not only has Tesco grown, but others have got pipelines of stores. There is 3 per cent growth in large stores every year, quite apart from all the small, modern stores that have come along. Although the Commission made suggestions for change, these have not undermined the basic conclusion that it is good for consumers.'[3]

Neville-Rolfe acknowledges the impact that supermarkets have had. 'Supermarkets have grown very strongly in the last ten to fifteen years, really on the back of changing lifestyles and a more egalitarian society. People vote with their feet and go and shop in attractive supermarkets with big ranges. But that obviously impacts on certain sectors of society less positively. The best small shops are always fine. But a number, especially the less clean, more expensive and less attractive ones, went out of business. That's a continuing trend. Suppliers that have supplied the growing supermarkets like Tesco have done well. But some, supplying less successful shops, have done less well. There has therefore been a debate about the relationship between suppliers and supermarkets.'[4]

Tesco went from hero to villain in parts of the UK media. Leahy's comments implicitly acknowledge that, for Tesco people, this was uncomfortable. 'In part it's an accident that media people tend to live in a small area of London: they don't see big hypermarkets or superstores, so the enormous social change in terms of the creation of those stores almost went unnoticed. But they do have local small shops. As Tesco started to move into Express [in the mid-nineties] they noticed it for the first time and started to ask questions about it.

'The other part of it is that it's a theme to make people read newspapers and watch television programmes. For many years the editorial theme was: "Here's Tesco, it's the underdog, it has come through, isn't that a good thing?" Now the theme is: "Tesco is too successful, isn't that a bad thing?"

'Tesco came from nothing and the people who work in Tesco largely came from nothing, so we don't rely on being on a pedestal. We don't go to work each day hoping to look good in the newspapers. We've got the advantage that we work with tens of thousands of ordinary British people and people around the world, and we serve millions of ordinary people, so we've got a much more reliable guide as to what Britain is thinking and what people's lives are like. So of course you listen to the media and the media has a view, but it isn't necessarily an accurate view of British life from the apartments of Notting Hill.'[5]

Tesco, however, could not ignore its new media image. 'Tesco is of great interest to people: they are going to write about us because if you put Tesco in the newspaper, people will read it,' says Neville-Rolfe.[6]

Take the PR campaign to find a motto for the UK launched by Gordon Brown, then prime minister, in November 2007: one jaded contributor submitted the mock-Latin line: 'Dipso fatso bingo asbo Tesco'. Cartoons abound – a moon landing with a query about the whereabouts of the nearest Tesco is typical. There is a film, most easily accessed through YouTube, spoofing a Tesco invasion of Denmark.

That is how central Tesco has become in British life: a by-product of decades of development in the supermarket as it reinvented itself over and over again to stay 'number one for customers'.

During the first decade of the twenty-first century, three national events have shown the role that supermarkets now have. 'Crises are dreadful,' acknowledges Neville-Rolfe, 'but they illustrate that supermarkets are at the heart of the community.'

It took a while, though, for Tesco to make its voice heard during the petrol strike of 2000. 'It was the only time, before David Cameron took over, that the Conservatives were ever ahead of Labour in the polls because Labour managed to get a strike in the refineries and lorry drivers wouldn't drive the tankers,' Neville-Rolfe recalls. 'The nation was forty-eight hours away from having no food. The government barely talked at all to the supermarkets. The DTI [Department of Trade and Industry] was talking to BP, but nobody was talking to us. We collaborated uncharacteristically with Sainsbury to make the government talk to us. Tony Blair got involved and they stitched something up and it went away, but it was very scary for a few days.

'The petrol drivers put cordons round the depots. The depots weren't designed to stop that and the police weren't very well geared up to come and stop it happening. It was in the media from the Friday and so by Sunday people were worried, so they all rushed off and topped up their cars, which made more of a problem. We set up a crisis team, though possibly not quite quickly enough, which met on the Monday morning. We have a special crisis room. It was a combination of people like me who pick up the media noise coming in, people in charge of lorries, stores and ordering. The worst point was the Monday afternoon when all the motorists were queuing up. One person in the crisis room passed a note to another saying the petrol station is open in Cheshunt and immediately three people left the room to go and pick up their petrol! We were working out whether rationing would be imposed.

'The government put in military-type contingency planning in

Whitehall. They asked us to put the price down, but I can't quite remember why. It was all back to normal by the Wednesday and Thursday.'[7]

It was one thing to deal with a shortlived crisis. Britain, though, would encounter much tougher challenges when its farming community was hit by a wave of foot-and-mouth disease. It was the first major outbreak since 1967. The first case was detected at an abattoir in Essex in February 2001, the next more than 300 miles away in Northumberland. Again, the authorities feared a significant impact on food supplies and consequent panic buying. More than 10 million animals were slaughtered during the next eleven months.

Neville-Rolfe, with her childhood roots in farming and her Civil Service career in agriculture and the environment, found this one the hardest to handle. 'The foot-and-mouth crisis was appalling. The authorities didn't ban the movement of cattle for about a week.

'We had crisis meetings two or three times every day, just below Board level. We issued internal communications updating stores, staff and suppliers. We had a problem in Northern Ireland because of the trade between [the Republic] and Britain. They wouldn't allow those imports. The certification process took weeks. It caused problems in those stores.'[8]

As well as responding operationally, Tesco had to ramp up its communications response. The press office 'was destabilized', recalls Neville-Rolfe, because media wanted comment from the country's biggest food retailer.

After these crises, Tesco set up a rapid-response strategy. Senior directors rehearse handling major operations, from a terrorist attack to an outbreak of SARS. 'You work out what weaknesses you have,' explains Neville-Rolfe. 'You can lose a company if you get it wrong in a crisis. Now we're international it is even more important. In a crisis people turn national again: they close their borders.'[9]

As Tesco operates in so many countries, there are few parts of the world where a disaster does not have some impact, from the 2004 tsunami which destroyed Pacific coastal areas across thousands of miles to the Japanese earthquake–tsunami in 2011 which killed 20,000 people and triggered a nuclear meltdown. At home, there were the less devastating but traumatic floods in Gloucestershire and Cumbria in 2010. In all such disasters Tesco people find themselves in or near the front line. People learned that practical help – boxes of bottled water or even, in Cumbria, building a temporary store – is useful and that targeted financial aid is appreciated.

The Boxing Day tsunami in 2004 and the following year's floods in the UK prompted Tesco and the Red Cross – the company's Charity of the Year in 2007 – to set up a special fund for the Red Cross to draw on in emergencies without having to go through red tape.

Tesco had become more than a chain of supermarkets to so many people that its directors would have to rethink its role in every society where it sold products and services. As with most modern corporations, it had to learn to answer to consumers for more than just the quality of its bread and butter.

Chapter 25

Power and Responsibility: Handing On the Baton

'I feel like I'm just picking up a baton, chiselled out of a piece of wood by Jack Cohen in Hackney . . . and now I've got it for a while and we know where we are headed.'

Philip Clarke[1]

Power in the form of success brought a challenge. It was not enough to say Tesco was good for customers because millions of them chose to shop there. 'Tesco had been very successful,' says Leahy. 'People started asking were we too successful and were other people paying an unreasonable price for our success. A sensible response was not just to pay it lip-service but to use the tools that had made Tesco successful to address this concern on behalf of some people,' said former chief executive Sir Terry, looking back on his career with the company in October 2011, six months after he retired.

'We took our Steering Wheel,[2] the way we had been able to focus on the important elements of our business that created our success: customers, how we organize work, how we lead people in the business, how we make and meet our financial targets. We added a fifth segment around community. If our core purpose was to create benefit for customers to earn their lifetime loyalty, could we also demonstrate that we created benefit for communities for these same customers as citizens in order to earn their loyalty, respect and

319

support? It put it at the centre of what Tesco does, rather than creating something on the edge of the business that might be photogenic but wasn't at the heart of the business.

'Its origins were in a Board discussion when some outside directors were concerned about the criticism we were receiving. Rather than protest that the criticism was unjustified, which would have become a sterile, redundant debate, I felt a more positive response would work better. Tesco is always better when it is doing something positive rather than when it is defending something that is negative.

'It was well understood by the business and by the Board and it did prove to be the case that engaging with people on positive issues worked better. It doesn't mean the negative issues go away, but slowly but surely people can see it in a more balanced context and see that, like most things, it is not all bad or all good but it is a complex mix.

'Our customers were very happy, but they pick up on these discussions and want to be reassured that Tesco does something for their local community on themes where they feel Tesco should be being a positive force, like diet and health, education and the environment. They want to see clearly that we are taking it seriously and making a contribution.'[3]

Since 2008 Tesco has been seen 'more in context', gaining some credit for creating tens of thousands of jobs, for example.

'In modern life businesses always have to explain themselves and how they operate and how they create benefit,' observes Leahy. 'This is particularly so in markets such as ours because you have creative destruction. You can only have a great success by winning and that means somebody loses. People feel very uncomfortable with winners and losers. You have to explain why, on balance, that is a good thing: there are costs but there are greater benefits. I profoundly believe that true competition – not managed or mock, but one in which businesses fight for a customer – empowers individual people in their lives, gives them choice and control, a voice, and that is a key part of democracy. Responsive businesses are a big part of serving society and citizens.'[4]

During Leahy's tenure, Tesco's response was to set out a strategy on climate change. 'I and everybody else at Tesco tried to run a good business that, with all those costs and benefits, is net beneficial to society. Then there was this price that you hadn't weighed in – a price so large that it might be unpayable by your children, and that was shocking.

'Good businesses are always about more than making money. They are about a worthwhile purpose. Making money is the end of the process, not the only part of the process.

'If you put it in market terms, you have to compete in a narrow sense to win customers and make money, but you also have to invest into the wider community and environment because you can't have successful business if you don't have successful communities to operate within, so you have to contribute to that as well. That is the best way to look at corporate social responsibility. Your policies have to be relevant in a long-term sense to your core business. So our investment into diet, health, education, the environment and local communities are relevant to our business. Climate change was very relevant.

'In January 2007 we said we were part of the problem: we sat at the heart of modern consumption. But we were also part of the solution: this challenge must be addressed not by trying to limit consumption – certainly in Asia that couldn't be done, because people would demand a better material existence – but instead by finding new solutions, a new type of consumption, that could be separated from consumption of fossil fuels and other finite natural resources.

'We set out a green revolution in consumption and said we would show we were serious: we would change our operations. We set the target to halve our carbon emission. We must have been one of the first big companies in the world to recognize the extent of the challenge and to make really significant targets for ourselves. It was a difficult time because people were sceptical, so not that open-minded, about anything that we might say. It received a muted response.'[5]

When, two years later, Tesco opened the world's first zero-carbon supermarket (in Ramsey, Cambridgeshire), the response was indeed low-key. 'We got on with it nevertheless,' continues Leahy. 'We have learned a lot. A modern economy is geared to respond to the desires and wishes of individual people. If you don't get them on board, if they don't desire to consume in a sustainable way, you can't make them. You can't ration, browbeat, tax or regulate, at least not in a modern economy. In Asia they are creating modern economies. There is no way you can turn round to them and say, "You can't have or aspire to the quality of life that the West has had." It is just not going to happen.'[6]

One of the threads of Tesco's newly expressed approach to communities generated more attention than some of its environmental initiatives: investing in regeneration led to the term 'Tesco Town'. The term is also applied to communities that some say have too many Tesco shops.

Some even claimed as far back as 2006, incorrectly, that Tesco was lending people money to buy homes it had built close to new stores. Tesco Bank lent its first mortgage in 2012.

'Tesco Town is an idea used by people to challenge Tesco,' observes Leahy. 'They do not actually exist. There are, though, regeneration schemes anchored on a large Tesco store and they include housing, other shops and a varying provision of amenities created in partnership with other businesses and organizations. Tesco has, in those twenty schemes, created hundreds of millions of pounds of investment into the most deprived places and thousands of jobs for people who had been long-term unemployed. For some, these are life-changing jobs. Other businesses should be asked to be similarly and directly involved in these places that have become disconnected. These are the places from which riots and social problems come. You can't have them cut off from aspiration and from prosperity.'[7]

Neville-Rolfe explains how Tesco took eighteen months – strengthening the community team with appointments from government and from non-governmental organizations to bring in expertise – to develop its ten-point community plan before going public with the strategy in January 2007.

On the eve of Leahy's big speech on climate change, M&S revealed its Plan A environmental campaign – causing some internal irritation about the timing.

Tesco pushed on with the strategy: customers would see an increase in locally sourced products (Tesco research suggested most of its customers defined 'local' as their county or, in the case of Scotland and Wales, their country) and six regional sourcing teams were set up to kick-start the programme. Customers would also see carbon-footprint labels on products – a scheme developed with the Carbon Trust (owing to its complexity, now under review). Schemes that worked better were the introduction of widespread recycling facilities in shops, especially before local authorities had developed viable collection schemes. Tesco's 'bag for life' project converted millions of shoppers who had been using plastic bags, though Tesco was criticized because it would not introduce a charge for carriers unless forced by legislation to do so (as in Wales and Ireland). Nor would it sign up to the *Daily Mail*'s campaign to introduce charges, with predictable headlines ensuing.

In January 2007, Leahy also announced an investment of £100 million in the community plan. Tesco also put £25 million into the Sustainable Consumption Institute, linked to Manchester University, which beat Oxford University in the bidding process, to research and explore technologies and techniques for reducing carbon emissions.

Another aspect of Tesco's community programme was its role as an employer and trainer: there are qualifications linked to NVQs as well as schemes for school-leavers, graduates or the long-term unemployed. Every employee has a personal development plan. Not everybody enjoys them, but the constant appraisal system attempts to keep to a minimum the people who are overlooked.

Although times have changed since Tesco first felt it had to challenge the assumption that a supermarket job was not a 'good' job, back when Cohen, Porter then MacLaurin were in charge, the company still has to work to demonstrate the value of these careers, to bring in fresh people and to look after those it has. Clarke says, 'In

Tesco we're basically all working-class people. We want somebody to be interested. That makes us want to go and do the job with a smile because we know somebody is caring about us.

'Cultures are different [but] all human beings want to be appreciated. We have an extraordinary responsibility to the millions of consumers we serve, but also to the 500,000 staff who every day have to do it. They say what they want is a manager who helps them, that they are paid fairly, recognized and appreciated and have a chance to get on. Those needs are echoed around the world.

'The greatest limiting factor to Tesco's growth is not our reputation; it is have we got enough talent? We have grown so fast that all our people have been pushed into jobs that few of us ever thought we could do. There is a big effort towards finding the leaders of tomorrow.

'I am a digital settler. I was born in an age when I was taught at a blackboard, not a whiteboard with an iPad. I have settled into the digital world. I was the chief information officer for Tesco for ten years. I've always had an affinity for technology, but I am a settler. We need a huge number of digital natives to be part of the leadership group of the future. This is the great talent challenge.'[8]

He observes that this is what MacLaurin and Malpas did when they brought on a new generation of store managers in the early 1990s. 'I have no doubt in my mind that Ian MacLaurin and David Malpas knew what they were doing. They had a very clear vision. They could see it would be possible to grow and be the leading retailer in the UK and they even harboured ambitions to go out of the UK. They were very deliberate about it. They were trying to find a group of men and women who could run the business in the future and nearly without exception my [2012] executive were found by Ian and David, fostered and nurtured by them, and then Terry Leahy took them on to a new level of learning and growth. It had been deliberate. The word I would use about that time was the intimacy, the fact that Ian MacLaurin would come to my store and ask me what I thought and come back to the office and tell people what I thought, know what I was doing and he was watching my career.

I didn't realize it at the time, but it was part of his plan. It is amazing to think they had the foresight.

'It is exactly what I am doing now. Finding the right team to do the right thing is what you have to do, and then bring them through in depth for the challenges that lie ahead and the opportunities, which are many.'[9]

It is again customers who have led Tesco rather than the other way around: the impact of social media and internet retailing demands transformation. The tapes which formed the basis of this story ended just before Tesco warned that profit growth in the year ahead would be minimal. The business also announced it would put the brakes on big stores in favour of small shops and it has increased its range of goods available online tenfold in less than twelve months. Clarke has initiated a reappraisal of pricing and promotion policies, with a renewed focus on Clubcard and customer-data analysis in the age of Facebook. Investment in technology is accelerating – from hand-held scanners (at Plymouth Extra and rolling out in Hungary) to virtual shops, such as the subway wall in South Korea that displays pictures of products, as if they were on shelves, which can be scanned using a mobile 'app', ready for delivery or customer collection. The customer of the future makes no distinction between a shop of bricks or retail through clicks. Tesco is reinventing itself to meet consumer demand, whatever its form.

'I feel like I'm just picking up a baton, chiselled out of a piece of wood by Jack Cohen in Hackney and handed on to Leslie Porter and then to Hyman Kreitman and then to Ian MacLaurin and then to Terry Leahy, and now I've got it for a while and we know where we are headed,' says Clarke. 'You have to do the right thing for your customers. You have to be part of your community. You have to have loyal and committed staff and you only get them if you treat them in the right way. The heart of Tesco is that core purpose and our Values, and they will stand us in good stead wherever we are, through thick and thin. That is the business I am privileged enough to lead.'[10]

Tesco today would in many ways be unrecognizable to Sir Jack Cohen. Shopping has transformed to keep up with social and technological changes, but the stories told by those who feature in this book demonstrate that in retail one aspect remains constant: survival depends upon keeping step with the customer – from barrow to Burnt Oak to Beijing.

The Making of Tesco in Dates

1919 Jack Cohen sets out his stall on a hired barrow in Well Street, Hackney.

1924 Cohen sells TESCO tea – a joint venture with importer T. E. Stockwell.

1930 Jack's daughter, Shirley, born at the family home in Gunton Road, Clapton.

1932 Tesco incorporated at Companies House on 28 January.

1934 Tesco headquarters established at Angel Road, Edmonton, and a warehouse is built.

1947 public listing on the London Stock Exchange, shares priced at 25p.

1949 the first self-service Tesco opens in St Peter's Street, St Albans in October; Tesco acquires Knowles Brothers chain of stores.

1950 Thomas Freake resigns from the Board after a row.

1951 Edgar Collar joins as executive director to run finances; Kevin Doherty joins Tesco.

1953–4 Britain comes off food rationing.

1954 Durbin's Stores, Ealing, acquired (£6,533).

1955 trading profits exceed £100,000 for the first time; nineteen Burnards stores acquired in June (£175,000).

1956 Tesco's first supermarket opens at Maldon, Essex; the Restrictive Trade Practices Act prohibits the collective enforcement of conditions regulating the resale price of goods.

1957 Tesco sells fresh meat in its stores; seventy stores and restaurants in London and the south-east bought from Williamsons Ltd.

1958 150 stores are now self-service.

1959 Ian MacLaurin joins Tesco – the first graduate management trainee; Leslie Porter joins on a salary of £3,000.

1960 Leicester Lee Circle opens, with a price war against RPM; expansion into the North of England after Liverpool-based Irwins store chain (212 shops) acquired.

1961 pre-tax profits exceed £1 million; the Cheltenham store is the first to have an escalator.

1962 John Gildersleeve joins Tesco as a trainee manager; Kayser Bondor (makers of stockings and tights) takes Tesco to court to enforce RPM.

1963 Edgar Collar dies in June; Pricerite chain launches Green Shield Stamps on 14 October and Tesco follows one week later.

1964 Tesco is among the first retailers to invest in a computer – an ICT 1300; acquisition of ninety-seven self-service stores from Charles Phillips & Co. and forty-nine cafés and bakeries from Bristol-based Cadena.

1965 Resale Price Maintenance abolished; Tesco has 12,000 staff; acquisition of forty-seven stores from Manchester-based Adsega.

1966 David Malpas joins Tesco as a graduate management trainee; Tesco opens fifty-one shops in one year; *Financial Times* puts it top of the UK company growth league.

1968 loss-making Victor Value acquired (including the former Anthony Jackson's chain); Tesco carries out rights issue in November; Crawley superstore opens in Surrey with 40,000 square feet of selling space; Sir Jack Cohen has a seventieth birthday party at London's Dorchester hotel and the TV show *This Is Your Life* is a surprise guest.

1969 McKinsey consultants invited in; Jack Cohen becomes Life President of Tesco; his elder son-in-law, Hyman Kreitman, becomes chairman; own-label beer launched; six staff training centres opened; Sir Save-a-Lot, Tesco's knight, falls off his horse at the opening of the shop in Rayleigh, Essex.

1970 Ian MacLaurin appointed to the main Board; McKinsey report shakes up the business.

1971 first official mention (in the Annual Report) that Tesco is looking at expansion into Europe.

1972 fresh bread baked in store at West Bromwich.

1973 on 1 April Tesco moves to New Tesco House, directly opposite its original headquarters in Delamare Road, Cheshunt; own-brand wine label De Georges is extended to include champagne and brandy; VAT arrives; by now a hundred shares bought in 1948 for £75 are worth £6,000. Hyman Kreitman resigns as chairman and is replaced by Leslie Porter. Ian MacLaurin becomes joint managing director; pension scheme upgraded; the first petrol stations open at stores.

1974–5 turnover exceeds £500 million, but profits dip for the first time in twenty-five years.

1976 lager added to Tesco own-label range and De Georges wine range relaunched; in February Tesco's first hypermarkets open at Irlam, Manchester, and Braintree, Essex; David Malpas promoted to run all of Tesco's retail operations.

1977 on 7 June Tesco exits Green Shield Stamps and launches Operation Checkout; Maidstone store fits the first 'merculator' moving ramp between floors; Leslie Porter president of the IGD.

1978 Tesco opens a store in Well Street, Hackney, where Jack started out on a market stall; Pitsea (Essex) superstore opens; two Debenhams stores acquired (Nottingham and Walkden, Manchester).

1979 on 1 January David Malpas joins the main Board as managing director; 24 March Sir Jack Cohen dies; Electronic Point of Sale (EPOS) (bar code) trial – 5,000 lines coded; first till receipts issued at Wellingborough store; Tesco buys 3 Guys stores in Republic of Ireland (converted the following year to Tesco); Terry Leahy joins Tesco.

1980 Cartier group of stores acquired in Kent; Board looks at America but 'walks firmly away'.

1982 checkouts are computerized (former Victor Value stores used to test the technology).

1984 John Gildersleeve appointed to the Board; home shopping, via Teletext, trialled at a library in Gateshead, Tyne and Wear, 'to serve the needs of the elderly and disabled'; community projects include the Wavendon All Music Plan, near Milton Keynes, and a Sunshine coach.

1985 Leslie Porter retires as executive chairman; Ian MacLaurin becomes executive chairman; Brent Park, Neasden, becomes the hundredth super-store; stores linked to distribution centres by computer; BAT looks at taking over Tesco; David Reid joins the company; Healthy Eating range launched.

1987 Sir Leslie Porter retires; Ian MacLaurin appointed non-executive chairman; Hillards acquired; profit-sharing scheme for staff introduced; bar-code scanning trial launched at Flitwick, Bedfordshire.

1988 Ian MacLaurin and USDAW general secretary Garfield Davies sign up for direct negotiating.

1990 Dudley Moore 'Our Man from Tesco' advertising campaign launches; Ian MacLaurin becomes a lord; Sir Leslie Porter retires completely from Tesco.

1992 Terry Leahy joins the Board as marketing director; Hoover Building, iconic art deco London landmark, bought and converted; Tesco acquires its own fleet of petrol tankers; Computers for Schools vouchers launched.

1993 Value brand launched; Tesco Metro launched in Covent Garden, London; French business Catteau acquired.

1994 fall in profits reported – the first for twenty years; in January the first Tesco store in Hungary opens following investment in S-Market shops; Tesco Express launched in Barnes, London; Every Little Helps strapline launched – 1.3 million more customers shop at Tesco between 1993 and 1995; One in Front queue-cutting campaign launched; William Low (Scottish stores chain) acquired; Terry Leahy becomes deputy managing director.

1995 Tesco acquires Savia chain of stores in southern Poland for £8 million; Clubcard launched; Dotty advertising campaign launches, running until 2004; Tesco overtakes J Sainsbury's market share; Tesco's first Charity of the Year campaign.

1996 twenty-four-hour trading allowed; Tesco buys Kmarts in Czech Republic and Slovakia.

1997 Terry Leahy appointed chief executive, Lord MacLaurin and David Malpas step down, John Gardiner appointed chairman; Dame Lucy Neville-Rolfe joins Tesco from the Civil Service; Tesco Personal Finance launches; Tesco returns to Republic of Ireland; Tesco Direct trials grocery home shopping.

1998 Tesco Extra launched at Pitsea, Essex; Tesco opens in Taiwan and Thailand; Tesco Finest brand launched; Catteau, France, sold to Promodes for £250 million; Nature's Choice range launched. Tesco Direct trial extends.

1999 mobile phones launched; Tesco goes into partnership with Samsung in South Korea.

2000 Tesco Direct grocery home delivery service re-launched as Tesco.com.

2001 Florence & Fred (now F&F) clothing range launched with the slogan 'Fashion in pence not pounds'.

2002 Tesco opens in Malaysia with local retailer Sime Darby; Free From food brand launched.

2003 Tesco opens in Turkey through acquisition of five Kipa shops, and also in Japan.

2004 Sir David Reid appointed chairman; Tesco opens in China as Hymall; Tesco Broadband launched and music downloads sold.

2005 profits exceed £2 billion.

2006 Lucy Neville-Rolfe appointed to Board as Tesco's first Corporate & Legal Affairs executive director; Clubcard launches 'green' points for re-using shopping bags; Tesco Direct launched for general merchandise, online sales.

2007 in November Tesco opens the first Fresh & Easy store in Hemet, California; ten-point community plan launched, as well as pledge to be a zero-carbon business by 2050.

2008 plans for cash-and-carry business in India with Star Bazaar announced; Tesco buys thirty-six hypermarkets in South Korea from Homever for £958 million from E.Land; other half of Tesco Personal Finance acquired from former partner Royal Bank of Scotland, forming Tesco Bank.

2009 Tesco.com's clothing arm launched online; first double Clubcard point promotion; Trading Fairly launched – a codified version of Tesco's sourcing practices; a skills academy opens in Bangladesh.

2010 world's first zero-carbon supermarket, Tesco at Ramsey, Cambridgeshire, opens; Tesco's first Lifespace mall opens in Qingdao, China; Leahy announces his decision to retire and names Philip Clarke as successor; Clubcard launches an app for mobile phones.

2011 Sir Terry Leahy retires, Philip Clarke becomes group chief executive; chairman Sir David Reid retires and is replaced by Sir Richard Broadbent; training academy opens at Incheon, South Korea; Fresh & Easy launches 'Friends' loyalty card; Bang Phra zero-carbon store opens in Thailand.

2012 first profits warning for twenty years; Tesco exits Japan; David Potts retires; new advertising agency, Wieden + Kennedy, appointed; Tesco announces strategic review of Fresh & Easy stores in US.

Notes

The many references to *Tesco: An Oral History* (see page 351), which was carried out by National Life Stories and is held in the oral history collections at the British Library, are abbreviated here as TAOH.

Foreword
1 Sir Terry Leahy, interviewed by Sarah Ryle, January 2011
2 Philip Clarke, speaking at Tesco's Company Conference, 18 October 2012
3 Philip Clarke interviewed by Sarah Ryle, TAOH, 4 January 2012, C1087/0047/0004
4 Sir Terry Leahy, interviewed by Sarah Ryle, January 2011

1 The Poor Shall Be Fed
1 Sir David Reid, interviewed by Niamh Dillon, TAOH, 18 October 2006, C1087/31/11
2 Dame Shirley Porter, interviewed by Niamh Dillon, TAOH, 1 December 2006, C1087/17/2
3 Ibid, C1087/17/5
4 Dame Shirley Porter, op. cit., 13 December 2005, C1087/17/4
5 Corina, Maurice, *Pile It High, Sell It Cheap: the Authorised Biography of Sir John Cohen*, London: Weidenfeld & Nicolson, 1971, pp. 36 and 38–9
6 Dame Shirley Porter, op. cit., 1 December 2005, C1087/17/1
7 Dame Shirley Porter, op. cit., 6 April 2006, C1087/17/5
8 Corina, op. cit., pp. 53–4
9 Ibid, pp. 73–4

2 Shopping through the Darkest Hour

1 Dame Shirley Porter, interviewed by Niamh Dillon, TAOH, 1 December 2005, C1087/17/1
2 Ibid
3 Ibid
4 Dame Shirley Porter, op. cit., 13 December 2005, C1087/17/3
5 Dame Shirley Porter, op. cit., 6 April 2006, C1087/17/5

3 Britain's Counter Revolution

1 Eddie Clark, interviewed by Niamh Dillon, TAOH, 1 June 2005, C1087/14/8b
2 Sir John Cohen, Tesco Annual Report, 1950
3 Dame Shirley Porter, interviewed by Niamh Dillon, TAOH, 1 December 2005, C1087/17/2
4 Eddie Clark, op. cit., C1087/14/2
5 Ibid, C1087/14/6
6 Ibid, C1087/14/7
7 Ibid, C1087/14/8
8 Eddie Clark, op. cit., 6 July 2005, C1087/14/13
9 Eddie Clark, op. cit., 1 June 2005, C1087/14/8
10 Ibid, C1087/14/9
11 Ibid, C1087/14/8

4 Gadgets and Groceries

1 Sir John Cohen, Tesco Annual Report, July 1959
2 Beryl Hinde, interviewed by Deborah Agulnik, 20 October 2003, TAOH, C1087/1/1
3 Ibid
4 Ibid
5 Ibid
6 Tesco Annual Report, 1959, introduction
7 This reference to Peckham threw the origins of the first Tesco store – long held to be Burnt Oak – into doubt and prompted fresh research for this book (see Author's Note, pages ix–x).
8 The European Free Trade Association (EFTA) came about after failed negotiations for an Organisation for European Economic Co-operation (OEEC) free trade area for countries not wishing to join the European Economic Community (EEC). The Outer Seven group, including the United Kingdom, signed the Stockholm Convention in November 1959 which established EFTA from May 1960. Members

committed to tariff reductions and quota liberalizations for industrial goods. The UK and Denmark left EFTA in January 1973 when they joined the EEC. Source: *Encyclopaedia Britannica*

5 A Successful Shambles

1 Lord MacLaurin, interviewed by Niamh Dillon, TAOH, 18 January 2006, C1087/22/4
2 Ibid
3 Lord MacLaurin, op. cit., 4 January 2006, C1087/22/1
4 Ibid, C1087/22/2
5 Ibid
6 Ibid
7 Lord MacLaurin, op. cit., 18 January 2006, C1087/22/4
8 Ibid
9 Ibid, C1087/22/3
10 Ibid, C1087/22/6
11 Lord MacLaurin, op. cit., 15 March 2006, C1087/22/8
12 Ibid
13 Ibid
14 Ibid
15 A muddle.
16 Lord MacLaurin, op. cit., 15 March 2006, C1087/22/8
17 Kevin Doherty, interviewed by Deborah Agulnik, TAOH, 1 March 2004, C1087/10/2 and 3
18 Ibid, C1087/10/2
19 Then Anthony Jackson's, a chain later bought by Victor Value, which in 1968 was itself bought by Tesco.
20 Kevin Doherty, op. cit., 16 January 2004, C1087/10/3
21 Ibid

6 The Best for Less from the Housewives' Friend

1 Dame Shirley Porter, interviewed by Niamh Dillon, TAOH, 15 August 2006, C1098/17/9

7 The 'Widening Front' and Stamp-collecting

1 Dame Shirley Porter, interviewed by Niamh Dillon, TAOH, 8 August 2006, C1098/17/7
2 Lord MacLaurin, interviewed by Niamh Dillon, TAOH, 15 March 2006, C1087/22/8
3 Dame Shirley Porter, op. cit., C1098/17/7b

4 Ibid
5 Lord MacLaurin, op. cit., 18 January 2006, C1087/22/4
6 John Gildersleeve, interviewed by Niamh Dillon, TAOH, 26 June 2005, C1087/30/2
7 Ibid, C1087/30/1
8 Ibid
9 Ibid
10 Ibid, C1087/30/2
11 Lord MacLaurin, op. cit., 15 March 2006, C1087/22/8
12 Corina, Maurice, *Pile It High, Sell It Cheap: the Authorised Biography of Sir John Cohen*, London: Weidenfeld & Nicolson, 1971, p. 26
13 Eddie Clark, interviewed by Niamh Dillon, TAOH, 6 July 2005, C1087/14/11
14 Tesco Annual Report, 1965

8 Growing Pains
1 Tesco Annual Report, 1965
2 David Malpas, interviewed by Niamh Dillon, TAOH, 13 January 2006, C1087/21/4
3 Eddie Clark, interviewed by Niamh Dillon, TAOH, 6 July 2005, C1087/14/12
4 David Malpas, op. cit., 12 April 2006, C1087/21/8
5 David Malpas, op. cit., 13 January 2006, C1087/21/4
6 David Malpas, op. cit., 3 January 2006, C1087/21/1
7 David Malpas, op. cit., 13 January 2006, C1087/21/4
8 David Malpas, op. cit., 3 January 2006, C1087/21/1
9 David Malpas, op. cit., 13 January 2006, C1087/21/2
10 Ibid, C1087/21/3
11 Ibid
12 Ibid
13 David Malpas, op. cit., 7 March 2006, C1087/21/4
14 David Malpas, op. cit., 13 January 2006, C1087/21/7
15 Harry Quinlan, interviewed by Deborah Agulnik, TAOH, 8 December 2003, C1087/7/3
16 Ibid
17 Ibid, C1087/7/2
18 Ibid, C1087/7/3

9 The Fight for Control

1 Lord MacLaurin, interviewed by Niamh Dillon, TAOH, 15 March 2006, C1087/22/10
2 Hyman Kreitman, Tesco Annual Report, 1971
3 Dame Shirley Porter, interviewed by Niamh Dillon, TAOH, 15 August 2006, C1098/17/9
4 David Malpas, interviewed by Niamh Dillon, TAOH, 7 March 2006, C1087/21/4
5 Lord MacLaurin, op. cit., C1087/22/10
6 Eddie Clark, interviewed by Niamh Dillon, TAOH, 6 July 2005, C1087/14/10
7 David Malpas, op. cit., 4 April 2006, C1087/21/8
8 Harry Quinlan, interviewed by Deborah Agulnik, TAOH, 8 December 2003, C1087/7/3
9 Lord MacLaurin, op. cit., 18 January 2006, C1087/22/5
10 David Malpas, op. cit., 12 April 2006, C1087/21/6
11 Ibid
12 Ibid, C1087/21/5
13 Powell, David, *Counter Revolution: The Tesco Story*, London: Grafton, 1991, chapter 9

10 The View from the Shop Floor

1 Joe Doody, interviewed by Niamh Dillon, TAOH, 28 June 2005, C1087/16/6
2 David Potts, interviewed by Niamh Dillon, TAOH, 18 May 2006, C1087/29/3
3 Ibid
4 Ibid
5 Ibid, C1087/29/2 and 3
6 David Malpas, interviewed by Niamh Dillon, TAOH, 12 April 2006, C1087/21/5
7 Joe Doody, op. cit., C1087/16/6
8 Ibid
9 Ibid
10 Ibid, C1087/16/7
11 Ibid
12 Ibid
13 Ibid
14 Ibid
15 Ibid, C1087/16/8

16 Ibid
17 John Gildersleeve, interviewed by Niamh Dillon, TAOH, 30 January 2005, C1087/30/3

11 Operation Checkout
1 Lord MacLaurin, interviewed by Niamh Dillon, TAOH, 15 March 2006, C1087/22/4
2 Kevin Doherty, interviewed by Niamh Dillon, TAOH, 30 March 2005, C1087/10/6
3 Lord MacLaurin, op. cit., C1087/22/3
4 David Malpas, interviewed by Niamh Dillon, TAOH, 7 March 2006, C1087/21/4
5 Lord MacLaurin, op. cit., 18 January 2006, C1087/22/4
6 David Malpas, op. cit., 13 January 2006, C1087/21/3
7 Lord MacLaurin, op. cit., 15 March 2006, C1087/22/4
8 Ibid
9 Kevin Doherty, op. cit., 30 March 2005, C1087/10/6
10 David Malpas, op. cit., 13 January 2006, C1087/21/3
11 Ibid
12 Kevin Doherty, op. cit., C1087/10/6
13 Mike Walastyan, interviewed by Niamh Dillon, TAOH, 29 March 2006, C1087/25/5
14 Victor Weeks, interviewed by Niamh Dillon, TAOH, 22 June 2005, C1087/11/7
15 Ibid, C1087/11/10
16 Ibid, C1087/11/3
17 David Malpas, op. cit., 12 April 2006, C1087/21/6a
18 Robin Gray, interviewed by Niamh Dillon, TAOH, 16 April 2007, C1087/37/3
19 David Malpas, op. cit., 12 April 2006, C1087/21/6
20 Morris, Steven, 'Bristol locals prepare for new fight after battle of Tesco', Guardian, 28 March 2012

12 High Street Wars
1 Sir Leslie Porter, Tesco Annual Report, 2 July 1978
2 David Malpas, interviewed by Niamh Dillon, TAOH, 12 April 2006, C1087/21/6b
3 Kevin Doherty, interviewed by Niamh Dillon, TAOH, 16 January 2004, C1087/10/3
4 Ibid

5 Dame Shirley Porter, interviewed by Niamh Dillon, TAOH, 6 April 2006, C1087/17/5

6 Sir Leslie Porter, Tesco Annual Report, 1979

7 Lord MacLaurin, interviewed by Niamh Dillon, TAOH, 15 March 2006, C1087/22/5a

8 David Malpas, op. cit., 12 April 2006, C1087/21/6b

9 David Malpas, op. cit., 12 April 2006, C1087/21/4b

10 Lord MacLaurin, op. cit., 15 March 2006, C1087/22/5a

11 David Malpas, op. cit., 12 April 2006, C1087/21/6b

12 Lord MacLaurin, op. cit., 15 March 2006, C1087/22/5a

13 John Gildersleeve, interviewed by Niamh Dillon, TAOH, 30 January 2007, C1087/30/3

14 Ibid

15 Lord MacLaurin, op. cit., 15 March 2006, C1087/22/5a

16 Lord MacLaurin, op. cit., 19 December 2006, C1087/22/6b

13 Managing Better

1 David Malpas, interviewed by Niamh Dillon, TAOH, 12 April 2006, C1087/21/4b

2 Sir Terry Leahy, interviewed by Niamh Dillon, TAOH, 8 September 2005, C1087/13/4a

3 John Gildersleeve, interviewed by Niamh Dillon, TAOH, 30 January 2007, C1087/30/3

4 Lord MacLaurin, interviewed by Niamh Dillon, TAOH, 15 March 2006, C1087/22/5b

5 Paul Nally interviewed by Niamh Dillon, TAOH, 19 October 2005, C1087/19/3

6 Harry Quinlan, interviewed by Deborah Agulnik, TAOH, 8 December 2003, C1087/07/3

7 David Malpas, op. cit., 12 April 2006, C1087/21/4b

8 Sir Terry Leahy, op. cit., 19 April 2005, C1087/13/2

9 Sir Terry Leahy, op. cit., 8 September 2005, C1087/13/3

10 Ibid

11 Ibid

12 Ibid

13 Sir Terry Leahy, op. cit., 8 September 2005, C1087/13/4

14 Sir Terry Leahy, op. cit., 8 September 2005, C1087/13/3

15 Ibid

16 Ibid

17 Ibid

18 Sir Terry Leahy, op. cit., 8 September 2005, C1087/13/4
19 Eddie Clark, interviewed by Niamh Dillon, TAOH, 1 June 2005, C1087/14/5
20 Sir Terry Leahy, op. cit., 8 September 2005, C1087/13/4
21 Ibid
22 Ibid
23 Ibid

14 Marketing for Beginners
 1 Sir Terry Leahy, interviewed by Niamh Dillon, TAOH, 8 September 2005, C1087/13/4
 2 Robin Gray, interviewed by Niamh Dillon, TAOH, 16 April 2007, C1087/37/2
 3 Ibid
 4 John Gildersleeve, interviewed by Niamh Dillon, TAOH, 30 January 2007, C1087/30/3
 5 Sir Terry Leahy, interviewed by Niamh Dillon, TAOH, 8 September 2005, C1087/13/14
 6 Robin Gray, op. cit., 20 April 2007, C1087/37/5
 7 Robin Gray, op. cit., 16 April 2007, C1087/37/1
 8 Tim Mason, interviewed by Sarah Ryle, TAOH, 5 October 2011, C1087/451
 9 Ibid
10 Ibid
11 Ibid
12 Ibid
13 Ibid
14 Ibid
15 George Marston, interviewed by Niamh Dillon, TAOH, 6 March 2007, C1087/36/1
16 George Marston, op. cit., 7 March 2007, C1087/36/4
17 George Marston, op. cit., 7 March 2007, C1087/36/7
18 Robin Gray, op. cit., 16 April 2007, C1087/37/2
19 Sir Terry Leahy, op. cit., 8 September 2005, C1087/13/4
20 Ibid
21 George Marston, op. cit., 6 March 2007, C1087/36/1
22 Robin Gray, op. cit., 16 April 2007, C1087/37/2

15 A Fresh Look at Food
 1 Sir Terry Leahy, interviewed by Niamh Dillon, TAOH, 5 December 2005, C1087/13/6

2   John Gildersleeve, interviewed by Niamh Dillon, TAOH, 30 January 2007, C1087/30/3

3   Sir Terry Leahy, op. cit., 5 December 2005, C1087/13/6

4   John Gildersleeve, op. cit., 30 January 2007, C1087/30/3

5   Sir Terry Leahy, op. cit., 27 October 2005, C1087/13/5

6   Ibid

7   Sir Terry Leahy, op. cit., 5 December 2005, C1087/13/6

8   George Marston, interviewed by Niamh Dillon, TAOH, 7 March 2007, C1087/36/4

9   Sir Terry Leahy, op. cit., 27 October 2005, C1087/13/5

10 Ibid

11 George Marston, op. cit., 7 March 2007, C1087/36/4

12 George Marston, op. cit., 7 March 2007, C1087/36/6

13 Ibid

14 Kevin Doherty, interviewed by Niamh Dillon, TAOH, 1 March 2005, C1087/10/6

15 Sir Terry Leahy, op. cit., 27 October 2005, C1087/13/5

16 John Gildersleeve, op. cit., 30 January 2007, C1087/30/3

17 Sir Terry Leahy, op. cit., 27 October 2005, C1087/13/5

18 John Gildersleeve, op. cit., 30 January 2007, C1087/30/3

19 Sir Terry Leahy, op. cit., 27 October 2005, C1087/13/5

20 Ibid

16 The Supply Side

1   John Gildersleeve, interviewed by Niamh Dillon, TAOH, 30 January 2007, C1087/30/3

2   Tim Mason, interviewed by Sarah Ryle, TAOH, 15 November 2011, C1087/45/2

3   Sir Terry Leahy, interviewed by Niamh Dillon, TAOH, 5 December 2005, C1087/13/6

4   Ibid

5   Ibid

6   Ibid

7   John Gildersleeve, op. cit., 30 January 2007, C1087/30/3

8   Ibid

9   Tim Mason, op. cit., 15 November 2011, C1087/45/2

10 Sir Terry Leahy, op. cit., 5 December 2005, C1087/13/6

11 Sir Terry Leahy, op. cit., 27 October 2005, C1087/13/5

12 Sir Terry Leahy, op. cit., 5 December 2005, C1087/13/6

13 Ibid

14 George Marston, interviewed by Niamh Dillon, TAOH, 7 March 2007, C1087/36/6
15 George Marston, op. cit., 21 March 2007, C1087/36/8
16 Tim Mason, op. cit., 5 October 2011, C1087/45/1
17 Ibid

17 Changing Times
1 Lord MacLaurin, interviewed by Niamh Dillon, TAOH, 14 March 2006, C1087/22/10
2 Dame Shirley Porter, interviewed by Niamh Dillon, TAOH, 15 August 2006, C1087/17/9
3 Lord MacLaurin, op. cit., 5 June 2007, C1087/22/14
4 Sir David Reid, interviewed by Niamh Dillon, TAOH, 6 September 2006, C1087/31/5
5 Sir David Reid, op. cit., 31 July 2006, C1087/31/3
6 Sir David Reid, op. cit., 31 July 2006, C1087/31/4
7 Sir David Reid, op. cit., 6 September 2006, C1087/31/5
8 Sir David Reid, op. cit., 18 September 2006, C1087/31/7
9 Sir David Reid, op. cit., 6 September 2006, C1087/31/6
10 Sir David Reid, op. cit., 18 September 2006, C1087/31/7
11 Ibid
12 Ibid
13 Lord MacLaurin, op. cit., 14 March 2006, C1087/22/10
14 Sir Terry Leahy, interviewed by Niamh Dillon, TAOH, 10 March 2007, C1087/13/10
15 Ibid
16 Ibid
17 George Marston, interviewed by Niamh Dillon, TAOH, 6 March 2007, C1087/36/1
18 Joe Doody, interviewed by Niamh Dillon, TAOH, 29 June 2005, C1087/16/10
19 Kevin Doherty, interviewed by Niamh Dillon, TAOH, 16 September 2005, C1087/10/9
20 Ibid
21 Kevin Doherty, op. cit., 16 September 2005, C1087/10/9 and C1087/10/10
22 Ian MacLaurin, Tesco Annual Report, 1991
23 Ibid
24 Robin Gray, interviewed by Niamh Dillon, TAOH, 16 April 2007, C1087/37/2

18 Bricks in the Wall

1   Sir Terry Leahy, interviewed by Niamh Dillon, TAOH, 5 December 2005, C1087/13/6
2   Tim Mason, interviewed by Sarah Ryle, TAOH, 15 November 2011, C1087/45/3
3   Ibid
4   Sir David Reid, interviewed by Niamh Dillon, TAOH, 18 October 2006, C1087/31/9
5   Jason Tarry, interviewed by Niamh Dillon, TAOH, 4 April 2007, C1087/38/1
6   Lord MacLaurin, interviewed by Niamh Dillon, TAOH, 19 December 2006, C1087/22/12
7   Sir Terry Leahy, op. cit., 5 December 2005, C1087/13/6
8   Sir Terry Leahy, op. cit., 5 December 2005, C1087/13/7
9   Ibid
10 David Malpas, interviewed by Niamh Dillon, TAOH, 12 April 2006, C1087/21/11
11 Sir Terry Leahy, op. cit., 5 December 2005, C1087/13/6
12 Ibid
13 Ibid
14 Ibid
15 Sir Terry Leahy, op. cit., 25 May 2006, C1087/13/8
16 Ibid
17 John Gildersleeve, interviewed by Niamh Dillon, TAOH, 30 January 2007, C1087/30/3
18 Sir Terry Leahy, op. cit., 5 December 2005, C1087/13/6
19 Ibid
20 Philip Clarke, interviewed by Sarah Ryle, TAOH, 12 December 2011, C1087/47/1
21 Ibid
22 Ibid
23 Ibid
24 Ibid
25 Ibid
26 Ibid
27 Ibid
28 Ibid
29 Ibid
30 Ibid
31 Ibid

32 Ibid
33 Ibid
34 Philip Clarke, interviewed by Sarah Ryle, TAOH, 12 December 2011, C1087/47/2
35 Ibid
36 Sir Terry Leahy, op. cit., 25 May 2006, C1087/13/8
37 Ibid
38 Ibid
39 Tim Mason, op. cit., 15 November 2011, C1087/45/3
40 Ibid
41 Sir David Reid, op. cit.,18 September 2006, C1087/31/8
42 David Malpas, op. cit., 12 April 2006, C1087/21/12
43 Sir Terry Leahy, op. cit., 25 May 2006, C1087/13/8
44 Ibid

19 The View from the Top

1 Lord MacLaurin, interviewed by Niamh Dillon, TAOH, 19 December 2006, C1087/22/12
2 Sir Terry Leahy, interviewed by Niamh Dillon, TAOH, 25 May 2006, C1087/13/8
3 Tim Mason, interviewed by Sarah Ryle, TAOH, 15 November 2011, C1087/45/3
4 Ibid
5 Robin Gray, interviewed by Niamh Dillon, TAOH, 16 April 2007, C1087/37/2 and C1087/37/3
6 Robin Gray, op. cit., 16 April 2007, C1087/37/3
7 Lord MacLaurin, op. cit., 19 December 2006, C1087/22/12
8 Sir David Reid, interviewed by Niamh Dillon, TAOH, 18 September 2006, C1087/31/7
9 David Malpas, interviewed by Niamh Dillon, TAOH, 12 April 2006, C1087/21/13
10 Lord MacLaurin, op. cit., 19 December 2006, C1087/22/12
11 Sir Terry Leahy, op. cit.,19 April 2005, C1087/13/1
12 Ibid
13 Sir Terry Leahy, op. cit., 19 April 2005, C1087/13/2
14 Ibid
15 Sir Terry Leahy, op. cit., 19 April 2005, C1087/13/3a
16 Sir Terry Leahy, op. cit., 8 September 2005, C1087/13/3
17 Ibid
18 Sir Terry Leahy, op. cit., 19 April 2005, C1087/13/2

19 Sir Terry Leahy, op. cit., 19 April 2005, C1087/13/3a
20 Sir Terry Leahy, op. cit., 8 September 2005, C1087/13/3
21 Sir Terry Leahy, op. cit., 8 September 2005, C1087/13/4
22 Ibid
23 Ibid
24 Sir Terry Leahy, op. cit., 5 December 2005, C1087/13/6
25 Sir Terry Leahy, op. cit., 25 May 2006, C1087/13/8
26 Sir David Reid, op. cit., 18 October 2006, C1087/31/9
27 Sir Terry Leahy, op. cit., 25 May 2006, C1087/13/8
28 Sir Terry Leahy, op. cit., 25 May 2006, C1087/13/9
29 Harvard Business School Press, Boston, 1996
30 HarperBusiness, London, 1994
31 Sir Terry Leahy, op. cit., 25 May 2006, C1087/13/9
32 Sir Terry Leahy, op. cit., 25 May 2006, C1087/13/8

20 New Tesco

1 Sir Terry Leahy, interviewed by Niamh Dillon, TAOH, 25 May 2006, C1087/13/9
2 Dame Lucy Neville-Rolfe, interviewed by Niamh Dillon, TAOH, 2 November 2007, C1087/15/2 [digital]
3 Gary Sargeant, interviewed by Niamh Dillon, TAOH, 21 September 2005, C1087/18/4
4 Sir Terry Leahy, op. cit., 25 May 2006, C1087/13/9
5 Sir Terry Leahy, op. cit., 29 March 2007, C1087/13/10
6 Ibid
7 Ibid
8 Ibid
9 Gary Sargeant, op. cit., 21 September 2005, C1087/18/4
10 Sir Terry Leahy, op. cit., 29 March 2007, C1087/13/10
11 George Marston, interviewed by Niamh Dillon, TAOH, 21 March 2007, C1087/36/11
12 Dame Lucy Neville-Rolfe, op. cit., 2 November 2007, C1087/15/2 [digital]
13 Dame Lucy Neville-Rolfe, op. cit., 1 April 2005, C1087/15/2 [tape]
14 Dame Lucy Neville-Rolfe, op. cit., 14 October 2005, C1087/15/4 [tape]
15 Ibid
16 Dame Lucy Neville-Rolfe, op. cit., 8 February 2008, C1087/15/4 [digital]
17 Dame Lucy Neville-Rolfe, op. cit., 2 November 2007, C1087/15/2 [digital]

18 Ibid
19 Ibid
20 Dame Lucy Neville-Rolfe, op. cit., 8 February 2008, C1087/15/4 [digital]
21 Dame Lucy Neville-Rolfe, op. cit., 8 February 2008, C1087/15/4
22 Dame Lucy Neville-Rolfe, op. cit., 2 November 2007, C1087/15/2 [digital]
23 Jason Tarry, interviewed by Niamh Dillon, TAOH, 5 April 2007, C1087/38/2
24 Ibid
25 Ibid
26 Dame Lucy Neville-Rolfe, op. cit., 2 November 2007, C1087/15/2 [digital]
27 Ibid
28 Ibid
29 Ibid
30 Ibid
31 Ibid
32 Ibid

21 Foreign Fields

1 Lord MacLaurin, interviewed by Niamh Dillon, TAOH, 19 December 2006, C1087/22/13
2 Sir Terry Leahy, interviewed by Niamh Dillon, TAOH, 29 March 2007, C1087/13/10
3 Lord MacLaurin, op. cit., 19 December 2006, C1087/22/13
4 Lord MacLaurin, Tesco Annual Report, 1993
5 Sir David Reid, interviewed by Niamh Dillon, TAOH, 18 October 2006, C1087/31/9
6 Ray Allcock, interviewed by Deborah Agulnik, TAOH, 4 November 2003, C1087/2/7
7 Mike Walastyan, interviewed by Niamh Dillon, TAOH, 29 March 2006, C1087/25/9
8 Ibid
9 Mike Walastyan, op. cit., 29 March 2006, C1087/25/9b
10 Ibid
11 Ray Allcock, op. cit., 4 November 2003, C1087/2/7
12 Ibid
13 Mike Walastyan, op. cit., 29 March 2006, C1087/25/10
14 Sir David Reid, op. cit., 18 October 2006, C1087/31/9

15 Lord MacLaurin, op. cit., 19 December 2006, C1087/22/13
16 Sir Terry Leahy, op. cit., 29 March 2007, C1087/13/10
17 Sir David Reid, op. cit., 18 October 2006, C1087/31/9
18 Kevin Doherty, interviewed by Niamh Dillon, TAOH, 16 September 2005, C1087/10/10b
19 Ibid
20 Kevin Doherty, op. cit., 16 September 2005, C1087/10/11
21 Kevin Doherty, op. cit., 16 September 2005, C1087/10/11a
22 Ibid
23 Ibid
24 Kevin Doherty, op. cit., 16 September 2005, C1087/10/11b
25 Ibid
26 Ibid
27 Kevin Doherty, op. cit., 16 September 2005, C1087/10/12
28 Ray Allcock, op. cit., 4 November 2003, C1087/2/8
29 Ibid
30 Ibid
31 Sir Terry Leahy, op. cit., 29 March 2007, C1087/13/11
32 David Potts, interviewed by Niamh Dillon, TAOH, 21 September 2006, C1087/29/4
33 Sir Terry Leahy, op. cit., 29 March 2007, C1087/13/10

22 Asian Tigers

1 Sir Terry Leahy, interviewed by Niamh Dillon, TAOH, 29 March 2007, C1087/13/10
2 Jason Tarry interviewed by Niamh Dillon, TAOH, 5 April 2007, C1087/38/2
3 Sir Terry Leahy, interviewed by Sarah Ryle, 20 October 2011, C1087/13/6 [digital]
4 Sir Terry Leahy, op. cit., 20 October 2011, C1087/13/6–8 [digital]
5 Sir Terry Leahy, op. cit., 20 October 2011, C1087/13/8 [digital]
6 Sir Terry Leahy, op. cit., 20 October 2011, C1087/13/46/6 [digital]
7 Sir Terry Leahy, op. cit., 29 March 2007, C1087/13/10
8 Sir David Reid, interviewed by Niamh Dillon, TAOH, 18 October 2006, C1087/31/9
9 Philip Clarke, interviewed by Sarah Ryle, TAOH, 4 January 2012, C1087/47/3
10 Ibid
11 Ibid
12 Sir Terry Leahy, op. cit., 20 October 2011, C1087/13/8 [digital]

13   Ibid
14   Philip Clarke, op. cit., 4 January 2012, C1087/47/3
15   Sir Terry Leahy, op. cit., 29 March 2007, C1087/13/11

23 The American Dream

1   Sir Terry Leahy, interviewed by Sarah Ryle, TAOH, 20 October 2011, C1087/13/1–5 [digital]
2   Tim Mason, interviewed by Sarah Ryle, TAOH, 5 October 2011, C1087/45/1
3   Sir Terry Leahy, op. cit., 20 October 2011, C1087/13/1–5 [digital]
4   Ibid
5   Gary Sargeant, interviewed by Niamh Dillon, TAOH, 21 September 2005, C1087/18/4
6   Tim Mason, op. cit., 5 October 2011, C1087/45/1
7   Sir Terry Leahy, op. cit., 20 October 2011, C1087/13/1–5 [digital]
8   Ibid
9   Ibid
10   Tim Mason, op. cit., 5 October 2011, C1087/45/1
11   Ibid
12   Ibid
13   Ibid
14   Sir Terry Leahy, op. cit., 20 October 2011, C1087/13/1–5 [digital]
15   Tim Mason, op. cit., 5 October 2011, C1087/45/1
16   Sir Terry Leahy, op. cit., 20 October 2011, C1087/13/1–5 [digital]
17   Ibid
18   Ibid
19   Ibid
20   Ibid
21   Sir Terry Leahy, op. cit., 20 October 2011, C1087/13/1–5 [digital]
22   Ibid
23   Tim Mason, op. cit., 5 October 2011, C1087/45/1

24 Success

1   Sir Terry Leahy, interviewed by Niamh Dillon, TAOH, 29 March 2007, C1087/13/10
2   Dame Lucy Neville-Rolfe, interviewed by Niamh Dillon, TAOH, 2 November 2007, C1087/15/2
3   Dame Lucy Neville-Rolfe, op. cit., 2 November 2007, C1087/15/2 [digital]
4   Ibid

5 Sir Terry Leahy, op. cit., 29 March 2007, C1087/13/10
6 Dame Lucy Neville-Rolfe, op. cit., 2 November 2007, C1087/15/2 [digital]
7 Dame Lucy Neville-Rolfe, op. cit., 2 November 2007, C1087/15/3 [digital]
8 Ibid
9 Ibid

25 Power and Responsibility

1 Philip Clarke, interviewed by Sarah Ryle, TAOH, 4 January 2012, C1087/47/3
2 Tesco's 'balanced scorecard' has four segments: customers, people, operations and finance, and each team and individual, from the chief executive to the checkout, has measurable objectives in each area.
3 Sir Terry Leahy, interviewed by Sarah Ryle, TAOH, 20 October 2011, C1087/13/9 [digital]
4 Ibid
5 Ibid
6 Ibid
7 Ibid
8 Philip Clarke, interviewed by Sarah Ryle, TAOH, 4 January 2012, C1087/47/3
9 Philip Clarke, interviewed by Sarah Ryle, TAOH, 12 December 2011, C1087/47/2
10 Philip Clarke, interviewed by Sarah Ryle, TAOH, 4 January 2012, C1087/47/3

Acknowledgements

Tesco: An Oral History was conducted by National Life Stories at the British Library between 2003 and 2007 and the principal interviewer was Niamh Dillon. The oral history materials are copyright of the British Library and the recordings can be accessed onsite at the Library (catalogue reference C1087). For more information, visit www.bl.uk.

There is yet another reason to be thankful for the British Library, as the following books were out of print and accessible only through its own collection: *Pile It High, Sell It Cheap: the Authorised Biography of Sir John Cohen*, Maurice Corina, London: Weidenfeld & Nicolson, 1971; *Counter Revolution: The Tesco Story*, David Powell, London: Grafton, 1991; and *Tiger By the Tail: A Life in Business from Tesco to Test Cricket*, Ian MacLaurin, London: Macmillan, 1999.

I am particularly grateful to the British Library's Oral History team, led by Dr Robert Perks and Niamh Dillon (the chief interviewer), whose helpful comments at reading stage were appreciated. Thanks are also due to my father, who applied invaluable subeditor's skills to the draft; to those other generous people who read the manuscript; to Sally Gaminara and the team at Transworld; to Nick Barratt, an archive expert, for his help in identifying which of three possibilities was the site of the first Tesco store (Burnt Oak); to Garry Blackman; to Sir Terry Leahy and Dame Lucy Neville-Rolfe, who saw the archive's possibilities and inspired this book; and to

Philip Clarke and my colleagues in Corporate Affairs and Legal Affairs for supporting the project. My family tolerated the process with good humour and love.

Picture Acknowledgements

All the images in the book have been kindly supplied by the Tesco Media Publishing Centre, except for the following photos in the illustration section:

Sir Jack Cohen returns to Frith Street: Getty Images

Sir Jack Cohen and Daisy Hyams, Well Street, 1978: Tesco Museum archive; artist's impression of Small Heath Store, Birmingham: Tesco annual report for 1963

Cartoon by Stuart Franklin, the *Sun*, 11 June 1977: the *Sun*/NI Syndication; Sir Jack Cohen raising a glass: Getty Images; artist's impression of New Tesco House: Tesco annual report for 1973

Lucy Neville-Rolfe: © Photoshot; Seacroft store, Leeds: Tesco annual report for 2000; Tesco advert featuring Dudley Moore: Tesco Museum archive; 'Computers for Schools' campaign: Tesco annual report for 1997

Tesco store, Beijing: © China Newscom/Photoshot

Index

Sarah Ryle works in Tesco's Corporate Affairs team. She read history at Oxford University and trained as a journalist on a local evening newspaper in Bath. She was a business and economics reporter at the *Guardian* for two years, and retail correspondent and consumer affairs correspondent at the *Observer* for eight years. She lives in London.